Exiles from Paradise

ZELDA AND SCOTT FITZGERALD

by Sara Mayfield

DELACORTE PRESS / NEW YORK, N.Y.

Typography and design by Barbara Cohen

FOR RICHARD KENNEDY
AND LURTON BLASSINGAME
WITH MY THANKS
AND MY DEVOTION

Contents

EXILES FROM PARADISE

Zelda and Scott Fitzgerald

*... il gardera toujours la nostalgie
de cette innocence première
et la souvenir de cette plenitude
d'autrefois; il se sentira en exil,
chassé de son paradis par les
démons d'un Esprit qui n'est pas
celui de son pays.*

Jean Onimus,
ALBERT CAMUS AND
CHRISTIANITY

1. Something Enchanted

I F THE BIRTH of that fabulous era known as the Jazz Age could be fixed arbitrarily, it would probably be placed in Montgomery, Alabama, on a sultry July evening in 1918. For that was the time and place in which the future laureate of that golden decade met the girl who was to help him celebrate it. It was a meeting, he said, about which there was "something enchanted."

On that memorable evening, Zelda Sayre had gone, as usual, to the Saturday night dance at the Montgomery Country Club. While she waltzed on its wide verandah, waiting there in the wings was the young man who was to do for her what Homer did for Helen of Troy. He was First Lieutenant F. Scott Fitzgerald of St. Paul, Minnesota, now stationed in Alabama at Camp Sheridan with the Forty-fifth Infantry, Ninth Division.

When Scott was ordered to Camp Sheridan, he had written to Lawton Campbell, a fellow Princetonian and a former Montgomerian, asking him to send him the names of the prettiest girls in the Cradle of the Confederacy. Lawton listed three of its most beautiful and popular debutantes for him, but Zelda was not one of them because she had grown up after Lawton left Montgomery. Scott had been rushing all three of the girls whose names had been sent him, and in the process, he had found their home town to be "a languid paradise of dreamy skies and firefly evenings . . . and especially of gracious, soft-voiced girls, who were brought up on memories instead of money."

Through the courtesy of one of his girls who took an active part in war work, particularly in the local efforts to provide wholesome entertainment for the officers stationed in the nearby cantonments at Camp Sheridan and Camp Taylor, Scott had secured a card to the Country Club. There he had spent many a relaxed and happy evening with his girls in the clubhouse, a rambling brown-shingled building, discreetly screened from the public eye by an impenetrable hedge of mock oranges.

However, since all Scott's girls had other dates on the fateful evening that he first met Zelda, he had escorted two of his superior officers to the dance. He had just arrived with them when he caught sight of a crowd of stags around a girl he did not know—a girl with the face of "a saint, a Viking Madonna." He stared at her as if he were bewitched. Then without troubling to excuse himself from his companions or to ask for an introduction to her, he strode over, cut in on her, and presented himself.

Zelda was only seventeen at the time. Not until July 24 would she be eighteen and old enough to put up her hair. Although she was sophisticated for her age, she still had the charm of an uninhibited, imaginative child. Her features were as perfect as those of a Gibson girl on a magazine cover. A summer tan gave her skin the color of a rose petal dipped in cream. Her hair had the sheen of spun gold. Wide and dark-lashed, her eyes seemed to change color with her prismatic moods; though in reality they were deep blue, at times they appeared to be green or even a dark Confederate gray. Her figure was slender and well-proportioned; and she was lithe, extraordinarily graceful, and a wonderful dancer.

Scott was not only fascinated by Zelda's beauty but he was also intrigued by her popularity. Before he could dance across the floor with her, one of her admirers would cut in and take her away from him. Not until the intermission did he have time enough with her to ask for her telephone number. She gave it to him, but when he wanted to make a late date with her, her eyes sparkled with mischief. "I never make late dates with fast workers," she replied.

Nevertheless, Scott had made an impression on Zelda. At the time, he was twenty-two years old—a blond Adonis in a Brooks Brothers uniform. Lawton Campbell recalls that when he first met Scott at Princeton in 1916, "he was the handsomest boy I'd ever seen. He had yellow hair and lavender eyes." Another Princeton friend insists that Scott "looked like a jonquil"—an apt simile in view of the color of his hair, which he wore parted in the middle and slicked down with tonic. His features were as regular and clear-cut as if they had been coined in a Greek mint. The summer maneuvers at Camp Sheridan had tanned his fair skin, but a small white scar shone in the middle of his forehead as if the gods had marked him for a stellar role. Scott carried himself well, with his shoulders back and his head held high. He rated himself as "an extremely good dancer." His walk was a slight swagger; he moved, Zelda once observed, "as if he secretly enjoyed the ability to fly but was walking as a compromise to convention," borne along by "some heavenly support beneath his shoulder blades."

When Scott called Zelda the day after the dance, he found that her date book was filled for weeks ahead. He was a Yankee, his family were in trade, and he was only a lieutenant in an infantry regiment, so he was no great catch by Zelda's standards. But Scott was persistent in anything that he set out to do. He called her so often during the next few days that he was to remember the Sayres' telephone number as long as he lived. When Zelda finally agreed to give him a date, she found that he was not only dashing and handsome but also intelligent and amusing. At Princeton he had acquired a polish, an urbanity, and a conscious charm that attracted her. After her first date with him, Zelda was frankly fascinated by him, although, as Scott admitted, she continued to hold him "firmly at bay." Always precise about dates, Fitzgerald noted in his Ledger that he fell in love with her on September 7, six weeks after he first met her at the Country Club dance. Eventually, she confessed that she returned his love, and the "romance of the century," as Scott called it, began for him.

There are more legends current in the Cradle of the Confederacy today about Scott and Zelda than about Jefferson Davis and Varina Howell. In Zelda's case, at least, the truths are more romantic, and certainly more engaging, than the fictions about her and her family that were to be invented by Scott and his apologists.

If there is a Confederate Establishment in the Deep South, Zelda came from the heart of it. Her mother's family, which belonged to the MacHen clan in Scotland, had taken the name of Machen before emigrating to Virginia early in the seventeenth century. From Virginia the Machens moved to Carolina and eventually to Kentucky. By 1802 Zelda's great-grandfather had settled in a Scotch colony on the Cumberland River. There he became a tobacco planter and prospered so well that before his death he was able to build a Presbyterian church for the colony.

His son, Willis B. Machen, who owned a tobacco plantation of three thousand acres, called Mineral Mount, on the river near Eddyville, began his distinguished career by practicing law there. A few years later, while serving in the Kentucky legislature, he helped write the state constitution. At the outbreak of the Civil War, he was made president of the Council of Ten, an advisory board formed by the governor of Kentucky to aid him in his decisions. Subsequently, Machen served as one of the two senators from Kentucky in the Confederate Congress. During the war, when his native state was torn between two rival governments, Senator Machen was forced to flee with a price on his head. He had married at the age of nineteen. Twice widowed before he was fifty, he married for a third time in 1858. Two years later Zelda's mother, Minnie Buckner Machen, was born in Eddyville on November 23, 1860. After her father fled to Canada, she, her mother, and the other children joined him there and remained with him until he was granted amnesty. The anxiety over his fate, the unaccustomed hardships, and the scant fare broke Mrs. Machen's health and brought on the death of Minnie's eldest sister.

When the war was over Minnie and her family returned to Mineral Mount. In 1872 her father was sent to the United States Senate, and she enjoyed the advantage of frequent visits to Washington. "The Wild Lily of the Cumberland," as her father called her, was talented as well as pretty and popular. She had a fine soprano voice; she played and sang at parties and, occasionally, gave free music lessons to her friends. Nor were her talents confined to music, for several of her stories were included in a volume devoted to Kentucky writers.

After graduating from the Montgomery Female College on June 26, 1878, Minnie spent a winter being "finished" in Philadelphia. There she took lessons in music and elocution. Her dramatic recitations impressed her elocution teacher, who arranged for her to read for Georgia Drew, the doyenne of the Barrymore-Drew theatrical clan. Minnie's tryout was successful, and she was offered a role in the play. But her father refused to allow her to accept it and ordered her to come home. For the Southern Democrats had begun to talk of nominating Senator Machen as their candidate for President, and in those Victorian times no Presidential candidate could afford to have a daughter who was an actress.

Doubtless one reason that Minnie had so few regrets about abandoning her dreams of a career on the stage was that she soon fell in love with Anthony Dickinson Sayre, whom she met at a New Year's ball while she was visiting a relative of hers in Montgomery. Anthony's mother, Musidora Morgan Sayre, was a sister of Senator John Tyler Morgan, one of Alabama's most distinguished men. Although Senator Morgan's formal schooling had been limited to three years, he was an outstanding statesman and a remarkably cultivated and intelligent man. "When I left school at the age of nine," he said, "I knew more Latin than anything else." He had already read *Historiae Sacrae*, the first six books of *Caesar*, the *Georgics*, the *Bucolics*, and the *Aeneid*. He had also dipped into Sallust and Horace. Many years later while Senator Morgan was in Paris, serving as chairman of the Bering Strait Commission, an Oxonian who was astonished by the Alabamian's erudition asked him where he had been educated. "At my mother's knee," he replied. "I never set foot upon a college campus until one day during the War of Secession, I had occasion to take my regiment behind the brick walls of the College of William and Mary to find protection from the Minié balls that were flying in our direction." After serving as a brigadier general in the Confederate Army, Morgan was elected to the United States Senate from Alabama. He served there from 1876 to 1907 and distinguished himself by the progressive measures he proposed, among which was one to build a canal across the hemispheric isthmus long before Theodore Roosevelt dreamed of the Panama Canal.

When Senator Morgan's nephew asked for Minnie's hand, Senator Machen could offer no objection, for Anthony Sayre was not only well born but he was also a young man of fine character and excellent position, who had already begun to make his mark in the world. His paternal ancestors had emigrated from England and settled on Long Island, where, in the early years of the seventeenth century, Thomas Sayre became one of the founders of the town of Southampton. But the Sayres soon began to move southward, first to Morristown, New Jersey, where they intermarried with some of the first families, then to Warren County, Ohio. Zelda's grandfather, Daniel Sayre, was born nearby in the frontier settlement of Franklin on January 13, 1808.

He and his elder brother, William, left Ohio for Alabama shortly after the territory became a state in 1819. The brothers first settled in Jacksonville, but before 1830 they had moved to Talladega. There Daniel edited the *Reporter* and later the *Beacon-Republican*, though he was a Whig who later turned Democrat. On November 26, 1835, at the age of twenty-seven, he married Musidora Morgan, a sister of Senator Morgan and a relative of the famous Confederate raider, John Hunt Morgan. Zelda's father, Anthony Dickinson Sayre, the youngest son of Daniel and Musidora Sayre, was born in Tuskegee on April 29, 1858.

Eventually, both Anthony's father and his Uncle William moved to Montgomery, where Daniel edited the *Post* and William practiced law. William prospered so well both as a planter and a lawyer that he soon bought a lot in a residential district near the Capitol grounds and, without the help of an architect, designed a beautiful mansion with fluted columns, liberty cap ventilators, and a parterre of boxwoods and magnolias. From these plans, he and his slaves built a home so imposing that at the outbreak of the Civil War, the Confederate government rented it for Jefferson Davis and made it the first White House of the Confederacy. A picture of the mansion appeared in *Harper's Weekly* for June 1, 1861, with a caption stating that it rented for five thousand dollars a year.

Anthony grew up in his father's large and comfortable, if less imposing, house on Court Street. Daniel, a studious and cultivated man who owned a fine library, saw to it that his children were properly educated. As a boy, Anthony attended a small private school. In 1878 he was graduated with honors in Greek and mathematics from Roanoke College in Salem, Virginia, where he was valedictorian of his class and where, in 1928, he was awarded the degree of Doctor of Laws. After his graduation, he spent a year teaching at Vanderbilt University before he returned to Montgomery to read law. In 1880 he was admitted to the bar and hung out his shingle. However, he spent comparatively few years as a practicing attorney, for in 1883 he was appointed clerk of the city court.

Assured of a regular income by the appointment, he and Minnie Machen were married the following year. The wedding took place at Mineral Mount on June 17, 1884. Thirteen months later, Marjorie, their eldest child, was born there in Eddyville. Meanwhile, Anthony and Minnie had been living in Montgomery in the old Sayre home on Court Street. But after his father's death, Anthony sold it and bought a cottage in a more venerable part of town, west of Sayre Street, which had been named for his Uncle William. Facing the cottage there was a pillared mansion, surrounded by gardens, fountains, and a grove of magnolias and water oaks; nearby were the rectory and the Church of the Holy Comforter, an Episcopal church attended by the Sayres and their relatives.

Anthony clung to that neighborhood long after the town began to move eastward because it was his family bailiwick. Another more practical attraction was that, in the days before automobiles and buses, it was near the streetcar line. For, a little past midnight on March 25, 1886, an event of worldwide interest had taken place in Montgomery. A mule-drawn car stopped on deserted Commerce Street. Two men unhitched the mules and connected the newly installed trolley to the power lines above it. Then they climbed aboard again and turned the switch. The car edged slowly forward, picked up momentum, and sailed past the fountain in Court Square. Next morning in the Montgomery *Advertiser*, the Sayres read that the first electric trolley car in America had made its trial run in the Cradle of the Confederacy, moving up and down Commerce Street "as easily and smoothly as a ghost in the moonlight."

Consequently, even after automobiles became common, Anthony, who was so nearsighted that he never learned to drive a car, declined to shift his home to a more fashionable section. Besides, he and Minnie were fond of the old neighborhood, and their first years in the cottage were both happy and fruitful.

They now had a son, Daniel, and another daughter, Rosalind. Marjorie was a frail, delicate little girl; but Daniel and Rosalind developed into fine, strong children. Miss Minnie used to say that Daniel was the healthiest, most beautiful boy she ever saw. Then came the first of the tragedies that were to overshadow her later years. One day Daniel was running about the house, laughing and playing; the next day he was stricken with spinal meningitis. After his death, Minnie lay with her face to the wall and refused to eat or see anyone. Finally, her family doctor forced his way in, turned her around, and made her look him in the eyes. "Minnie, I know how you feel," he said. "But you have to live for the living, and you have two little girls in the next room who need you very much." After the first shock of grief passed, she found courage to follow his advice. Before long, she had another little boy and two more little girls to live for. The Sayres' family Bible records that Clotilde was born in 1891; Anthony, in 1894; and Zelda, their sixth and last child, on Tuesday, July 24, 1900, at five forty A.M.

When his family began to increase, Anthony sold his cottage and rented a larger one in the same neighborhood. In addition to his own family, his mother and brother made their home with him. Then, after Senator Machen was thrown from his buggy and killed, his grief-stricken wife died; and his youngest daughter, Miss Minnie's sister, came to live with them. During Zelda's childhood, there were ten members of her family living under one roof.

Although her father had prospered, having been made first a member of the legislature and then president of the state senate, he had heavy financial burdens during his early years. But after Governor B. B. Comer appointed him to the Supreme Court in 1909, he had a salary of sixty-five hundred dollars a year, the equivalent of three times that amount today, and he could well have afforded to build or buy a home in the elite neighborhoods of Perry Street and Cloverdale. Instead, he rented a large, comfortable house in which Zelda grew up, at Six Pleasant Avenue, not far from the cottage in which he was living.

At that time in Montgomery, the status symbols were blood and breeding, not cars and houses. Absorbed in his legal work, Judge Sayre had no interest in material things. All his life he had an aversion to debts and mortgages, to the acquisition of property, to the cares and perils of possessions, and to the attention they required. A street address meant nothing to him, for he knew that his presence was sufficient to make any neighborhood respected; so he continued to rent Six Pleasant Avenue until his death.

A Montgomerian once described the Sayres' home there as "a pleasant house on a pleasant street, filled with pleasant people." Zelda said that it was a house that had an "affinity for light" because of its many windows. It was a square, gray frame house, with green shutters. Built in the early years of the twentieth century, it was distinguished by its freedom from the gingerbread work that was characteristic of the older houses in that part of town. One flight of steps led up from the sidewalk to the front yard; another flight led from the yard to the deep porch that ran across the front of the house. Miss Minnie had trained Virginia creepers and clematis vines on wires to screen the porch from the western sun. In summer, at one end of the cool, shady gallery, as she called it, she entertained her callers and the judge read the evening paper; at the other end, Zelda used the creaking swing as a meeting place for her friends.

The rooms of the house were kept cool in summer by their high ceilings and green shutters and heated in the winter by coal fireplaces. Downstairs the polished pine floors were covered with Oriental rugs. The front and back halls were separated by red-velvet portieres, which also served as stage curtains for Zelda's dramatic performances. Both halls were lined with glass-doored bookcases filled with encyclopedias; sets of Shakespeare, Fielding, Thackeray, Dickens, Scott, Ouida, and Mark Twain; dictionaries; Latin and Greek classics; as well as histories and the children's old schoolbooks. In the library, there were more books, a piano, a victrola, and a large collection of records that included popular, classical, and operatic music—Bach, Brahms, Beethoven, Schumann, Chopin, Kreisler, Caruso, Scotti, Mary Garden, and Geraldine Farrar. The living room was furnished with inherited pieces of rosewood and mahogany. Among them were Daniel Sayre's marble-topped table and Senator Machen's carved secretary. On the way up the Cumberland River to Fort Donaldson, a Yankee gunboat had fired at the Confederate flag flying from the Machen home and nicked a corner of the secretary, about which Minnie had too much sentiment to have it repaired. One of Musidora Morgan's wedding gifts, a mezzotint of Napoleon bidding farewell to his army, hung on the living-room wall, while over the mantelpiece there was an oil portrait of Miss Minnie's mother. On the opposite side of the hall, there was a large dining room, which was also furnished with family heirlooms, and an adjoining pantry and kitchen.

There were five bedrooms upstairs—comfortable and cheerful, with starched muslin curtains that let in the sunlight, freshly papered walls, and rag rugs covering the Japanese matting on the floors. They were informally and conservatively decorated, not by whims of a professional decorator but by Miss Minnie's innate good taste. Zelda's bedroom was the front one above the porch. It overlooked the grounds of the landlady's estate, a large white house surrounded by boxwood, crepe myrtle, camellias, and kiss-me-at-the-gate. Behind it, there was a pigeon cote, a greenhouse, a grape arbor, and an orchard, where flowers were planted among the fruit trees. Zelda's bedroom was the smallest in the house, but it commanded the finest view. A large wardrobe compensated for its lack of a closet. The bed was painted white and covered with a Marseilles counterpane. Flanking the bed stood a slender slat-backed rocking chair and a small desk inherited from her grandmother Sayre. The walls were papered with a pink floral design on a white background, which matched the chintz-covered dressing table between the front windows. Years later Zelda was to remember the colors of that little room and its garden view in her paintings, and the patter of rain on the tin roof under its windows in her autobiographical novel, *Save Me the Waltz*.

Between keeping house, rearing four daughters and a son, continuing her music and her reading, and tending the pink geraniums, the yellow peonies, the purple verbenas, and the potted ferns of which Judge Sayre was so proud, Miss Minnie was kept busy at home. Although she had a cook, a laundress, a yardman, and a nurse for the children, she had little time for clubs and parties. Besides, as she once said, "Montgomerians are fiercely jealous of their privacy." So she and the judge led quiet, uneventful lives at home with their children—until Zelda came along.

When Zelda was born, Marjorie was fourteen; Rosalind, eleven; Clotilde, nine; and Anthony, six. On the whole, all the young Sayres, including Zelda, were good children—a healthy, happy brood, handsome, high-spirited, and well-formed. They grew up without getting into serious trouble or suffering any severe illnesses. Zelda's childhood diseases were confined to measles and chicken pox, and her only physical defect was not revealed until after her death, when a specialist to whom she had gone for treatment of her sinus trouble told Miss Minnie that Zelda had no retina in one eye. The defect in her eye probably explained why she sometimes squinted when looking at things. As she grew older, she frequently complained of eyestrain, but she refused to wear glasses or to make use of her lorgnette.

As the baby of the family, Zelda became her mother's favorite. Miss Minnie, she claimed, had breast-fed her until she was old enough to bite a chicken bone in two. Accustomed to the abundance of plantation life at Mineral Mount, Miss Minnie set such a lavish table that Judge Sayre complained she would send them to the poor house. Even so, Zelda was finicky about her food, and if she did not like what she saw on her plate, she would sulk and refuse to eat. At such times, Miss Minnie would humor her by finding something in the icebox or the pantry that Zelda could not resist. Since the Sayres were more affluent in Zelda's childhood than they had been when her elder sisters came along, she had more than they did in the way of dancing lessons, party dresses, and trips to the circus. But she was never as spoiled at home as Scott liked to believe.

Whether from a lack of discipline in her early years, a biological mutation, or the unconscious influence of her name, taken from that of a gypsy queen that her mother had run across in a novel, from the beginning Zelda was like a wild grapevine grafted onto the traditional stock in a Confederate vineyard, and one with a rare, intoxicating flavor of its own.

Her mother had been carefully schooled in the axioms of Victorian etiquette that we called the "no ladies": no lady ever sits with her limbs crossed (and limbs, it was; legs was still a four-letter word); no lady ever lets her back touch the back of the chair; no lady ever goes out without a clean linen handkerchief in her purse; no lady ever leaves the house until the last button on her gloves is fastened; no lady ever lets her bare foot touch the bare floor, and so forth.

Miss Minnie tried dutifully to instill these rules of conduct in her daughters. Zelda's sisters, who were more conventional than she was, endeavored to follow their mother's precepts, but Zelda saw more humor than value in such old-fashioned notions and not only laughed at them but also deliberately defied them. She went barefoot, climbed trees, and fought in chinaberry wars. Once, while Anthony and his friends were trying to build a radio station in the backyard, she created so much static that a free-for-all between her and the boys broke the peace of the neighborhood.

Her rebellion against parental discipline began in her cradle; her revolt against conventional authority, on the day she entered Chilton Grammar School, which had been named for her great uncle, but which was later known as Sayre Street School. After her first day of classes there, she came home, declared that it was worse than prison, and refused to go back until Judge Sayre threatened to use the peach-tree switch that he kept in the hall closet. Disciplining her was impossible for Miss Minnie and difficult for the judge because, despite her rebelliousness, she was a lovable, appealing child, who, though she sometimes defied her parents, adored them as long as she lived.

Even as a child, she had magic, a charm and sweetness as spontaneous as the sparkle of champagne. Edmund Wilson once observed that the "fairies had been tipsy at the christening of Zelda . . . and had heedlessly squandered on her, with a minimum of stabilizing qualities, choice gifts." She was capricious and imaginative and, like all imaginative children, given to exaggeration. For example, once when her mother asked her why she was working so hard at a trench in her sandpile, she replied in all seriousness, "I'm digging me an en-NOR-mous river."

The original amusements that she devised fascinated other children. She invented games for them to play, told them enthralling stories, and led them about like the little Pied Piper that she was. Even after she was grown, she would spend hours playing with the little girl next door. Years later the child said, "I used to love to play with Zelda. She didn't look down on me as little but made me feel as big as she." Although my first and last memories of Zelda are separated by forty years, they have a common denominator in the impression of her as a rare person, compassionate, thoughtful, and tender, especially with children.

Between her house and mine stood the red-brick masses and the playgrounds of the Chilton School. The grounds of the school were surrounded by a low wall, where our nurses used to sit with us after they had bathed and dressed us for the afternoon. In those days, Sayre Street Hill, which ran from the Chilton School to the Jewish synagogue, was to the intrepid roller-skaters of 1910 what the runs of St. Moritz are to ski buffs today—a test of nerve and skill. I watched Zelda sweep down and make an easy, graceful turn just in time to avoid the cobblestones in front of the synagogue. On being given my first pair of skates, I decided that I could do it, too. Shrugging off my nurse's warning that I was a novice on skates and too young to "follow after" Zelda, who was five years my senior, I took off down the hill. Faster and faster, I careened along with no idea how to stop, headed straight for the cobblestones and a bad fall. Zelda overtook me, going at breakneck speed. Some fifty feet short of disaster, she put her arm around me and swung me out of danger. "Listen," she said, "you'll break your neck. Wait till a dray comes along to pull us back up the hill; then you can go down holding on to me until you learn how to make the turn."

From then on I "followed after" Zelda in the neighborhood games. Her house was a mecca for her playmates. There were costume plays, with the back hall for a stage. Behind her house lay a large open field that provided green moss to carpet shadow boxes, low-limbed sugarberry trees in which to build houses, and a grapevine for the forerunners of Tarzan to swing on. Although we were required to be home by dark, on the long summer evenings we were allowed to "play out" in the twilight after supper—a great time for playing I-spy, hide-and-seek, and prisoner's base, or for catching fireflies to put in bottles, or for waiting for the workmen to put new carbons in the arc lights and give us the old ones. Sometimes, before the Country Club or Bell Street pools were built, we would slip off to Catoma Creek or go swimming in the Y.W.C.A.'s musty, chlorinated pool, where Zelda had taught me how to dive. Then, when the weather began to get cool, we would rifle the pantry for cookouts behind our carriage house.

In one of his periods of affluence, my grandfather had given my mother an elegant brougham and a pair of spanking bays. Promptly, the next Saturday, Zelda came over to see "Miss Susie's glass carriage," as she called it. "If I had a pumpkin and a magic wand, I bet I could make me one," she observed.

While the coachman was hitching up, we opened the doors to see the steps let down, bounced on the cushions, and climbed up on the box. Zelda was a daredevil as well as a tomboy. "Let's take a ride," she suggested, gathering up the reins.

"All right." I took the whip.

"Naw, you don't. You chillun can't handle dem horses. Come down off dat box, don't I'll call yo mama," the coachman shouted after us. He tried to grab the bridle of the horse nearest him, but he was too late. Down the driveway we plunged, and had Zelda been as expert with the reins as I was with the whip, that probably would have been our last ride. Luckily for us, she cut too short as she turned out the drive, and the rear wheel struck the carriage block and stopped us long enough for the coachman to overtake us. He caught the reins that Zelda dropped as the jolt all but knocked us off the box; and, beyond a bent axle, there was no damage done.

My father and Zelda's were on the Supreme Court of Alabama together for almost twenty years, and they frequently played chess together in the evenings. We were then living on Court Street, a few blocks from the Sayres and near enough for Zelda to run over to watch the game after she finished her lessons. She would stand for a while with her feet apart and her hands behind her back, studying the board as if she were deeply interested in the strategy. Then she would call me aside and whisper, "Deck the heeltaps." It was some time before I discovered that what she was bidding for were the remains of the mint juleps with which Father and Judge Sayre began their games. Zelda's ploy was to have me take the silver julep cups back to the pantry before the butler came for the tray so that she could drain the heeltaps and eat the bourbon-flavored mint while Judge Sayre was too absorbed in figuring out where to move his knight to notice what she was doing.

The judge might have been another Paul Morphy had he concentrated on chess instead of law. Father once said that Judge Sayre had the most brilliant mind he had ever known. He had an encyclopedic store of general knowledge; he was an authority on Coke and Blackstone; his opinions were never overruled; his decisions were used in textbooks from Harvard to Alabama. His word was law—to everybody except Zelda. "Old Dick," as she called him, foreshortening his middle name, had a dignity and a reserve that presented an irresistible temptation to her; she could never resist teasing him when he found himself checkmated or spilled his coffee in concentrating on the chessboard.

Zelda shrugged off her father's reprimands with a lighthearted "Ishkabibble," for he was not the stern disciplinarian that he has been depicted as being. He had instilled his own principles of honor, integrity, and kindness into his children, and he expected them to be guided by them. But if they were guilty of misconduct, he punished them because Miss Minnie was too soft-hearted to do it. Although his parental authority sometimes irked Zelda, she looked up to him and respected him as she did no other man. His conduct was impeccable; he never smoked, and drank only an occasional mint julep or eggnog; his personal habits were Spartan, even austere. He was a selfless man, who lived for his family and his work. To Zelda, as Alabama said of Judge Beggs in *Save Me the Waltz*, her father "was a living fortress" in a time when all too many people hewed "the battlements of life from compromise, erecting their impregnable keeps from judicious submissions, fabricating their philosophical drawbridges from emotional retractions, and scalding marauders in the boiling oil of sour grapes."

Noble Seay, who was secretary of the Supreme Court from 1915 to 1922, remembers Judge Sayre as "one of the most honorable and courteous gentlemen I ever knew. He did rough drafts of his opinions in pencil on a foolscap pad, but when he wrote a letter, which he seldom did, his handwriting looked like copperplate script, precise, neat, and correct as the judge himself." Some people, he added, thought the judge was unapproachable, probably because he was very nearsighted and often did not recognize his friends on the street unless he was wearing his pince-nez. He would ride the streetcar to the Capitol in the morning, but in the evening he walked as far as the Court Square fountain and caught the trolley there. On the way he would stop and chat with everyone he knew. In fact, despite his quiet, reserved manner, he was a gracious man with a keen sense of humor and a genial wit. "I'll never forget an opinion that Judge Sayre wrote," Mr. Seay continued. "The case involved the title to some real estate that depended upon a conveyance, made by a man to his wife before, as the judge put it, 'they had settled down between the cold sheets of matrimony.'"

"Judge Sayre thought it was ungentlemanly and beneath his dignity to go out on the streets and ask for votes," Judge Robert Harwood said, "so his friends had to campaign for him and work like the devil to keep him from being defeated." Evidently, they worked loyally and well, for Judge Sayre served on the Supreme Court from 1909 until his death in 1931.

Perhaps, unfortunately for Zelda, the judge's "superiority absolved his children from the early social efforts necessary in life to construct strongholds for themselves." She had inherited blue blood, a brilliant mind, and, if not riches, at least social and economic security, but she never acquired the defense mechanisms necessary to protect herself from the people she charmed —and whose pursuit of her hastened her downfall.

In the Montgomery of her childhood, Zelda had no need of defense mechanisms. Like Rome, the capital of Alabama was built upon the seven hills, and, like Rome, it had a classical dignity, a respect for law and order, for authority and degree. Its sleepy oak-vaulted streets held no threat of violence by day or terror by night.

Montgomery was the heart of the Deep South, and the fountain on Court Square was the heart of Montgomery. From it radiated the main streets of the town. Above Court Square, which had been paved with cobblestones that had been brought over as ballast in the sailing ships, the streets running north and south were named for the naval heroes of the United States; those running east and west, for its Presidents. On the corner of Court Square and Commerce Street, which led down to the river, stood the Moses Building, a six-story building with a tall pyramidal tower, where Judge Sayre had his office in the early days.

From his office windows, Zelda could watch the circus parades when Ringling Brothers came to town, see the steamboats loading at the slides along the river, or look across the street at the people coming and going from the Exchange Hotel. It was a historic old hostelry that appealed to her imagination. From its balcony on February 16, 1861, William L. Yancey had introduced Jefferson Davis, President-elect of the Confederacy, to the crowd in the square below by crying out, "The man and the hour have met." After the war Sidney Lanier, whose family owned the hotel, acted as night clerk there and amused the guests by playing his silver flute for them. Across from the Exchange stood the Winter Building, from which the orders to fire on Fort Sumter had been sent; below it on Commerce Street a tablet marked the site of Freeney's Tavern, where Montgomerians had entertained Lafayette when he visited their city in 1825.

If she looked in the opposite direction, Zelda could see the slender spire of St. John's Episcopal Church, the cathedral of the Confederacy, where Jefferson Davis and his wife had attended services. To the southeast of the church, at the end of Dexter Avenue, rose the steep slopes of Goat Hill. Originally, Andrew Dexter had built a shelter there for his goats, by means of which a young nephew of Dr. Lyman Beecher, the Boston theologian, found a novel method of distributing the innumerable religious tracts that his uncle sent him. He caught as many of the goats as he could, stuck a tract on each of their horns, and sent them forth to spread the Gospel. Subsequently, when the most beautiful Statehouse in the South had been built there, crowning the green hillock with a magnificent Greek Revival building, the Capitol complex retained the name of Goat Hill. In Zelda's childhood she found Goat Hill a more fascinating place than Oak Park, Pickett Springs, or the fair grounds. The imposing dome of the Capitol and its gleaming white porticos, supported by Corinthian and Doric columns, held her spellbound. The piles of Minié balls at the top of the long flight of stone steps that led up to it, the cannons mounted on the lawn, the Confederate Monument on the north side, and the great circular staircase in the rotunda served her and Tallulah Bankhead, who was then living in Montgomery with her aunt, as a gymnasium for their athletic performances.

Father and Judge Sayre had their offices on the second floor of the Capitol, just above the Department of Archives and History, over which my cousin, Dr. Thomas M. Owen, and his wife, Marie Bankhead, Tallulah's aunt, presided. Consequently, I had a ringside seat for Zelda's and Tallu's performances on Goat Hill. Even in those days, both of them had a dash, a style, and a daring that left me wide-eyed and open-mouthed with admiration, for Zelda and Dutch, as we called Tallulah, were personalities and performers long before they became famous. Tallulah specialized in cart wheels, back bends, mimicry, and song-and-dance routines. Although Zelda never learned to play the piano or even the ukulele, she loved to sing and dance. She began taking dancing lessons when she was in her nonage and became a star in the local dance recitals. When she appeared in one of them at the Grand Theater, she and two other little girls in pointed hats and pink tarleton tutus came on stage jumping ropes. One of the other performers, Elizabeth Crommelin, remembers that when the ropes knocked off their hats, she and her companion fled into the wings in tears; but before Zelda could retreat, her feet tangled in her rope; and she took a pratfall. She sat there for a moment and laughed. Then, quick-witted even as a child, she scrambled up and took one tumble after another until her pratfalls appeared to be part of her act and won a round of applause.

Zelda was ingenious as well as quick-witted. She invented a novel way of escaping the tedium of baby-sitting with Noonie, her young niece, by climbing up a tree with the child and leaving her there, too high for the little girl to come down alone. "Listen," she would say, "you just stay right there till I get back, and I'll buy you some candy." Then Zelda would go off to a movie. When she returned with a bag of peppermint jawbreakers, she would make Noonie "cross her heart and swear not to tell" before she would give her the candy.

As a member of the Montgomery Board of Education, Judge Sayre felt that his children should be educated in the public schools, so Zelda did not go to Miss Gussie Woodruff's dames' school with Tallulah and me or to the Margaret Booth School, a finishing school for girls run by Lawton Campbell's aunt. Moreover, Zelda pitied us for being incarcerated there without any boys around to make life interesting.

After she graduated from the Sayre Street Grammar School, Zelda entered Sidney Lanier High School, where she took four years of the classic curriculum—history, English literature, mathematics, geography, physiology, physics, chemistry, French, and Latin. Her schoolmates there recall that she usually wore blue or white middy blouses to school. They found her amusing, vivacious, outgoing, and full of mischief. Her boon companions in her high-school days were Eleanor Browder, who looked like one of Modigliani's better models, and Livye Hart, whose dark gypsy coloring contrasted with Zelda's blond beauty. On Friday nights, the three of them went with their dates to the teen-age dances over May's confectionery—famed for the pineapple drops and sugared perfume balls of which Zelda was so fond—or to the pavilions at Oak Park and Pickett Springs. Only later did she and the crowd of which she was the ringleader and center of attention begin to go to the dances at the Country Club and in the auditorium over the old city hall, an ancient building that Zelda described in *Save Me the Waltz*:

> It was from there the first Alabama regiment had left for the Civil War. The narrow balcony sagged on spindle iron pillars and there were holes in the floor. The sloping stairs led down through the city markets: Plymouth Rocks in cages, fish and icy sawdust from the butcher shop, garlands of negro shoes and a doorway full of army overcoats.

At the end of her senior year at Sidney Lanier, Zelda made a speech in a wartime pageant given before the Rotary Club, in which she was supposed to say, "In these peaceful pursuits, I have been interrupted by the tragedy of war." At "I have been interrupted," she faltered and repeated like a record stuck in a worn groove, "interrupted . . . interrupted . . . interrupted . . ." Not at all abashed, with one of her brilliant smiles, she bowed her way toward the wings and brought down the house with her exit line, "Gentlemen, I have been permanently interrupted."

By the time Zelda finished high school, she was the only child at home. Marjorie, Rosalind, and Clotilde had married; Anthony had gone to work in Mobile as a civil engineer; and the pleasant house on Pleasant Avenue seemed deserted and lonely to Zelda.

Before her marriage to Minor W. Brinson, Marjorie had taught school and amused herself by making delicate pen-and-ink sketches. After Rosalind graduated from Sidney Lanier, she worked as society editor of the Montgomery *Journal* until her marriage in 1917 to Newman Smith. Two months later Clotilde married John M. Palmer. Zelda wanted to have a good time with her crowd before she settled down to work or marriage. Some critics have thought it odd that she never took a job. Since it was unnecessary for any of the Sayre girls to go to work, Marjorie and Rosalind worked because they wanted to, and Montgomerians found it equally odd that they did.

As Zelda pointed out, " 'Those girls,' people said, 'think they can do anything and get away with it.' " At least, Zelda was convinced that she could, and her pranks and quips made the neighbors' tongues wag. She was, in her own phrase, "an excitement-eater." One of her favorite stories about herself involved her efforts to break the monotony of a hot, still, summer afternoon such as she described so vividly in *Save Me the Waltz*:

> She had a strong sense of her own insignificance; of her life's slipping by while June bugs covered the moist fruit in the fig trees with the motionless activity of clustering flies on an open sore. The barrenness of the dry bermuda grass about the pecan trees crawled imperceptibly with tawny caterpillars. The matlike vines dried in the autumn heat and hung like empty locust shells from the burned thickets about the pillars of the house. The sun sagged yellow over the grass plots and bruised itself on the clotted cotton-fields. The fertile fields that grew things in other seasons spread flat from the roads and lay prone in ribbed fans of broken discouragements. Birds sang dissonantly. Not a mule in the fields nor a human being on the sandy roads could have borne the heat between the concave clay banks and the mediant cypress swamps that divided the camp from the town—privates died of sunstroke.

On this particular afternoon, everyone else in Montgomery seemed to be taking a nap. In desperation, Zelda called the fire department to come at once. "I didn't want to set the house on

Something Enchanted · 21

fire," she said, "yet I didn't want to disappoint the firemen, so I just climbed up on the roof, kicked the ladder down, and let the heroes rescue me."

After the outbreak of World War I, the Yankee soldiers invaded Montgomery for a second time. To the dismay of her family and friends, Zelda immediately struck up an *entente cordiale* with the officers in the cantonments. Miss Minnie shook her head over some of Zelda's new admirers. "The bottom rail's on top now," she sighed. When the young officers with whom Zelda was going to a dance stopped in front of her house and blew for her to join them in the car, Judge Sayre declared that no gentleman would call for a lady in any such manner and forbade her to go with them until they came properly to the door to escort her to the car. If Zelda was irked by her father's old-fashioned ideas, she was also a bit ashamed of some of her friends when she compared them with him.

Steeped in their classical manners and Confederate traditions, the old families in Montgomery were as startled by the new wave of Yankee ideas and customs as their descendants are today by hippie culture and psychedelic parties. Prewar Montgomery moved to the stately measures of the minuet. With the arrival of the cantonments, the tempo was stepped up. Two years before, *Variety* had reported the discovery in Chicago of the so-called "jazz band," which "seldom plays regulated music." Dixieland jazz, said to have originated in Storyville, the red-light district of New Orleans, was nothing new in Montgomery; but it was strictly tabooed there by the better class of whites—and blacks—until the Yankee soldiers' enthusiasm for it elevated it, along with the Shimmy, the Bunny Hug, and the Buzzard Lope, from the brothel to the ballroom. However, unthinkable as it might be to the elder generation that gently bred girls, psychically laced into the "no ladies" stays, should take to such outlandish steps and to such syncopated music, they nevertheless adopted both with the same gusto that teen-agers of the sixties had for the Slop, the Mashed Potato, and rock bands.

Zelda would have been the last to deny that she danced cheek to cheek and did the Shimmy, the Charleston, and the Black Bottom. If she gave a demonstration of the Hula at a midterm dance at the University of Alabama, had not Alice Roosevelt, the President's daughter, been similarly criticized for doing the same thing at a party in Hawaii? She rode behind her admirers from Camp Sheridan on their motorcycles with her arms around them, raised her hemlines to the knee, bobbed her hair, smoked, tippled, and kissed the boys good-bye. In her autobiographical novel, she tells of kissing an officer whom she calls "Dogface," who had asked her to marry him. When she turned him down, he asked, "Then why did you kiss me?"

"Because," she replied, "I had never kissed a man with a moustache before."

Again, there was her account of the night on which Judge Sayre saw her kiss her date good night. He ordered her to come in the house. "I won't have you carrying on in any such fashion, you little hussy," he said.

"Ishkabibble," Zelda retorted. "Isn't that the way hussies do?"

She spoke for herself in her "Eulogy of the Flapper" when she said:

> She flirted because it was fun to flirt and wore a one-piece bathing suit because she had a good figure, she covered her face with paint and powder because she didn't need it and she refused to be bored because she wasn't boring. She was conscious that the things she did were the things she had always wanted to do.

Zelda had a pink Annette Kellermann bathing suit, a daring thing in the pre-bikini days; but she swam in it at Roquemore's gravel pit, and not in the nude as the scandalmongers said. It is true, however, that once when her beaux slipped off from her because they wanted to swim in the buff, she followed them to the spot where they had undressed and tied their clothes in knots. One of Scott's biographers has alleged that "she was not above taking a swig of corn liquor when men circulated the bottle." But Zelda had champagne tastes, and she is far more likely to have sent one of them to fetch her a split of Pommery or a Sazarac cocktail than to have offended her nose with raw corn liquor, which smells, at best, as if it had been once drunk and involuntarily returned. Further, the evidence is against Scott and his critics when they intimate that Zelda was "a speed." Flirtation was an old Southern custom; "going the limit" was not. Zelda was a reigning beauty and "a knockout" in the paleolithic slang of the day, far too popular to have to "put out" for her beaux, far too shrewd in the tactics and strategy of popularity to grant her favors to one suitor and thereby alienate a regiment of them.

The foundation of the Confederates' house was land. Men of property insisted on the chastity of their womenfolk to insure the legitimacy of their heirs and assigns. Consequently, the technique of Southern ladies was to proceed so far and no farther; their brinksmanship did not "go the limit." Men have a word for such restraint, but no gentleman would use it of a lady, and this is no place for it. As long as she retained the equivocal virtue of "a technical virgin," under the "New Freedom" even a *jeune fille bien élevée* could proceed quite a distance, if she kept quiet about it. The sin was in the saying. Frequently, the gossip about Zelda snowballed from her own stories of her escapades. The aura of excitement that she created for herself drew admirers to her as the perfume of a flower does the bees.

Undeniably, as one of Scott's critics, Dr. John Kuehl, has pointed out in *The Apprentice Fiction of F. Scott Fitzgerald*, Zelda became the prototypal heroine, the *femme fatale*—as Scott himself became the hero, the *homme manqué*—of his fiction. On the other hand, she was never *La Belle Dame sans Merci* or the heartless charmer that Scott in his jealousy sometimes imagined her to be. Nor was she the "speed" that she liked to have people think her. She was simply an unusually attractive young girl, having a good time with her crowd—and usually in a crowd. Her friend and contemporary, Judge John P. Kohn, says that she was "attractive, vivacious, daring—and a dashing type. No one to my knowledge ever questioned her good reputation as to morals."

The Montgomery blades who rushed her, year in and year out, were all wellborn and wealthy. Among them were Leon Ruth, Peyton Spottswood Mathis, John Allen Sellers, Dan Cody, and Lloyd Hooper. By their reports, much of the criticism of Zelda was the malicious flowering of envy, jealousy, and disprized love. Hobart Fulton, a young newspaperman, who was working on the Montgomery *Advertiser* in Zelda's youth, called her ". . . one of the South's truly fine examples of feminine brains, beauty, and charm."

The pranks that gave rise to the talk about her were mischievous rather than vicious. For instance, one night when Lloyd Hooper had taken her to a dance, she pretended to be drunk and fell down on the floor. Since Lloyd could not rouse her, he picked her up and carried her to his car. Before he could open the door, she doubled up laughing at him for being taken in by her joke. Again, George Mark Wood has never forgotten how she startled him on a house party that he and she attended at White Water Lake. George was late in arriving. As he came up on the porch, someone yelled, "My God, look at Zelda Sayre! She hasn't got on a stitch!" George ran down through the thicket of elderberries to the lake. When he looked up and saw Zelda, she was standing on the diving board—wearing the pink one-piece bathing suit.

"She was the most popular girl at every dance," George added; "but it was no fun to dance with her, for you couldn't take two steps before somebody cut in on you." Although he knew her all her life, and they went around in the same crowd, he never dated her because he was working his way up in the bond business and did not feel that he had money enough to compete with the rich playboys who surrounded her.

One of her wealthy admirers had a Stutz Bearcat with a spotlight on the windshield—the ultimate status symbol in the teen-age world of that day. Zelda liked to borrow the car at night so that she could throw the light on the boys lounging in front of Harry's Place, the local "jelly joint," to see who was dating and who was not. Another favorite target for her spotlight was the couples parked in Boodler's Bend, a lovers' lane in a pecan orchard at the end of Court Street. Many of her choice stories were about her adventures in riding by Madam Helen St. Clair's studio and throwing the spotlight on boys that she knew as they entered the brothel.

In *Save Me the Waltz*, Zelda described a hot, humid summer in Montgomery, during which she could find nothing more exciting to do than to get another girl drunk by filling her bottle with gin at a baby party:

> "I'm so tired of just sitting on the porch and having dates and watching things rot."
>
> "It seems that you have plenty to do without corrupting others," her father said.

"Nothing to do but drink and make love," she commented privately.

When Zelda tired of courting, she used to borrow the Stutz Bearcat, fill it with her girlfriends, and take them for a ride. Sometimes they sang bawdy ballads, such as "Colombo," "Willie, the Weeper," or "The Bastard King of England." But if the evening star had risen and the blue dusk fallen, and the air was cool and damp and nostalgic with the fragrance of bays and magnolias, they would launch into "My Man," "Three o'Clock in the Morning," or some of the more plaintive songs that Montgomerians used to sing in those days:

> Sometimes between long shadows on the grass,
> The little truant waves of sunlight pass.

Or

> You said, and your voice was fretful,
> My mourning days are few.
> You called me 'Old Forgetful.'
> My God, if you only knew.

And so the summers passed for Zelda until she met Scott Fitzgerald, and he pointed out to her the way to a larger, more exciting life. As she danced with him that fall at the Beauvoir Club to the music of a ragtime band, she caught the beat and swing of the fabulous decade that lay ahead of her.

2. Spires and Gargoyles

A FELLOW PRINCETONIAN, Dale Warren, whose room in Little Hall faced the one occupied by Fitzgerald during his last year at the university, has described Scott as "definitely a status seeker," which he undeniably was. Consequently, he was utterly incapable of understanding the Sayres' complete lack of any social or financial pretense. Sure of their own position, and too sure of it to share Scott's "awe of high society" or his "reverence for the very rich," they lived simply, comfortably, and conservatively—so conservatively that they were sometimes embarrassed by Scott's imitations of Trimalchio.

Scott's lapses into ostentation and arrogance grew out of a deep-seated inferiority complex, which he himself once tried to analyze in a letter to John O'Hara:

> I am half black Irish and half old American stock with the usual exaggerated ancestral pretensions. The black Irish half of the family had the money and looked down on the Maryland side of the family who had, and really had, that certain series of reticences and obligations that go under the poor old shattered word "breeding" (modern form "inhibitions"). So being born in that atmosphere of crack, wisecrack and countercrack I developed a two-cylinder inferiority complex. So if I were elected King of Scotland

tomorrow after graduating from Eton, Magdalene to Guards, with an embryonic history which tied me to the Plantagenets, I would still be a parvenu. I spent my youth in alternately crawling in front of kitchen maids and insulting the great.

Fitzgerald had inherited an Irish imagination from his mother's side of the family along with all the "exaggerated ancestral pretensions" of his father's side. As a child, unable to come to terms with the shabby gentility of his parents' lives, he pretended that he was not their son, but the son of a king. To the astonishment of his playmates, he told them that he had been found on his mother's doorstep wrapped in a blanket to which was pinned a note that bore the royal arms of the House of Stuart.

The first time that I met Scott was in September 1918. Sara Haardt—later to become Mrs. H. L. Mencken—and I had stopped under the portico of the Capitol to chat with the watchman, Captain Paul Sanguinetti, a Corsican who had been a drummer boy in the Confederate Army. While we were talking to him, Zelda brought Scott out to show him the golden star on the steps that marked the spot where Jefferson Davis had taken office. She had no sooner introduced him to the three of us than he began to tell Captain Sanguinetti how his father, Edward Fitzgerald, who was then living near Rockville, Maryland, had rowed the Confederate scouts across the river to join General Jubal A. Early's troops as they marched toward Washington. Subsequently, on finding that I had spent the summer at Fort Howard, Lieutenant Fitzgerald told me that he was a great-grandson of Francis Scott Key, who had written "The Star-Spangled Banner" after watching the bombardment of Fort McHenry, which lies just across the Patapsco River from Fort Howard.

Like John Fitzgerald Kennedy, Scott claimed that his father's family could trace their ancestry back through a long line of Irish earls to the famous Gherardini brothers who had fled from Tuscany to the Emerald Isle after Dante was exiled from Florence. In this claim—as I discovered while I was doing research in the Florentine archives on Elizabeta Gherardini, better known today as Mona Lisa Gioconda—there was a great deal more truth than in Scott's version of his relationship to the author of "The Star-Spangled Banner." Francis Scott Key was actually a very distant relative, since he was merely the brother of Edward Fitzgerald's great-great-grandfather.

While Scott was quicker to bring up his family tree than any Confederate or New Englander, there was one of his father's relatives that I never heard him mention. This was Mrs. Mary Surratt, who was hanged after the assassination of President Lincoln as an accomplice of his murderer, John Wilkes Booth. Andrew Turnbull says that after Scott became famous, Edward Fitzgerald, who always believed that Mrs. Surratt was innocent, wanted Scott to write a book exonerating her; but Scott declined to do it because he said that she was either guilty or a fool, and in neither case was he interested.

In a moment of truth, however, Scott did confess that his family was "strictly 1850 potato famine Irish." His maternal grandfather, Phillip Francis McQuillan, was born in County Fermanagh, Ireland. At the age of nine, "P.F.," as he was called, immigrated to this country with his parents, who settled in Galena, Illinois, in 1845. As a young man "P. F." worked as a clerk in a clothing store there until he decided to seek his fortune in the booming Minnesota Territory that had just opened up in the North. The luck of the Irish was with him, and two years after he went to work in a grocery store in St. Paul, he was able to set up a business of his own. He began by trading supplies to the Indians in exchange for furs and deer hides, but he soon became a wholesale grocery dealer. By 1867 the firm of McQuillan and Beaupré was one of the largest wholesale companies in the Midwest, and the imposing four-story building that "P. F." built to house it was known as "The McQuillan Block."

Meanwhile, "P. F." had married his Galena sweetheart, Louisa Allen, and acquired a stable of horses, a pack of blooded foxhounds, and a Victorian mansion not far from that of the empire builder, James J. Hill, on St. Paul's fashionable Summit Avenue. There Louisa bore him five children, the eldest of whom was Molly McQuillan, Scott's mother. Molly was seventeen when her father died suddenly of Bright's disease. Although he was still a relatively young man, he left an estate of $266,289.49, which was quite a fortune in 1877.

Molly and Edward Fitzgerald were married in February 1890. They lived comfortably, even affluently, during the first years of their marriage. She and Edward were able to make a grand tour of Europe on their honeymoon, before they returned to settle down quietly in St. Paul; but during the depression of 1893, the small wicker-furniture factory of which Edward Fitzgerald was manager went bankrupt, and he was forced to take a job as a soap salesman for Procter and Gamble in Syracuse, New York. He began to drink more than he should have. Molly lost the two baby daughters that she had borne him before Scott arrived. She and Edward were so depressed and in such financial difficulties that she went home to St. Paul to have her third child.

Her first and only son, Francis Scott Key Fitzgerald, was born in a three-story brick house at 481 Laurel Avenue in St. Paul, on September 24, 1896, at 3:30 P.M. To Molly's delight, Scott was a sound, strapping baby. His baby book notes that he weighed ten pounds and six ounces at birth. The same source records that his first word was "Up!"—an utterance that was as prophetic of his early rise to fame as another one of his childish sayings was of the cause of his downfall: "Mother, when I get to be a big boy can I have all the things I oughtn't to have?"

In contrast to his mother, who had spent her childhood surrounded with every luxury and had made four trips abroad before she went again to spend her honeymoon there with Edward Fitzgerald, the McQuillans' money and their mansion with its towering cupola, stained-glass windows, and walks bordered with conch shells were the only affluent memories of Scott's early years.

In 1897 the Fitzgeralds' fortunes were at such low ebb that there was no way that little Scott could go except "Up!" His early childhood memories were shadowed by his moves from one town to another and from cheap flats and dreary boarding houses to run-down hotels. In Scott's Ledger, which is now in the Firestone Library at Princeton, he made a significant record of his first seven years:

1897 Dec. Bronchitis. A specialist was summoned but as his advice was not followed the child pulled through.
1898 Apr. Tiring of St. Paul he went east to Buffalo, New York, where with his parents, he installed himself at the Lennox.

Jan. He put on bloomers and went to Washington to spend the winter at the Cairo Hotel.

Apr. He returned to Buffalo and moved into a flat at Summer Street and Elmwood Ave.

June A persistent cough drove him to Orchard Park, New York. His mother feared consumption for him.

1899 Aug. He returned to St. Paul, visiting his grandmother McQuillan in her house on Summit Avenue near Dale Street.

1900 Jan. His mother presented him with a sister who lived only an hour.

Feb. He celebrated the new century by swallowing a penny and catching the measles. He got rid of both of them.

Mar. His parents sent him to school but he wept and wailed so they took him out again after one morning.

Sept. He had a party to celebrate his birthday. He wore a sailor suit about this time & told enormous lies to elder people about being really the owner of a real yatch [sic].

1901 Jan. He now went to Sarycuse [sic] where he took Mrs. Peck's apartment on East Genesee Street.

July His sister Annabel was born. His first certain memory is the sight of her howling on a bed.

Aug. Again he went to Atlantic City—where some Freudean [sic] complex refused to let him display his *feet*, so he refused to swim, concealing the real reason. They thought he feared the water. In reality he craved it. Also he attended the Buffalo exposition, the Pan American.

1902 Jan. He now moved from East Genessee Street to the "Kassou" on James Street. He remembers Jack Butler who had two or three fascinating books about the civil war [sic] and he remembers hitting a delivery boy with a stone and cutting his head.

May He went to Randolph to his aunt Elisa Delihant's place in Montgomery County, Maryland, where he made friends with a colored boy, name forgotten— name Ambrose.

Sept. He entered Miss Goodyear's school and he and another little girl, name unknown, worked out the phonetic spelling of C-A-T, thus becoming the stars of the primary class.

1903 Jan. Naturally he moved again—this time to a flat on East Willow Street. He begins to remember many things, a filthy vacant lot, the haunt of dead cats, a hair-raising buckboard, the little girl whose father was in prison for telling lies, a Rabelasian [*sic*] incident with Jack Butler, a blow with a baseball bat from the same boy—son of an army officer—which left a scar that will always shine in the middle of his forehead, a history of the United States which father [*sic*] brought me; he became a child of the American Revolution. Also he boxed with Edgar Miller the grocery man's son, egged on by his father. His nurse pierced her ear for rings and he howled.

Apr. He went south to Randolph again where he was a ribbon holder with Jack Garland at his Cousin Cecilia's wedding. After the wedding he turned on his two black friends Roscoe and Forrest and with the help of a bigger boy tried to tie them up with ropes. He remembers crying one day in fury over the irrevocability of a decision—he had decided once too often that he did *not* want to go down town. He found his father's soap boxes and apricots quite diverting. He went on a trip with his father.

July He wandered off on the Fourth of July & was spanked in consequence, so he sat on the porch with his breeches down and watched the fireworks. On Sunday mornings he walked down town in his long trousers with his little cane and had his shoes shined with his father. There was also a boy named Arnold who went barefooted [*sic*] in his yard and peeled plums.

Sept. He had a birthday party to which no one came. He moved to Buffalo, New York, possibly in consequence where he had a dog named "Beautiful Joe", a black cocker spaniel, and also a bycycle—a girl's bycycle [*sic*]. He was sent to school at the Holy Angel's convent under the arrangement that he need only go half a day and was allowed to choose which half. He lived at 29 Irving Place. . . . He remembers 'Nana',

Annabelle's nurse. . . . He remembers the attic where
he had a red sash with which he acted Paul Revere
. . . He fell under the spell of a Catholic preacher,
Father Fallon, of the Church of the Holy Angels. . . .

After his father was fired from his job with Procter and Gamble
in 1908, Scott was to remember many years later, according to
his own account: "That morning he [Edward Fitzgerald] had
gone out a comparatively young man, a man full of strength, full
of confidence. He came home that evening an old man, a completely broken man. He had lost his essential drive, his immacu-
lateness of purpose. He was a failure the rest of his days." But in
a sense, his father's dismissal came as a blessing to Scott because
the Fitzgeralds packed up and moved back to St. Paul. There
they rented a house at 599 Summit Avenue. The McQuillans
secured Edward Fitzgerald a job in the wholesale grocery business. Scott's mother entered him in St. Paul Academy, a fashionable day school, and in Professor Baker's dancing class, where
Fitzgerald formed the friendships that gave him the entree into
the higher echelons of St. Paul society that he so longed to have.

As Edmund Wilson, Scott's "intellectual conscience," observed,
"Fitzgerald is as much of the middle west of large cities and
country clubs as Sinclair Lewis is of the middle west of the
prairies and little towns." But, as Wilson pointed out, that milieu
was, despite its "sensitivity and eagerness for life without a sound
base of culture and taste; a brilliant structure of hotels and exhilarating social activities built not on the eighteenth century but
simply on the prairie."

At St. Paul Scott learned little Latin and less Greek, but he
went out for sports, starred in dramatics, and published his first
short stories in the school magazine, *Now and Then.* For all his
literary and dramatic triumphs, however, his years at St. Paul
were not particularly happy ones. For one thing, his multifold
extracurricular activities played havoc with his grades. Again, he
was far from popular with his schoolmates. One of them declared
that Fitzgerald "fairly effervesced with suppressed knowledge,
most of it erroneous." Another asked somewhat truculently
whether someone would not volunteer to "poison Scottie or find
some way to shut his mouth." Further, among the wealthy and

aristocratic boys there, Scott felt embarrassed by his father's failure and his mother's lack of style and grace.

Molly McQuillan was as gauche as she was kindly. Physically,
she was not attractive. Stout and broad for her height, she walked
with the unsteady gait of a turkey hen. Her clothes looked as if
they had come out of the ark. One of Scott's teachers described
her as "dressed like the devil and always coming apart." The
plumes of her ancient bonnets were forever awry and drooping as
though they had just been rained on. Her long, full skirts trailed
behind her, and their hems were always gray with the prairie
dust. Her hair would not stay up, and it sprouted in wisps that,
Andrew Turnbull reports, made the neighbors warn their daughters, "For heaven's sake comb up your hair or you'll look like Mrs.
Fitzgerald." There were dark circles around her pale-blue eyes.
Her sallow skin was prematurely wrinkled, and her upper lip
fitted down over her lower one like the lid of an old-fashioned
syrup pitcher. Her neighbors considered her decidedly eccentric,
Scott's schoolmates openly made fun of her, and he thought of her
as "an old peasant."

All things considered, Fitzgerald was not unhappy when his
low marks at St. Paul made it apparent that he could not enter
college unless some drastic changes were made; so his Aunt Annabelle offered to send him to Newman, a Catholic preparatory
school near Hackensack, New Jersey. There he was almost as
unpopular with his fellow students as he had been at St. Paul
Academy. The reasons for this are obvious in a curiously objective
self-appraisal that he later made:

> I had a definite philosophy which was a sort of aristocratic
> egotism. I considered that I was a fortunate youth capable of
> expansion to any extent for good or evil. I based this, not on latent
> strength, but upon facility and superior mentality. I thought there
> was nothing I could not do, except, perhaps, become a mechanical
> genius; still I traced special lines in which I considered I must
> excel, even in the eyes of others. *First:* Physically—I marked my-
> self handsome; of great athletic *possibilities*, and an extremely
> good dancer. Here I gave myself about eighty percent. *Second:*
> Socially—In this respect, my condition was, perhaps, magnetism,
> poise, and the ability to dominate others. Also I was sure that I

exercised a subtle fascination over women. *Third:* Mentally—Here I was sure that I had a clear field in the world. I was vain of having so much, of being so talented, ingenuous and quick to learn.

To balance this I had several things on the other side. *First:* Morally—I thought I was rather worse than most boys, due to latent unscrupulousness and the desire to influence people in some way, even for evil. I knew I was rather cold; capable of being cruel; lacked a sense of honor, and was mordantly selfish. *Second:* Psychologically—Much as I influenced others, I was by no means the "Captain of my Fate." I had a curious cross section of weakness running through my character. I was liable to be swept off my poise into a timid stupidity. I knew I was "fresh" and not popular with older boys. I knew I was completely the slave of my own moods, and often dropped into a surly sensitiveness most unprepossessing to others. *Third:* Generally—I knew that at bottom I lacked the essentials. At the least crisis, I knew I had no real courage, perseverance or self-respect.

So you see I looked at myself in two ways. There seemed to have been a conspiracy to spoil me and all my inordinate vanity was absorbed from that. All this was on the surface, however, and liable to be toppled over at one blow by an unpleasant remark or a missed tackle; and underneath it, came my own sense of lack of courage and stability. If I may push it farther still, I should say that, underneath the whole thing lay a sense of infinite possibilities that was always with me whether vanity or shame was my mood.

The most important event of Scott's years at Newman was not his modest triumph on the football field or his literary and dramatic achievements but his meeting with a man who was to be one of the formative influences of his life and to whom he paid tribute in the portrait of Father Darcy in *This Side of Paradise.* This was Father Sigourney Webster Fay, a Philadelphian who had left the Episcopal Church to become a Catholic and who brought to it all the ardor of a recent convert. Father Fay was a trustee of the Newman School, and he was soon to become its headmaster.

Although he was twenty-one years older than Scott, he soon became one of Fitzgerald's closest friends. Sigourney Fay was an intellectual and a priest, as well as a gourmet, a connoisseur of wines, a man of the world, and a friend of Shane Leslie, Henry Adams, and Cardinal Gibbons. He liked to say Mass in Greek and Celtic, to play the piano and sing sentimental songs, to gossip about the great and near great, and to tell sophisticated jokes.

Father Fay was almost an albino; his hair and eyelashes were snow-white, though he was only thirty-seven at the time that Scott first met him. His body was as soft and round as a butter-ball, his *embonpoint* bulged under his cassock, and his multiple chins cascaded over his clerical collar. He wore thick-lensed glasses; and the eyes behind them were red-rimmed and watery, but they often danced with merriment. His voice was high-pitched, and his conversation was punctuated with shrill giggles. If young Fitzgerald was at first startled by Fay's appearance, the priest soon won him over with his joviality and sympathy. He talked so fluently, so wisely, and so well, that he soon charmed Scott, who became his protégé, over whom he brooded and yearned as if Fitzgerald were his own son.

He understood Scott's virtues as well as his foibles. He once wrote him, "There are deep things in us and you know what they are as well as I do. We have great faith, and we have a terrible honesty at the bottom of us that all our sophistry cannot destroy, and a kind of childlike simplicity that is the only thing that saves us from downright wickedness." Scott had been drifting away from his Catholic upbringing, but under Father Fay's influence he felt a resurgent faith in the Church.

During Fitzgerald's last year at Newman, his financial situation was relieved by the death of his Grandmother McQuillan, who left a small legacy that enabled him to go to college. He had always longed to go to Princeton, but Princeton turned him down because of his low grades at Newman. With a determination that was characteristic of him in his youth, Scott then applied to take the entrance exams at Princeton. After he failed, he went to Princeton in September and took the re-exams, which he also failed to pass. Finally, he appeared before the Admissions Committee to appeal his case and, as he often said, literally talked his way into Princeton.

On September 24, 1913, his seventeenth birthday, he wired his mother: ADMITTED SEND FOOTBALL PADS AND SHOES

IMMEDIATELY PLEASE WAIT TRUNK. The football pads were doubtless the ones that he referred to ruefully almost twenty years later as "the shoulder pads worn for one day on the Princeton freshman football field." He told Andrew Turnbull that he actually "stuck it out three days and withdrew semi-honorably with an ankle injury." The Princeton squad was no place for a boy who was only five feet, eight inches tall, and who weighed less than a hundred and forty pounds.

After he found that he was too light for the football squad, he began to look for some other way to make a place in the sun for himself by analyzing the social structure of the campus and the relative merits of the clubs.

As soon as his trunk arrived, he put up his pennants and settled himself in "The Morgue," an off-campus rooming house at 15 University Place. Then he went over to sign up for the Triangle Club, a musical comedy group. He was given a part in the "all girl chorus line" of the next play, and during his freshman and sophomore years his collegiate interests were centered in the Triangle Club and its shows.

At the beginning of his second year, he moved from "The Morgue," where he lived with nine other freshmen, to a single room at 107 Patton Hall so as to have the peace and quiet in which to work on the Triangle show, *Fie! Fie! Fi-Fi!* Gregarious though he was, Scott discovered early that writers, with the exception of newspaper people, can work only in silence and solitude. Consequently, when he moved again in his junior year, he again found a single room, this time in Little Hall.

Scott's new room was on the second floor, overlooking the beautiful neo-Gothic campus in the direction of Blair Arch and the gymnasium, giving him a superb view of its "romantic battlements with their spires and gargoyles." However, the interior of the dormitory was not so attractive, particularly after Fitzgerald fell into the habit of scrawling notes on the walls of its murky hallway to Dale Warren, the occupant of the room across from his, who recalls:

> The messages usually read "Dale Warren wake me up at 7 sharp" or "D. W. don't forget to wake me" or "Don't let me miss my 8 o'clock." At first they concluded with a "Signed F. S. F."

Then with a mere "S." Then there was no signature at all. The scribbles were anywhere from two to six inches high with total disregard for alignment, and were often superimposed on one another. . . .

When one wall got used up he began on the other, but by that time I had taken my assignment as routine. My procedure was to shake and yank the prostrate figure on the bed, sometimes applying a wet towel, and after that to begin a search for socks, shoes and other articles that were scattered all over. He would pull on something while I would help him pull on something else. A razor was an unnecessary hurdle. . . .

Gradually I learned that my charge had come to Princeton by way of . . . Newman School, that his athletic ambitions had soon been squelched—the cult of the campus athlete was still in its heyday—but that he was now a "Big Man" in more refined circles: he was a leading light in the Triangle Club, and had been elected to the editorial board of the *Tiger.* He was a member of the Cottage Club. I also learned that he had missed class so often that he was close to the maximum number of cuts allowed, that he had forfeited his chance to participate in the extracurricular activities by which he set such store. . . .

To add to his sorrows that spring, Ginevra King, a beautiful brunette from a wealthy Chicago family, with whom he had fallen deeply in love at Christmas, began to write him about the well-heeled blades from Yale and Harvard who were showing her attentions that Scott could not afford in his straitened circumstances. It was then that he began to carouse in a way that temporarily put an end to his career at Princeton. In his account of Scott's junior year there, Dale Warren said:

Occasionally, I was conscious of his stumbling down the corridor when he came in, or dropping his pencil. His few hours' sleep seldom refreshed him, and I began to suspect that the morning haze might well be due to a beery night at the "Nass", Princeton's nearest equivalent to a den of iniquity. Once or twice I found him lying fully or partly clothed on top of the rumpled bedspread. One morning when he was not there at all I assumed that he was out-of-town, but later learned through the grapevine that he had spent the small hours of the night on the dewy grass somewhere out behind the Peacock Inn.

Number 32, Scott's room for a brief tenure, was the usual con-
glomeration of miscellaneous and probably secondhand furniture,
such a boon to undergraduates in an era when taste and any
pretense to elegance was considered effete. A Morris chair and
undoubtedly a few "mission" pieces. For all I remember, there may
have been a Maxfield Parrish on the walls and a banner or two,
but certainly not the array of pin-up girls of today. . . .

For all its convention and casual disarray, Number 32 differed in
certain respects from the typical student's room. There were very
adult books that I had never heard of, and that were certainly not
curricular reading. There were papers of various sorts and shapes
and sizes with writing on them, piled on the desk and chairs, even
mixed up with socks and shoes and crumpled pajamas on the floor.
The wastebasket overflowed. Obviously when other students were
reading their history assignments or plugging away at calculus, he
was experimenting with Triangle lyrics, working over a skit for the
Tiger or a piece for the highbrow *Lit* [*The Nassau Literary Magazine*].

As a result of his work on the *Nassau Lit*, Fitzgerald came
under the influence of Edmund Wilson, who was then its editor.
Wilson was more mature and far more widely read and cultivated
than Scott, though he was only a class ahead of him. Fitzgerald
admired his erudition and deferred to his taste and judgment in
literary matters. Through his friendship with Wilson and John
Peale Bishop, Scott began to take an interest in prosody and to
write serious poetry of his own. That, however, did not prevent
him from writing the witty lyrics for *Fie! Fie! Fi-Fi!*—the Triangle show, in which he competed with Lawton Campbell for the
privilege of writing the script, only to have Walker Ellis rewrite
the book and sign it, leaving Scott only credit for the lyrics.

In later years, whenever Scott wanted to provoke Zelda, he had
only to bring out the photographs of him taken for that Triangle
show. Dale Warren says:

> I remember a day in the ramshackle offices of the *Daily Prince-
> tonian* . . . when one of the editors, Alec McKaig, blew in flourish-
> ing a sheaf of glossies of a breath-taking siren, and asked us to
> name her. One said Marilyn Miller, another Justine Johnson, and a
> third Ann Pennington. We were all wrong. It was F. Scott Fitzger-
> ald photographed as a chorus girl to publicize the upcoming
> Triangle Show.

Turnbull notes that people remarked that Scott and Zelda "looked enough alike to be brother and sister . . . ." Although there was a slight resemblance between them in that they were both blond and handsome, with clear features and a well-scrubbed look, their likeness to each other was not sufficient to explain the old Triangle photograph of Scott as a chorus girl that recently appeared in a French magazine, *Marie Soir*, captioned as Zelda Sayre, the girl that Scott Fitzgerald fell in love with.

The Triangle show opened without Scott, Warren continued:

> Ironically, although he had written most of it, he had been declared ineligible [because of his grades] to take part or to go on the coveted Christmas trip [with the Triangle Show].
>
> Disappointment, discouragement, overindulgence, late hours with pencil and paper, and increased worry over his academic standing all ganged up and in November landed him in the infirmary, knowing that he would have to repeat his junior year. To save face, always important to him, he voluntarily "withdrew" until the following fall, and went home to St. Paul to recuperate and lick his far too many wounds.

Scott returned to Princeton after his first "crack-up," saddened by the loss of Ginevra King, who had thrown him over for a wealthy suitor, sobered by the failures of the past year, which had cost him a chance at the Triangle presidency, and confused by the latent Catholicism that Father Fay had stirred in him. For a time, he went to Mass regularly and kept the fast days. He even began to talk of taking the orders and becoming a priest. But after the United States declared war on Germany and his fellow Princetonians began to apply for commissions, Scott changed his mind and decided to go into the army. Since he could not apply for a commission until he reached the age of twenty-one, Father Fay, who hoped to be sent on a secret mission to Russia, suggested that Scott go with him as his aide. To the disappointment of both of them, the priest's plans fell through, and Fitzgerald stayed on at Princeton.

During his last year there, at Father Fay's instance, Scott began a novel called "The Romantic Egotist." He frequently visited Fay at Newman to talk about the progress of the novel or to sit by the fire and sip port while the priest either read aloud from his favorite poets, Wilde and Swinburne, or told some of the after-dinner stories that had given him the reputation of a brilliant raconteur. Father Fay introduced his protégé to Shane Leslie, who was not only the son of a baronet and a cousin of the Churchills but who had also attended Eton and Cambridge, had studied at the Sorbonne, and had known Tolstoy and Rupert Brooke—all of which added up to make him "the most romantic figure" the young man from Minnesota had ever met.

Fay took Scott up the Hudson River to visit the wealthy and beautiful Mrs. Winthrop Chanler, who had built a private chapel on the grounds of her estate for the priest's use. Mrs. Chanler was a cousin of Edith Wharton, the mother of Teddy Chanler, and a friend of Stephen Parrott, whom Scott had known at Newman. All that went into the mill was grist for Scott. Before many months, Stephen, who was known in college as "Peevie," appeared in *This Side of Paradise* as Stephen Palms, Mrs. Chanler as Mrs. Lawrence, and Fay as Father Darcy.

At the end of October the arrival of Fitzgerald's commission cut short his visits to Father Fay, his trips to New York for tea dances at the Plaza and the Club de Vingt with a girl from Westover or Farmington "collected from under the clock at the Biltmore," his hilarious evenings with companions at Bustanoby's or Reisenweber's, his curfew nightcaps at the Nass, and his quiet strolls along the banks of the old canal, reading poetry or humming "Poor Butterfly" and "Love Sends a Little Gift of Roses." It was the end of many things, and he expressed the nostalgia he felt at leaving the spires and gargoyles of Princeton in the epilogue to Book One of *This Side of Paradise*, a prose version of a poem of his that had been printed in *The Nassau Literary Magazine* in May 1917.

Nevertheless, Fitzgerald lost no time in signing his oath of allegiance and sending it back because, as he wrote his mother on November 14, 1917, his pay began the day he signed it. Then he ordered a uniform from Brooks Brothers and joined the campus drill squad. Dale Warren said:

> In his uniform he [Scott] looked every inch the officer, a contrast indeed to the "chorus girl" pictures of two years before. Much has been made of his effeminate appearance, but feminine would be closer to the mark, as it was of John Barrymore of the striking and

quite similar profile. He was blonde, pale, sallow, and often looked "washed-out," but with it all went a buoyancy and tensile strength. An agile and adroit parlor-snake if there was ever one, but yet something more.

In November Fitzgerald was ordered to report to Fort Leavenworth for his officers' training. Before he left Princeton, he took the manuscript of "The Romantic Egotist" to Dean Gauss, whom he had asked to recommend it to Scribner's, Gauss's publisher. After reading it Gauss not only refused to do this but tried to persuade Fitzgerald not to publish it. Scott replied that he wanted to see it published before he was killed in the war and took the manuscript with him to the training camp.

Fort Leavenworth was a dusty post in the midst of a Kansas prairie. To "an adroit and agile parlor-snake" the training there was durance vile. He had to sleep on an army cot in the barracks with fifteen men and keep all his clothes, souvenirs, books, and papers in a locker at the foot of his bed. His captain was a hard-working, hard-driving West Pointer, Ike Eisenhower. Ike brooked no nonsense from a trainee with more literary than military ambition, who scribbled away at a novel during the lectures on "Small Problems of Infantry," and who concealed pieces of stove pipe in his field kit to lighten the load. Despite the fact that Captain Eisenhower constantly put him on report and penalized him, Scott made the best of his three months at Fort Leavenworth. He spent his spare time working on his novel in the smoke-filled officers' club, unfazed by the chatter, the rattling of ice in the glasses, or the rustling of newspapers around the table. "I would begin work at it every Saturday afternoon at one and work like mad until midnight," he said. "Then I would work on it from six Sunday morning until six Sunday night, when I had to report back to barracks." In this way he had finished "The Romantic Egotist" before he left Fort Leavenworth and sent the manuscript to Shane Leslie, who, at Father Fay's request, had promised to submit it to Scribner's. But before forwarding it to the publishers, Leslie had to spend ten days correcting the grammar, spelling, and punctuation.

In February Scott was sent to Camp Taylor, Kentucky. Ten weeks later he was ordered to Camp Gordon, Georgia. In June he was transferred to Camp Sheridan, near Montgomery, Alabama. The South was terra incognita to Scott; Montgomery both puzzled and fascinated him. The telluric unity of the planter's world lay concealed by the sharp contrasts that met his eyes. A brilliant sun cast high lights and deep shadows. Broad savannas suddenly became rolling hills. Tropical vegetation—century plants, palmettos, bananas, and night-blooming cereus grew side by side with tulips, violets, roses, and other homely flowers.

As the first capital of the Confederate States of America, Montgomery was an international city, coequal with London, Rome, or Athens—and in the eyes of its proud citizens, *primus inter pares*. In Zelda's youth it combined the attractions of North and South, city and country, white and Negro, a former world capital and a quaint Southern town. Scott definitely preferred the variety of Montgomery to the monotony of Camp Sheridan, and he spent all his spare time in town. He was constantly in search of some amusement to divert his mind from his troubles. For shortly after having arrived at the camp, a letter overtook him announcing Ginevra King's marriage. Then, in August, Scribner's sent back "The Romantic Egotist," suggesting that he make a number of revisions and return it to them. Scott made the corrections that they had asked for and sent the manuscript back to them, but they again rejected it. The first time I saw him, he told me that he wanted Mencken to see "The Romantic Egotist," and he was thinking of sending the manuscript to *The Smart Set*, which H.L. was then editing. However, no record exists to show that Mencken ever saw it until it was rewritten and published as *This Side of Paradise*.

On January 10, 1919, while Scott was sitting with Zelda on a sofa before the fire in her living room, he suddenly began to shiver with a premonition of disaster. Next morning he received a telegram informing him that Fay had died of influenza during the epidemic. Denied the devotion that Fay had lavished on him, Scott became increasingly dependent on Zelda for love and affection.

To add to his troubles that winter, Peyton Mathis and John Sellers, who had been dating Sara Haardt all summer, returned to rushing Zelda as soon as Sara went back to Goucher College in

September. Rich and inseparable, Peyton and John were known as "The Gold Dust Twins." Peyton, who had all the charm of an older man with a romantic past, was the proprietor of the Montgomery Marble Works and creator of such distinguished monuments in Oakwood Cemetery as "The Broken Column" and "The Wings of Death." John was learning to class and staple cotton in his father's firm, Sellers Orum. He was tall, blond, immaculate, and distinguished by what Peyton called "maxillary regions similar to a Pontiac chief's." His mother was dead, but the wife of his father's partner was one of the Twenty-Twos, the Montgomery equivalent of New York's Four Hundred, which by local standards made John highly eligible.

Both he and Peyton had what Scott considered the two top things: great animal magnetism and money. The pay check of F. "Scotch" Fitzgerald, as they called him, was a hundred and forty-one dollars a month. A bottle of bonded whiskey cost ten dollars; a dinner at the Pickwick Cafe, a minimum of six; and taxis, a dollar a mile. To make the competition stiffer, Peyton and John had cars. They could drive Zelda to Oakwood Cemetery to admire the art of the Montgomery Marble Works; but when she took Scott there to show him the Confederate graves, she had to walk. Like all Southern gentlemen, Peyton and John were past masters at putting their girls on pedestals, glorifying them, and abasing themselves; while on the evening that Scott carved his legend on the pillars of the Montgomery Country Club, he made his initials very large and Zelda's very small—a trifling thing, but one that was still rankling in her, when in *Save Me the Waltz*, she said, "David, David, David, Knight, Knight, Knight, and Miss Alabama Nobody."

If possible, Scott was less popular with Zelda's Montgomery beaux than were the other Yankee officers who courted her. With his masterly command of invective, "The Pride of the Confederacy," as Sara Haardt called Peyton, expressed his distaste for all the Northern invaders and his hope that the Confederates could keep the traditions of the Old South intact. If he owned heaven and were Czar of the Yankees, he once said, he would abdicate and go to hell. In October he and John were happy to hear that Scott's unit had been sent to Camp Mills, Long Island, and ordered overseas—thus relieving them of the competition of a young man who confessed in his Notebooks:

> Scott Fitzgerald so they say,
> Goes a-courting night and day.

The armistice was signed while Fitzgerald awaited his embarkation orders at Camp Mills. His disappointment at not getting overseas sent him off on a drinking marathon. Scott's conduct was so erratic that his commanding officer confined him to quarters. He slipped off, went AWOL to New York, and liquidated his sorrows at the Knickerbocker Bar. In his absence, his unit was ordered back to Camp Sheridan and entrained for Montgomery, leaving him stranded in New York. To the amazement of his comrades, when their troop train pulled into Washington, Scott was sitting there on a baggage truck beside the track, with two girls and a bottle, waiting for them—but not impatiently.

On his return to Montgomery, Scott explained to Zelda that he had commandeered a locomotive to take him to Washington on the plea that he was a courier with important papers to deliver to the White House. And another of Scott's fabrications about himself passed into legend.

The series of personal disasters that made up Fitzgerald's military career ended, not with a bang but with a minor triumph and a major contretemps. Back at Camp Sheridan, he entered upon "a haughty career as aide-de-camp" to the commanding general. Scott was "the army's worst," he unblushingly admitted, in that "pleasant chatty sinecure," won him by his good looks and parlor graces rather than by proficiency in military arts and sciences. Although his accomplishments did not include even a rudimentary knowledge of horsemanship, to the amusement of Montgomerians and despite the crossed infantry rifles on the collar of his tunic, he insisted on wearing the boots and spurs to which he was entitled as a member of a headquarters company. Shortly after he became aide to the general, he appeared on horseback in a dress parade. At last he had a chance to use his spurs and did such a thorough job of it that his horse reared and threw him. A sergeant was assigned to teach him to ride, but he never learned to be at home in the saddle.

Scott drank frequently now; after each spree there was a quarrel with Zelda, who in these days was incontestably the saner, soberer, better integrated, and better adjusted of the two. On Friday afternoons they went to the vaudeville at the Grand Theater and sat in the gilt-and-red plush box across from ours. Zelda was gay and animated; Scott sulky, morose, and jealous.

During Scott's absence at Camp Mills, Zelda had become the reigning prom queen in the Deep South. She made the dances at the University of Alabama, at Marion Institute, at the University of Georgia, and Sewanee. At Auburn she was so popular that her admirers founded a fraternity, called Zeta Sigma, in which the qualifications for membership consisted of a pledge of devotion to Zelda and proof that the candidates had had at least one date with her in Montgomery. The young aviators from Camp Taylor whom she had met at the Country Club dances looped and barrel-rolled their planes over her home to attract her attention until the neighbors complained of having their houses buzzed. After one of her beaux was killed in stunting for her benefit, the commanding officer at Camp Taylor forbade further such aerial methods of courtship. Meanwhile, not to be outdone by the aviators' gallantries, a squad of infantrymen from Camp Sheridan marched up and down Pleasant Avenue and executed a drill for her benefit in front of her house. When Montgomery celebrated the Armistice with victory marches, parades, and lanes of flowers held by young girls, Zelda attracted more attention from the soldiers than did the generals and politicians in the stands. At the street dance that concluded the Armistice Day festivities, the military police had to break up the stag lines that crowded around her.

At first, Scott had been pleased by such evidences of her popularity. But after she broke a date with him to attend the governor's inaugural ball with a local beau and compounded that crime by accepting a bid from a famous quarterback to attend the Washington's Birthday dances at Auburn, Fitzgerald showed his jealousy by denouncing her pranks, which had once delighted him, and taxing her with being a "speed." Although Zelda insisted that her admirers at Auburn were friends, not sweethearts (and at least two of them later protested that while she was full of life and fun, she was not considered "wild"), Scott persisted in believing otherwise.

He was discharged from the army on February 14, 1919, and

when he left Montgomery for New York four days later, he was still in a dark mood. For he felt that his efforts to win Zelda had been frustrated by the local competition. Dan Cody, whose father was president of the Union Bank and Trust, had tossed his hat into the ring. Lloyd Hooper, the handsome scion of one of the wealthiest, most aristocratic families in the Black Belt, announced that he would marry any girl who liked Cabell's *Jurgen* and could sing second part. Zelda fulfilled his requirements, and Lloyd won great favor with her by diving into the Alabama River in a new white linen suit to retrieve her hat, which she had dropped in the water.

Scott's reaction to his rivals and their demands on Zelda's attention embittered him as deeply as did his awareness of the difference between Zelda's background and his, of her complete security as Judge Sayre's daughter, and of the uncertainty that would face her as the wife of an unpublished author—all he could offer her at the moment. Further, Scott had always longed to be a football hero, and when he discovered that the famous Auburn quarterback had given Zelda his gold football, Fitzgerald's smouldering jealousy exploded into rage. He forgot himself, and when she resisted his attempts to kiss her into contrition and compliance, he hurled violent charges at her. Just before he left for New York, and after an epic quarrel, she broke her engagement to him. Scott wrote a friend that it was "a great tragedy" to him and that unless Zelda would someday marry him, he would never marry at all.

"Zelda was cagey about throwing her lot in with me before I was a money-maker," he recorded in his Notebooks. "She was young and in a period when any exploiter or middle-man seemed a better risk than a worker in the arts." Even though their quarrel was patched up, Zelda, the more innately prudent and sensible of the two, refused to marry him until he had visible means of supporting her.

John Dearborn, who was then at Sewanee, asked Jordan Prince, a friend of Zelda's, up to the midterm dances. Jordan accepted and asked if she could bring another girl. To Scott's annoyance, she took Zelda with her to Sewanee. There was snow on the ground there, and it was very cold. After the dance, John, who had gotten Jordan another date and escorted Zelda to the dance, took her back to the ATO house, where they piled on more logs and spent the rest of the night sitting before the fire, talking. John still maintains that Zelda was the most charming woman he ever knew. He was so entranced with her that he said it was daylight before he knew it.

In the course of the evening, he added, Zelda told him that she did not think that she was really in love with Scott in a romantic way, but that she felt it was her mission in life to help him realize his potential as a writer. This is a more likely explanation of Zelda's marriage to Scott than those given by some of his biographers who claim that she was madly in love with him and insinuated that he had seduced her before her marriage to him—an assumption based, as far as I know, on nothing more than the fact that in *The Great Gatsby*, Scott has Daisy seduced by Gatsby before her marriage. Hence, it is impossible to tell whether Scott's irresistible impulse to ask his friends intrusive questions about their premarital relations with each other derived from a need to justify his own actions or his resentment over Zelda's having held him "firmly at bay."

Disgruntled as Scott was with Zelda when he left Montgomery, he wired her as soon as he arrived in New York, telling her that he hoped she would soon be with him there. He continued to be optimistic about their future together, though his prospects were not bright nor his surroundings inviting. After an abortive experience as a newspaper man, he secured a job writing slogans for street-car advertisements for the Barron Collier agency at twenty dollars a week. On that salary he could not even stay on at the Allerton, the men's hotel where he first stopped, so he moved to a cheap room in "a high, horrible apartment house in the middle of nowhere" at 200 Claremont Avenue.

For a while Zelda attempted to reassure him and encourage him by writing him every day. Her letters were filled with extravagant protestations of her love for him, her need of him, and her impatience at having to wait for him to make his fortune before marrying him. But she continued to go to proms, to have dates with other men, and to write ardent letters to several "other fiancés." Unaware that it was customary for Southern belles to have as many strings to their bow as they could string along, Scott took her avowals at their face value and sent Zelda his mother's engagement ring—a diamond by no means as big as the Ritz. Zelda wrote him a rapturous letter about it and wore it to the Saturday night dance at the Country Club—or so she told Scott. But she soon relegated it to her trophy box because she did not like to wear rings. Moreover, to exhibit it flagrantly would have impeded her conquests at home.

Oblivious of the conventions of courtly love in the Deep South in the days before "going steady" was dreamed of, Scott continued to make plans for marrying Zelda. He wrote to Judge Sayre and had his mother write to Zelda. But neither she, nor her family, nor her friends took her engagement seriously. Alarmed by the change in the tone of her letters and the accounts of her escapades, probably invented to amuse him, Scott made a trip to Montgomery in April and another in May in an effort to find out where he stood. But Zelda declined to commit herself any more definitely than she had already done.

She had been having a wonderful time. When Les Mysterieuse, an exclusive Mardi Gras club in Montgomery, gave a "Folly Ball," she had been chosen to play the part of Folly in the skit that Rosalind and Mrs. Sayre had written to be given during the intermission. Zelda had been to Auburn again and was just recovering from a "wholesome amour" with its "startling quarterback." Now, she was looking for new fields of conquest and planning to go to the commencement dances at Georgia Tech. When she wrote Scott about the dates, dances, and parties that consumed her time, and he replied so often by saying that he used to wonder why they locked princesses in towers, she wounded his literary vanity by telling him that he had written her the same thing six times and that she was tired of it. To increase the injury, after her trip to Georgia Tech, she put the wrong photograph in the wrong envelope and sent Scott a picture of herself, which he claimed to have paid for, tenderly inscribed to a famous Atlanta golfer whose fraternity pin she was wearing. Although Scott eventually forgave her for her error, his romance with her continued to be an off again, on again, gone again affair.

That spring, when Rosalind's and Clotilde's husbands, who had been serving as officers in the American Expeditionary Forces in Europe, returned to the States, their wives joined them in New York. Left in Montgomery without her sisters and without Scott, Zelda became fretful, for she, too, longed for the opportunities of a larger stage. Even commencement at Auburn, where she confessed to Scott that she and Eleanor Browder had more " 'best friends' than Solomon had wives," seemed dull and tedious to an impatient Zelda.

Although Scott was even more impatient to have her with him, he could not provide for her and she refused to marry him until he could do so. The manuscripts of his stories came back as fast as he mailed them out. He had a frieze of rejection slips pinned up around the walls of his dismal room on Claremont Avenue. Then one morning he received another one in a mail that brought no letter from Alabama. After a day spent in drinking martinis with two of his college friends, he tried to jump out of a window of the Princeton Club, but was deterred from doing so by his companions.

In June Mencken accepted "Babes in the Woods" for *The Smart Set* and sent Scott thirty dollars for it, which he promptly invested in a magenta feather fan for Zelda and a pair of white trousers for himself. Encouraged now by his prospects, he took a train to Montgomery. There he tried to persuade Zelda to marry him at once with frantic pleas and hysterical threats. But, unimpressed by them or by his ability to support her on his miniscule salary and the occasional sale of a story, she broke her engagement to him again and returned his ring.

On his return to New York, Fitzgerald found little consolation and little additional income from the sale of "The Debutante" to *The Smart Set*. Strangely enough, despite the fact that Mencken bought the first two stories that Scott ever sold, he later claimed, "It was not until I got the proofs of my book [*This Side of Paradise*] from the publisher that I learned of Mencken. I happened across *The Smart Set* one day and thought, 'Here's a man I ought to know, I guess I'll stick it in the proof sheets.'" It was an odd story for him to tell, particularly since it was after an epic bender to celebrate Mencken's acceptance of "The Debutante" that Scott retreated to his home in St. Paul on July 1 to recuperate and to revise "The Romantic Egotist" into *This Side of Paradise*, which was not accepted until September 1919, much less published.

As soon as he arrived in St. Paul, Scott secluded himself in his parents' home, one of eight units in a block of row houses that looked like an illustration of one of Grimm's fairy tales. Built in 1899, the brownstone facades of the eight units incorporated a variety of designs, featuring recessed doorways and bay windows, flanked at the corners of the block by octagonal turrets, so sharp-pointed that they appeared to have been patterned after witches' hats. Scott described himself to Alida Bigelow, one of his girls from St. Paul, as working

> In a house below the average
> On a street above the average
> In a room below the roof
> With a lot above the ears. . . .

His mother brought his meals up to his attic room, where he wrestled with his novel fifteen hours a day. He worked methodically from outlines of the chapters pinned to the curtains, revising old material and adding new. With the exception of Father Joe Barron, a Catholic priest who served as dean of students at St. Paul Academy, and Donald Ogden Stewart, Scott saw few people. Stewart once told me:

> I was a clerk in the office of the American Telephone Company in Minneapolis in 1919. That is where I first met Scott as I was living in a boarding house in St. Paul, and he had just come back from his army camp in Alabama, full of Zelda and literary ambition. I didn't meet Zelda until a year or two later, but in St. Paul, Scott showed me a shoe box, full of handwritten-in-pencil manuscript of a novel called *This Side of Paradise*. Fortunately, I liked it very much, so that our friendship deepened over the years.

In the revisions of his novel, Scott had used parts of both "Babes in the Woods" and "The Debutante," as well as portions of Zelda's love letters from other men and parts of her diary, which he had borrowed and taken to New York with him. There he had shown the diary to Stephen Parrott, who thought that it was worth publishing. So did Scott. Next he showed it to George

Jean Nathan, *The Smart Set*'s critic, who agreed to take it for that magazine on the condition that he was to be introduced to the girl who had written it. But instead of rewriting it for Nathan as "The Journal of a Young Girl," as he had originally intended, Scott incorporated the better parts of the diary into *This Side of Paradise*, and Zelda quipped, "Plagiarism begins at home."

But however often Scott thought or talked of Zelda, he had not written her since he left New York, though, obviously, he had not forgotten her. Nor did he ever forget or forgive the suffering that she had caused him by breaking her engagement to him. For twenty years later he was to say:

> A man does not recover from such jolts. . . . I had again over extended my flank. It was one of those tragic loves doomed for lack of money, and one day the girl closed it out on the basis of common sense. During a long summer of despair I wrote a novel instead of letters, so it came out all right, but it came out all right for a different person. The man with the jingle of money in his pocket who married the girl a year later would always cherish an abiding distrust, and animosity towards the leisure class—not the conviction of a revolutionist but the smouldering hate of a peasant. In the years since I have never been able to stop wondering where my friends' money came from, nor to stop thinking that at one time a sort of *droit de seigneur* might have been exercised to give one of them my girl.

3. This Side of Paradise

IMMEDIATELY after Scribner's accepted *This Side of Paradise*, Scott wrote Zelda the news and asked if he might see her again. She replied casually that she would be glad to have him come down and reminded him to bring a bottle of gin, adding that she had not had a drink all summer. In November Scott rode the day coach to Montgomery. Just before he arrived, he tipped the porter and arranged to descend from the vestibule of the Pullman. Despite his depleted bank balance, he was in high spirits. He already had begun another novel, "The Demon Lover," and he was convinced that he was going to be a successful novelist. In a matter of weeks he persuaded Zelda that he was destined to become a great writer, who could open for her the glittering gates to fame and wealth.

But Zelda was still reluctant to set a date for the wedding. Her hesitancy was due as much to her reluctance to leave her familiar world and to her doubts as to what life would be like with Scott as to his lack of money. So it was not until early in January that Zelda finally agreed to marry him. Judge and Mrs. Sayre still opposed the match. Scott, they felt, was unstable and unreliable; further, they were still dubious about his ability to provide for Zelda. Besides, she was an Episcopalian; he, a Catholic. However, if Scott did not have what he considered "the two top things, great animal magnetism and money," he had the next best, good looks and intelligence; better, perhaps, for the business in hand, he had an Irish talent for blarney when he chose to use it. So, in the end, he got "the top girl" and won her parents over.

"Zelda has had several admirers," Miss Minnie wrote him in one of the understatements of all time, "but you seem to be the only one to make anything like a permanent impression. . . . A good Catholic is as good as any other good man and that is good enough. It will take more than the Pope to make Zelda good; you will have to call on God Almighty direct."

Once his engagement to Zelda had been informally announced again, Scott went to New Orleans. He took a room in a cheap boardinghouse at 2900 Prytania Street and tried to work on "The Demon Lover." But between visits to Montgomery to see Zelda and to take her a shaker of her favorite Sazarac cocktails, he made little progress on the new novel. In February, however, his story "Head and Shoulders" was published in *The Saturday Evening Post*, and the movie rights to it were sold to Metro for twenty-five hundred dollars. On March 26 Scribner's published *This Side of Paradise*. The laureate of the Jazz Age had begun to win recognition.

Scott sent an advance copy of his novel to Mencken with the admission that "it derives from Mackenzie, Wells, and Tarkington." Mencken said it was the best American novel that he had read lately and gave it a highly favorable review in the August 1920 issue of *The Smart Set*.

Fitzgerald was on the crest of the wave. On March 28, 1920 there appeared on the society page of the Montgomery *Advertiser* a formal notice:

> Judge and Mrs. A. D. Sayre announce the engagement of their daughter, Zelda, to Francis Scott Fitzgerald, of New York, the marriage to take place at an early date.

Scott sent her a corsage of orchids—her first one—to commemorate the event. The announcement came as a bolt out of the blue to her other beaux. Two of them, one in Montgomery and one in Auburn, who had expected to marry Zelda, refused to believe their eyes when it was published. Few, if any, of her friends had ever thought that she would marry Scott. Indeed, less than three years after her marriage to him, Zelda told Rosalind, "I never did want to marry Scott." However that may have been, the following week the *Advertiser* revealed that

> Mrs. M. W. Brinson (Marjorie Sayre Brinson) accompanied by her sister, Miss Zelda Sayre, have gone to New York City, and while there will be guests of Mrs. J. M. Palmer, formerly Miss Clotilde Sayre.

There were a number of reasons why Scott and Zelda had decided to be married in New York. For one thing, it was the easiest way to avoid the turmoil and expense of a wedding in Montgomery; for another, Scott insisted on being married in the Catholic Church; and he favored St. Patrick's Cathedral because he had a cousin, a priest—a monsignor, in fact—on the staff there who would marry them. Zelda's family had always attended the Church of the Holy Comforter in Montgomery; Marjorie had been married there, Rosalind had sung in the choir there, and Zelda had been baptized there—a little on the late side—in 1910. Although she went regularly to Sunday school at the Holy Comforter, a search of the church records does not reveal that she was ever confirmed. Apparently, Zelda had no particular sentiment about being married at home or in the Church of the Holy Comforter and no objection to a Catholic ceremony. Doubtless she thought that it would be more exciting to be married in New York. Rosalind was living there; Clotilde, in nearby Tarrytown; and Marjorie was going along with Zelda to chaperone her on the trip, so the Sayres felt that it was all very proper.

A crowd of Zelda's friends, laden with flowers for her, saw her off at the station. She was wearing a Confederate gray suit almost the color of her eyes, and some of the people with her thought that they had never seen her look so beautiful before. Rosalind and Newman Smith met Zelda and Marjorie at Pennsylvania Station, but instead of going to Clotilde's, they stayed at the Biltmore Hotel, where Scott had made reservations for them.

Fortunately, Judge and Mrs. Sayre decided not to go with them, for what they would have found would have shocked them.

Fame and fortune had come to Scott almost overnight. In the money now, and out to prove it, ostentatiously and alcoholically, he had gone on a monumental spree. Bellboys were called up to bathe him. After one of his luxurious baths, he left the taps on and flooded the hotel. He used five-dollar bills to light his cigarettes and folded five-hundred-dollar ones to show the figures when he wore them in his vest pockets.

After Zelda arrived, Scott, who had not communicated with Rosalind and Clotilde before, phoned to tell them that the wedding was to take place the next day. Then, fancying himself a Pygmalion, he inspected the bride's trousseau, made short shrift of her small-town frills and furbelows, and sent her to Fifth Avenue with one of his former girls, who helped to outfit Zelda with a wardrobe that he considered more suitable for New York.

Nevertheless, Zelda wore her spring suit to the wedding, ornamented only by the corsage that Scott had sent her. Rosalind, Newman, and Ludlow Fowler, a fellow Princetonian who was to act as Scott's best man, met Scott, Zelda, and Marjorie at the rectory on April 3, 1920. Clotilde and her husband had been invited and arrived from Tarrytown at the appointed hour, but too late for the service, for Scott had become fidgety and impatient and instructed the priest to proceed without them. There was no music, no flowers, no photographers, and no luncheon afterwards. The marriage as reported by the Montgomery *Advertiser* of April 7, 1920, was indeed a quiet affair:

> Miss Zelda Sayre, the lovely and attractive daughter of Judge and Mrs. A. D. Sayre, of Montgomery, was married Saturday at high noon in New York City to Francis Scott Fitzgerald, son of Mr. and Mrs. Edward Fitzgerald, of Minnesota, at the Rectory of St. Patrick's Cathedral. The marriage was the culmination of a romance that was begun when Lieutenant Fitzgerald was stationed at Camp Sheridan with the Ninth Division.

The Fitzgeralds' honeymoon at the Biltmore was so hilarious that it was cut short by the request of the management. The bride and groom then moved to the Commodore. They spent the rest of their honeymoon going to the midnight roofs, the follies and the plays, and a great many parties with Ludlow Fowler.

At a luncheon at the Fowlers' home, Zelda was intrigued to find that there was an elevator in the house, the first one she had ever seen in a private house. The impression that the Fowlers' affluence made on Scott germinated five years later in his story "The Rich Boy." In it he describes its protagonist, Anson Hunter, who was drawn from Fowler, in what Scott, in an undated letter, told him was an unsparing but sympathetic way. He depicts Fowler as a convivial, bawdy young man of great wealth, with scores of friends for whom he had done many kindnesses, but whom he occasionally embarrassed by "his burst of rough conversation or his habit of getting drunk whenever and wherever he liked." Scott assumed that "The rich are different from you and me. They possess and enjoy early, and it does something to them, makes them soft where we are hard, and cynical where we are trustful. They think, deep in their hearts, that they are better than we are because we had to discover the compensations and refuges of life for ourselves"—an unsparing and hardly a sympathetic portrait.

If Scott was critical of rich boys, he was by no means averse to consorting with them. On the weekend of April 25 he, Zelda, Fowler, and two other men drove to Princeton, where the Fitzgeralds were to chaperone a house party at the Cottage Club. Harvey Firestone took them down in his eye-stopping new automobile, a bright robin's-egg blue car. The party began with stirrup cups before they left New York, and Scott reported that "not one of us drew a sober breath." Scott startled his old club by introducing Zelda at the Cottage Club as his mistress. "It was," he added, "the damnedest party ever held in Princeton and everybody in the University will agree"—a doubtful assertion in view of the more sensational one that followed it.

A week later Scott went back to Princeton with John Peale Bishop and Edmund Wilson to a banquet given for the veterans of the *Nassau Lit* staff. After a few drinks they decided to celebrate the vernal season with appropriate rites of spring, and before leaving New York they borrowed lyres, pipes of Pan, laurel wreaths, and other props from the Greenwich Village Players. On arriving in Princeton they stopped first at the dean's house to crown Christian Gauss with a gilt wreath. Scott delivered an extempore oration. In conclusion he boasted, "We are going to give American literature a boost such as it has never known."

"Who can tell?" Dean Gauss replied. "You may give it a fatal shove."

Unperturbed by the dean's retort, with a laurel wreath cocked over one eye, the Boswell of the Beautiful and Damned danced into the Cottage Club, playing the pipes of Pan. When the club revoked the engraved silver platter which it had presented to him, Scott flew into a rage and struck out blindly at his fellow members. He was finally corralled by half a dozen of the shocked Cottagers, thrown out a rear window, and suspended from the club.

Hurt and sobered, Fitzgerald went back to New York, where he and Zelda bought a secondhand Marmon and departed for Rye. Finding it a dull place, they headed north to Lake Champlain. Zelda loved to swim, dive, and sunbathe, but since it was still too cold there for such sports, she and Scott went back to Westport. There they rented the Burritt Wakeman place, a secluded, gray-shingled cottage, guarded by a statue of a Minuteman, with a small garden and a beach of its own on the Sound.

In June the *Metropolitan* advanced Fitzgerald seven thousand dollars for serial rights to an unwritten novel, then entitled "The Flight of the Rocket." Scott tried valiantly to work on the new book, which eventually became *The Beautiful and Damned.* But he and Zelda soon found Westport depressing and began commuting to parties in Gotham to break the monotony of suburbia.

Early in August they met Zelda's parents at the station in New York to escort them to Westport for a visit. Zelda's report of the debacle there in *Save Me the Waltz*, she once told me, was almost a literal account of their visit. When Judge and Mrs. Sayre arrived, Scott and Zelda had two dollars between them. Fortunately, Judge Sayre insisted on paying the taxi. "Where's your sister?" he inquired. Zelda hesitated to tell him, but finally she revealed that the last time Clotilde visited them, she had borrowed the Fitzgeralds' best suitcase and carried away the baby's wet diapers in it. Relations had been strained between the Palmers and the Fitzgeralds ever since Scott had ordered the wedding to proceed before Clotilde and her husband arrived. After the episode of the diapers, the Fitzgeralds had seen little of them.

The Fitzgeralds arrived in Westport with Zelda's parents to find two drunken friends of Scott's asleep in the hammock. Unluckily, they did not stay asleep, for at dinner the two men staggered in to do a carmagnole around the table and invite the Fitzgeralds and the Sayres to join in the dance. Since the intruders, too, were out of pocket, Zelda borrowed twenty dollars from her mother to speed them on their way to a roadhouse, only to have them return at three o'clock in the morning. Scott evolved a novel method of keeping them from waking Judge and Mrs. Sayre; he fed them gin to keep them quiet and tomato juice to sober them up. Then Scott began to drink with them. By the time Zelda had dressed and come down, the kitchen was a shambles; bloated cigarettes overflowed the ashtrays; the place smelled like a saloon; rings of gin and orange juice made unappetizing designs on the table. As Zelda tried to take the gin bottle from Scott, he fended her off; she backed against the doorjamb, and the swinging door caught her full in the face. Her nose bled down the front of her dress; her eyes began to swell. It was daylight before Scott finally sent his unwelcome guests off to sleep at the inn and began to treat Zelda's injuries.

Zelda applied a heavy coat of make-up in an effort to conceal her black eyes, but they were all too obvious to her parents when they came down to breakfast. Judge Sayre stared at her in chilly silence. Feeling as he did about drinking parties, and especially those that involved Zelda, when he finally spoke, he was exceedingly mild.

In a letter to Ludlow Fowler, postmarked August 6, 1920, Zelda told him:

> Mama and Daddy are here this week and I can't tell you how glad I was to see them—however, I feel very festive and I guess it's hardly conventional or according to Hoyle to take one's family on a celebration that I feel in dire need of. It's been a wild summer, thank God, and I have several anecdotes collected from the wreckage that I'm saving to tell you—At present, I'm hardly able to sit down owing to an injury sustained in the course of one of Nathan's parties in N.Y. I cut my tail on a broken bottle and can't possibly sit on the three stitches that are in it now—The bottle was bath salts—I was boiled—The place was a bathtub somewhere. None of us remember the exact locality.

But Zelda's festive mood vanished when her father showed his disapproval of the surprise party that had met him in Westport by leaving sooner than he had expected to. After the departure of her parents, she was "desolate." To cheer her up Scott took her down to New York for another round of gaiety with his literary friends.

Between them, Scott and Zelda had taken the New York literati by storm. Before his marriage, Fitzgerald, accompanied by John Peale Bishop, had laid siege to George Jean Nathan's apartment at the Royalton until the drama critic finally asked them in to have a drink. Through Nathan, Scott met Carl Van Vechten, who remembers a party at Theodore Dreiser's on St. Luke's Place, which Scott crashed, credentialed only by the bottle of hot champagne that he brought along. His antics that evening furnished the other guests with gossip for a week. Ernest Boyd, Llewelyn Powys, Carl Van Vechten, Burton Rascoe, Sherwood Anderson, and H. L. Mencken all wrote conflicting stories of Dreiser's soiree, but the consensus was that it had been a very dull evening until Fitzgerald arrived to enliven it.

At the end of July Nathan laid in three cases of gin and invited Scott and Zelda down to New York to a party at which Mencken was to be present. Although Scott resented Nathan's attention to Zelda, particularly his facetiously affectionate billets doux to her, one of which had prompted Fitzgerald to throw a roundhouse right at George Jean, Scott forgave him and decided to go because Mencken, whom he said he had rather have like his work than anyone in the country, was also to be there.

After the party Nathan visited the Fitzgeralds in Westport. When he told Mencken that Scott's Japanese butler, Tana, was in reality a German spy, the Sage of Baltimore was intrigued. He promptly began to forward bundles of German newspapers to Lieutenant Emil Tannenbaum in care of the Fitzgeralds in Westport, which immediately set off rumors of an espionage ring there, to the amusement of Mencken and Nathan.

At dinner in New York about this time, Scott and Zelda met Nathan's longtime friend, Lillian Gish, who recalls:

> We were at a large round table, with them, Fannie Hurst and other writers here in New York at that time. They were both so beautiful, so blond, so clean and clear—And drinking strait [*sic*] whiskey out of tall tumblers. Dorothy [Miss Gish's sister] and I were fascinated—then we became friends. . . .

Zelda could do outlandish things—say anything. It was never offensive when Zelda did it, as you felt she couldn't help it, and was not doing it for effect.

Toward the end of the summer, when they tired of partying, the Fitzgeralds drove down to Montgomery in their ramshackle Marmon. Their cars, Zelda said, were always secondhand and romantic. It was this particular back number that prompted Scott to write, "The Cruise of the Rolling Junk." On the way south they packed their luggage with table silver, towels, and the big square pincushions from the hotels where they stopped. At the New Willard in Washington, they noted that the electric fans blew the smell of peaches and hot biscuits and the cindery aroma of traveling salesmen down the halls. The hotel in Richmond had long-unopened rooms and statues of the gods lost somewhere along its echoing corridors. In the O'Henry Hotel in Greenville, they found that the bathtubs ran red mud instead of water. There were so many smells and so much organdy in the dresses of the girls, they said, that they did not feel inclined to linger.

Since neither of the Fitzgeralds was an expert driver, they had a wild, hazardous trip through the country. They arrived full of stories of their weird experiences and covered with dust. To their dismay, they found that Judge and Mrs. Sayre were out of town and Six Pleasant Avenue was securely locked. So they drove over to Livye Hart's house. At the sight of them, Livye could not repress her laughter. Zelda had on a plaid, accordion-pleated skirt and a vivid green jacket with a beret to match; Scott wore a linen duster, a cap, and goggles; but the smart cut of their clothes served only to make their road-stained and bedraggled condition ridiculous.

News of their arrival brought more invitations than they could accept, and a friend of Zelda's solved the problem of living quarters by organizing a house party for them in her spacious Victorian house. After Scott and Zelda had bathed and changed, they joined their hosts and the other guests at the Country Club. They appeared on the golf course wearing matching white linen knickerbocker suits. Their idea in having the matching suits made was to present a united front, not to create a sensation. Nevertheless, they electrified the bystanders. Peyton Mathis took one look at

Zelda and infuriated her by asking, "What's happened to you? You went away in long skirts and you've come back in short pants."

Whenever they wore the knickerbocker suits, the conversation buzzing around them gave way to an uncomfortable silence as they came within earshot. Accustomed as they were to being the observed of all observers, the disapproving stares of the elder generation vexed them and chilled their enthusiasm for the celebrations that had been planned in their honor.

Scott felt that Zelda's hometown had never properly appreciated him. It was a political, not a literary, town, and perhaps at the time it did not appreciate him. That trip to Montgomery, Scott noted, was the most unpleasant one that he and Zelda ever took. "Never knew what a trial a tour was. The joys of motoring are more or less fictitious," Zelda wrote Ludlow Fowler. "We had to leave the car in Ala—"

Not only had Scott's attitude toward his "paradise" in Montgomery begun to change but also the relationship between him and Zelda had altered. Although he still loved her desperately, the ardor of his courtship had worn off, and he could not keep up the constant wooing if he was to work on his book. Her zest for guests and parties frequently interfered with the progress of his book. He began to be uneasy about what she was doing while he was engrossed in writing.

Zelda's youth, beauty, and wit attracted men as flames do moths. She flirted with Nathan, bantered with Carl Van Vechten, and drank toasts to them out of her slipper. She danced on table tops to the cheers of Scott's Princeton friends; and one of them, Alex McKaig, who was then in the advertising business in New York, declared that she was the most brilliant and beautiful young woman he had ever known. Her mind was undisciplined, he added, but her intuition was marvelous. The trouble was, he decided, that Scott was absorbed in her personality, and she unfortunately was the stronger of the two. He also remarked that she furnished Fitzgerald with all the copy for his feminine characters. Scott, he said, had even confessed in his presence that Zelda's ideas were responsible for his stories "The Ice Palace" and "The Jelly Bean," as well as for the new novel he was writing.

Lawton Campbell, then a witty, charming young-man-about-town, an executive of General Foods, and the author of two Broadway plays, *Solid South* and *Immoral Isabella*, saw the Fitzgeralds frequently in New York. "Of all the people who ever came out of Alabama," he once said, "I think Zelda Sayre Fitzgerald and Tallulah Bankhead the most fascinating." To him Zelda appeared to be more innately brilliant than Scott. "I have always thought," he continued, "that Zelda did more for Scott than Scott did for Zelda. I have seen him many times write down the things she said on scraps of paper or the backs of envelopes. *The Beautiful and Damned* was pure Zelda."

Although he was still proud of her popularity, Scott began to resent the attention and adulation that his friends showed Zelda. Not only was he jealous of her but he was also irritated with her for wanting to buy an expensive coat when he was out of pocket and impatient at her deficiencies as a housekeeper. Zelda had been waited on hand and foot all her life; she liked to entertain and to cook; but she had never before had to clean house, hang up her clothes, or remember to send out the laundry. In the South in those days, young ladies in her position were not expected to darn socks, wash dishes, and make up beds, and she balked at the chores that women in Scott's native Minnesota accepted as part of the marriage contract.

Shortly after they returned from Montgomery, the resentment between them that had been smoldering flared out in a serious quarrel. Scott came back from New York on a train that almost killed Zelda, who was walking along the tracks. Fitzgerald had boarded the train without money or a ticket. The conductor threatened to throw him off but finally agreed to let him stay on when Scott promised to pay him upon his arrival in Westport. After Scott tore into Zelda for walking the tracks, she refused to give him the money for his ticket, and they joined in a verbal battle that was to continue intermittently for two decades. But in the early years passionate reconciliations swiftly followed their tiffs. In *The Beautiful and Damned* there is a letter that is probably a paraphrase of one that Zelda wrote Scott after their quarrel at the railroad station, for it is written in her idiom rather than his:

I look down the tracks and see you coming—and out of every haze
& mist your darling rumpled trousers are hurrying to me—without
you dearest, dearest, I couldn't see or hear or feel or think—or live
—I love you so and I'm never in all our lives going to let us be
apart another night. It's like begging for mercy of a storm or
killing Beauty or growing old, without you. . . . Goofo, you've got
to try to feel how much I love you—how inanimate I am when
you're gone—I can't even hate these damnable people—Nobody's
got any right to live but us—and they're dirtying up our world and
I can't hate them because I want you so. Come Quick—Come
Quick to me—I could never do without you if you hated me and
were covered with sores like a leper—and if you ran away with
another woman and starved and beat me—I would still want you.
I *know*.

Despite the fact that during the lulls between parties and quarrels, Scott had worked well on *The Beautiful and Damned*, the
Fitzgeralds' summer of rusticating had not been a success; Westport was too hectic on the weekends and too dull between them.
So in November, when "the late autumn made the country
dreary," they took an apartment in a brownstone house in New
York at 35 West Fifty-ninth Street.

There it was hectic all week, for the apartment was near the
Plaza Hotel and Scott competed with the bartender of the Palm
Room for the patronage of literary and theatrical people. Ever
since the Blackfriars, the dramatic club at the University of Alabama, had produced his sketch, *The Debutante*, Scott had felt the
lure of the theater, especially since he had learned that plays
usually took less time to write than novels and made more money.
So he began to cultivate friendships with Charles MacArthur and
Helen Hayes, Anita Loos, and Lillian Hellman. He saw Nathan
and Lillian Gish frequently, and Lawton Campbell dropped in
now and then.

Lawton arrived one day to take Scott and Zelda to lunch, only
to find them just getting out of bed. Their apartment looked as if
a cyclone had struck it. Books, papers, and ashtrays littered the
floor; tall glasses sat in white rings on mahogany tables, and dirty
dishes overflowed the sink—evidence of the party the night before. Scott and Zelda met Lawton looking like a pair of heavy-

eyed, uncombed Sealyham terriers. While Scott dressed, Zelda retired to take a tub, leaving the bathroom door open so as not to miss the conversation—or rather, so as to join in it. Before Scott could finish detailing one of their escapades, she would urge him to tell about another. "Goofo, does Lawton know about what happened to us at the Plantation?" and "Tell Lawton what I said when the house detective knocked on the door."

Though they were constantly in touch with Mencken by mail, they partied with him very little after they returned to New York. When Fitzgerald's first book of short stories, *Flappers and Philosophers*, was published by Scribner's in August 1920, Scott sent H. L. an advance copy, in which he had noted the stories that he considered worth reading. In November Mencken reviewed it in *The Smart Set*, calling it "a sandwich made up of two thick and tasteless chunks of *Kriegsbrot* with a couple of excellent sardines between." Scott retaliated by reviewing Mencken's *Prejudices: Second Series* in *The Bookman*. Although it was entitled "The Baltimore Anti-Christ," tongue-in-cheek H. L. called it an "encomium," for which he thanked Scott profusely and asked when he would see him and "the fair Madonna," as he called Zelda. Before Scott finished *The Beautiful and Damned*, Mencken suggested that they should have a *sub rosa* conference, in which he would reveal to Fitzgerald (who had modeled the protagonist of his new novel on Nathan), a highly discreditable but very dramatic and completely fictitious episode in George Jean's life. The drama critic, Mencken alleged, had been forced to flee New York and hide out in Union Hill, New Jersey, after an affair with La Shapiro, a typical Grand Street flapper. Nathan's treatment of her, H. L. added, was indefensible. But she took Chichester's Family Pills, the child was stillborn, and she subsequently married Irving Blumblatt, the lawyer.

As soon as they were settled in the apartment, the Fitzgeralds asked Mencken and Nathan over for drinks one evening. When Scott explained that he had not intended his review of *Prejudices* to drench Mencken with vaseline, oleomargarine, mayonnaise, and cocoa butter, as H. L. claimed that it did, the Sage assured him that he was grateful for being anointed by him. But he baffled Scott by suggesting that an intellectual aristocracy might be a panacea for the shortcomings of American art. "What on earth does he mean by that?" Fitzgerald demanded. Obviously, he intended to warn Scott that the way to make a literary reputation was not to arrive at a party on the hood of a taxi with Zelda cheering from the roof, to be escorted out of the theater at the *Scandals* for trying to outdo the strippers by shucking off his clothes in an orchestra seat, or to stand on his head in the lobby of the Biltmore when he discovered that he had not been mentioned in the papers for a week.

That winter was a mad, gay, glorious time for Scott and Zelda. There were parties with Mencken and Nathan, parties with Edna Ferber and Dorothy Parker, and parties with Edmund Wilson and John Peale Bishop, who were then both on the editorial staff of *Vanity Fair*. When Donald Ogden Stewart arrived, there were more parties with him. Scott introduced him to the literati. "When I lost my job in a Dayton, Ohio bank a year or so after 1919," Stewart said, "it was Scott in New York who took me around to see Edmund Wilson, who was editor of *Vanity Fair*, and that is how I became a writer instead of a banker. I have been terribly grateful to him for this and other kindnesses. He was a very kind and generous person."

In fact, Scott was so generous that he soon ran out of funds. Neither he nor Zelda had ever had any experience in handling money. Maxwell Perkins, Scott's editor at Scribner's, to whom he appealed for a loan, blamed Zelda for Fitzgerald's financial crisis. "She wanted everything," Perkins complained. Money ran through her fingers, as it did through Scott's, but she had nothing to spend except what he gave her. In fact, she did not even have a bank account of her own. Scott wanted her to be dependent on him, and he needed the sense of power over her that he derived from giving her money. One day she took Rosalind to lunch at the Plaza. When she went to pay the bill, she pulled out a roll of bills the size of a baseball. "Zelda," Rosalind exclaimed, "why on earth are you carrying that much money around with you?"

"Because," she explained, "Scott gave it to me as I went out the door, so what else could I do with it but bring it along."

In addition to *This Side of Paradise*, Scott had had sixteen short stories and two articles published in 1920. Although he had earned almost twenty thousand dollars in that year, by December he was overdrawn at the bank. His unpaid bills amounted to more than six hundred dollars. He owed his agent considerably more than that for advances against stories that he had been unable to write. *The Beautiful and Damned* was still unfinished, and the bank had refused him a loan. He abjectly offered Scribner's his next ten books as security on a sixteen-hundred-dollar loan.

With the till empty, Zelda was forced to use her ingenuity to conjure up a Christmas present for Scott; so she wrote James Branch Cabell a letter in which she enclosed a snapshot of herself, asking him to do a favor for her. Under the pretense of intoxication, she confessed, she had attempted to carry off Nathan's first edition of *Jurgen*; but she had come off with a fencing foil instead, which she would gladly exchange for a copy of Cabell's book. Intrigued by her picture, the author of *Jurgen* replied with a gracious note and sent her an autographed copy of the book. To Scott it was the one bright spot in a dreary Christmas.

Late in April Fitzgerald finished *The Beautiful and Damned.* By that time Zelda had discovered that she was pregnant. She and Scott were both tired of the chaos and disorder of their New York apartment and of the steady stream of guests, usually inebriated, who filled it. Since they had long wanted to go to Europe, they decided that it would be easier to see the Continent before the baby came than afterward. Besides, they told themselves, they could live more cheaply there.

The night before they were to sail, despite Lawton Campbell's intervention, Scott had attempted to fight a rear-guard action against a bouncer at the Jungle Club, who had tried to throw him out. Zelda egged Scott on as he flailed at his opponent. But before Lawton could get him out, the bouncer had given him a merciless beating. Scott awoke next morning with a bandaged head, a black eye, and so many bruises and abrasions that he and Zelda had to cancel their sailing and postpone their trip to Europe for a week.

4. The Beautiful and Damned

ON MAY 3, 1921, the Fitzgeralds sailed for England on the *Aquitania*. Before Scott unpacked his luggage, he checked all the important names on the passenger list—including his own—but the celebrities aboard were distressingly few and far between.

In London, Tallulah, who was then the toast of the town, introduced the Fitzgeralds to the Marchioness of Milford Haven; but that, Scott said indignantly, was as near to royalty as they came. However, John Galsworthy invited them to dinner with St. John Ervine; Lady Randolph Churchill entertained them; and Shane Leslie took them on a tour of the Limehouse district. Wapping, the Hindus, and the royal processions pleased them more than the other sights of London. Buckingham Palace appealed to Zelda as a "Town Hall with redskins walking around it," her way of describing the scarlet-coated guards.

In "Show Mr. and Mrs. F. to Number—," they recorded that the staff of the Cecil Hotel, where they stopped in London, was "respectful." But that of the St. James and Albany in Paris was not. Scott smelled up their room with an uncured goat skin and left melting ice cream outside its windows. After Zelda, who tired of waiting for the elevator, began to make a habit of lashing it to the gate on her floor with her belt, the management asked them to leave.

Scott scoured the city in vain, looking for Edmund Wilson, whom he had hoped to meet there but who had failed to register at the American Express. Before they departed for Italy, Scott and Zelda waited in the rain in front of Anatole France's house for hours, hoping to catch a glimpse of him. When he failed to appear, they left Paris in disgust. They found the City of Light a bore and a disappointment because they knew no one there.

Italy pleased them little more than England or France. Its treasures left them cold; sightseeing was not their dish; they preferred people to art and architecture. St. Mark's impressed them less than a gambling machine in the Royal Danieli Hôtel in Venice and the gold-braided officers from an American destroyer in the harbor there. But they "had fun in a gondola feeling like a soft Italian song." In Florence they noted only that "bamboo curtains and an asthma patient complaining of the green plush and an ebony piano were all equally embalmed in the formal parlors of the Hôtel d'Italie." The glories of the Eternal City were unnoted; they only remarked that "there were fleas on the gilded filigree of the Grand Hôtel in Rome; the clerks said it was the flea season." Their dream of spending a year in Italy was rudely shattered by the parasites and the heat.

After their whirlwind tour of the Continent, the Fitzgeralds returned to London. From the Hotel Cecil there, Scott wrote Wilson:

> God damn the continent of Europe. It is of merely antiquarian interest. Rome is only a few years behind Tyre and Babylon. . . . France makes me sick. Its silly pose as the thing the world has to save. I think it's a shame that England and America didn't let Germany conquer Europe. It's the only thing that would have saved the fleet of tottering old wrecks. My reactions were all philistine, anti-socialistic, provincial and racially snobbish. I believe at last in the white man's burden. We are as far above the modern Frenchman as he is above the Negro. Even in art! Italy has no one. When Anatole France dies French literature will be a silly jealous rehashing of literary quarrels. They are through and done. You may have spoken in jest about New York as the capital of culture but in 25 years it will be just as London is now. Culture follows money and all the refinements of aestheticism can't stave

off its seat (Christ! what a metaphor). We will be the Romans in the next generation as the British are now.

This Side of Paradise had just been published in England. Half the reviews were favorable, but at least a fourth of them implied that Scott had read Compton Mackenzie's *Sinister Street* once too often. Fitzgerald grumbled, "I doubt that it will sell fifteen hundred copies here." He was so low in funds that he had to borrow twenty pounds from Scribner's representative in London. England failed to live up to what he and Zelda had expected of it. "Claridge's in London," they remarked, "served strawberries in a gold dish, but the room was an inside room and gray all day, and the waiter didn't care whether we left or not, and he was our only contact." They did not have enough friends in London to have a pleasant time. However, they did have dinner again with Galsworthy the night before they left. But Scott was also disappointed in him because he said he could not stand Galsworthy's pessimism, which was unrelieved by either irony or bitterness. Although they had announced that they intended to spend a year in England, they took a train for Liverpool and sailed for home from there on July 9.

When they landed in New York, Scott told the ship's reporters that he had had a rotten time. Europe, he added, was "a vastly overestimated place." In the tone of a man condemned to penal servitude, Scott wrote Edmund Wilson that he was going down "to the Sahara of the Bozart [Montgomery] for life." Zelda not only wanted her child to be born there but she also wanted to settle down and buy a house in her hometown.

Unfortunately for her plans, they arrived in the midst of a heat wave. Little tornadoes of dust whirled up from between the rows of cotton that fanned out in the fields along the railroad track. The air in the old Union Station seemed to be coming from a blast furnace. Waves of Lazy Lawrence danced off the melting asphalt on Court Square. Despite the rainbow spray from the garden hoses whirling over the seared lawns, all the flowers along Sayre Street, except the metallic zinnias, the hardy cannas, and the scarlet hibiscus had been burned toast brown by the incandescent sun. Banana plants, drooping under their sweet burden, waved their ragged yellow arms in a languid, half-hearted welcome.

The Fitzgeralds stayed with Zelda's parents at Six Pleasant Avenue. Judge and Mrs. Sayre greeted Scott courteously, but he had never been at ease with them. Now, after the "happening" to which he had treated them at Westport, he was distinctly uncomfortable around them. Because Judge Sayre felt that since he had to sit in judgment on cases involving violations of the prohibition laws, he should uphold them at home, there was not so much as a dram of blackberry wine in his house. All Scott could get from the bootleggers was raw moonshine, colored and bottled as Canadian Club or White Horse, which he swigged alone in the locker room of the Country Club and tried to conceal its stench by chewing Sen-Sen before he went back to the Sayres' for dinner. Often as not, he would stay downtown and call Zelda to join him at the Elite Cafe, which to his irritation she called the *Ee*lite, as all Montgomerians did. Scott ascribed their pronunciation to ignorance, unaware that it derived its name not from the French *élite* but from a Greek word meaning "joy." However it was pronounced, the Elite served the best food to be found in any restaurant between Baltimore and New Orleans and provided teacups to camouflage the cocktails that their friends brought when they met them. Lloyd Hooper often met Scott and Zelda there to have a shrimp cocktail and a steak while they mapped plans for the evening.

When they tired of dancing and the vaudeville, Lloyd proposed to take them on a house party at his mother's beautiful old home in Selma. They drove over in Lloyd's car, with the avowed intention of spending a quiet and restful weekend in the Black Belt. But Scott's discovery of the Hoopers' prewar cellar primed a four-day celebration of his escape from the drought on Pleasant Avenue. Since Zelda's pregnancy was too far advanced for her to join wholeheartedly in the wassailing, she sulked on a sofa in the corner and, for once, refused to dance. For want of a better partner Scott unearthed a fitter's dummy in Mrs. Hooper's sewing room. As he waltzed it around the drawing room, the neighbors' eyes bulged, and word went round that the Hooper's famous guest was dancing with a naked woman. Half a dozen of Lloyd's friends dropped in to see what was going on and stayed until the "quiet and restful" trip ended in a rout.

The weekend grew in the telling, and Scott and Zelda were still full of it when they came to tea at our house a few days later. After they had regaled us with stories about it, Scott began to inspect the house. There was a Rembrandt Peale portrait of a dark Byronic gentleman in a black redingote and white stock in the library. "Who is that?" Scott wanted to know.

"One of my forebears," my mother replied.

"He looks very distinguished. What did he do?"

"He was a federal judge."

"Here in Alabama?"

"Yes. He was sent out by President Madison to settle the land claims with the Indians before Alabama became a state."

"It's a fine portrait," he observed. "Why don't you have that tear in it mended."

"Because it was made by a Yankee bayonet," she told him.

"You sound like Zelda's mother," he laughed. "You people down here cherish your scars, don't you?"

"I suppose so," she admitted with a smile. "Like the Bourbons, *nous n'avons rien appris ni rien oublié.*"

"Scott's changed," Zelda pointed out. "He used to love to go to the cemetery to see the Confederate graves and say he loved the South, but now he wants to get as far away from it as he can."

Although Scott politely protested that his feeling about the South had not altered, he had already decided that the dignified, *dolce far niente* life there was not for him. He had tried to work in the morning in the Sayres' library under the electric fan, but the breeze from it was like the blast from a blowtorch. The heat sapped his energy and his flow of ideas. His inability to work irritated and alarmed him. While he was idling around the house, looking for something to divert him, he found a play that Miss Minnie had written about Mary, Queen of Scots. Thinking that it had Broadway possibilities, he set out to revise it; but he bogged down in the middle of the first act, took it off with him, and eventually lost it.

The rainy season set in at the end of July; instead of relieving the heat, the humidity increased its discomforts. The ceiling fans merely stirred the steaming air. To add to Scott's malaise, Judge Sayre never appeared at the table or left the house without his coat, so Scott felt obliged to wear one, too. Cooped up in the house by one torrential downpour after another, with his shirt sticking to his back and stinging with heat rash, he grew irritable with Zelda, and she taxed him for quarreling with her in order to break the monotony. When it did slack up, the golf course was too soggy to play, and Zelda's condition barred her from the tennis court and the swimming pool.

His vexation was increased when he discovered that Scribner's advertising of *This Side of Paradise* was negligible in comparison with the sales campaign that Knopf was staging for Floyd Dell's *Mooncalf*, another book about an adolescent. In writing Max Perkins, Fitzgerald complained that upon its publication *Mooncalf* had been advertised in Montgomery, while *This Side of Paradise*, which had sold over fifty copies on the strength of Zelda's reputation, had never had a single advertisement in the local papers.

By the first week in August, Scott was so wilted and fed up with the South that he decided to settle permanently in St. Paul. Through some friends there, Mr. and Mrs. Oscar Kalman, he arranged to rent a house at Dellwood, a resort on White Bear Lake. After less than a month in Montgomery, he and Zelda left for Minnesota.

Dellwood proved to be cooler but more distracting than the Cradle of the Confederacy. After a heartwarming welcome by the Kalmans, Father Joe Barron, Tubby Washington, and Tom Boyd, the proprietor of the Kilmarnock Book Shop, who toasted Scott as the hometown boy who had made good, Fitzgerald tried to settle down to work. But he and Zelda had the gift of creating an atmosphere of excitement and charm wherever they went. Consequently, they were in great demand, and Scott's determination to begin a play of his own withered steadily under the warmth of his friends' attentions. The satisfaction of returning home as "St. Paul's first successful novelist" soon wore off. The daily round of golf, tennis, and parties left him tired and bored. From Dellwood he wrote Perkins on August 25:

> Hope you are enjoying New Hampshire—you probably are. I'm having a hell of a time because I've loafed for five months and I

want to get to work. Loafing puts me in this particularly obnoxious and abominable gloom. My third novel if I ever write another one, will I'm sure be black as death with gloom. I should like to sit down with ½ dozen chosen companions and drink myself to death but I am sick alike of life, liquor and literature. If it wasn't for Zelda I think I'd disappear out of sight for three years. Ship as a sailor or something and get hard—I'm sick of the flabby semi-intellectual softness in which I flounder with my generation.

In October Scott and Zelda moved to the Commodore Hotel in St. Paul until the Kalmans could find a place for them to live. As soon as they had leased a house at 626 Goodrich Avenue, Scott rented a bare office in the business section of the city and buckled down to the job of revising *The Beautiful and Damned*. Alone in the house all day, Zelda felt deserted and homesick. After she had written Teddy Chanler a description of her "lone wolf poignancy," Scott chaffed her by adding, "Poor battered little Zelda. Think of a bright girl like her running on about 'lone wolf poignancy.' It brings tears to my eyes." She knew few people in St. Paul; and in her first meeting with Scott's parents, she failed to establish any sort of rapport with them. She put his mother down as a character; and his father, with his flowing cravats, his white-piped vests, his Vandyke beard, and his cane, struck her as an ineffectual cardboard figure cut out in a bygone age. Although she was unfailingly courteous and kind to them, and they to her, she probably could not avoid seeing them through Scott's eyes.

Mrs. Fitzgerald and Mrs. Sayre had each sent her some clothes for the baby, but beyond that no preparations had been made for the child's arrival. When Sandra Kalman discovered that there was not even a diaper on hand, she took Scott and Zelda out to buy a stock of them, a bassinet, a baby bed, and a bathtub. Then she arranged for a doctor, a nurse, and a hospital room for Zelda. That done, the Fitzgeralds waited impatiently for the baby to come.

Their daughter, Frances Scott Key Fitzgerald, was born on October 26, 1921. The Kalmans went to the hospital with them and tried to calm a pale and anxious Scott, who paced the floor outside the delivery room, lighting one cigarette from another and swearing that he would kill himself if Zelda died. But the delivery was not a difficult one, and Scott reported to Edmund Wilson that

Zelda had come through it without a scratch, and he had awarded her a *croix de guerre* with palm.

No matter what was taking place in the periphery of Scott's consciousness, at its center there was always a writer. As soon as he was allowed to see Zelda, he took a notebook with him and recorded her first words as she came out from under the anesthetic: "Goofo, I'm drunk. Mark Twain. Isn't she smart—she has the hiccups. I hope it's beautiful and a fool—a beautiful little fool." Zelda had already learned the penalty that a woman pays for being beautiful and intelligent.

Although she was disappointed that her first and only child was not a son, Zelda wrote Ludlow Fowler that she found Scottie, as she called the baby, very cute and became devoted to her. She was such a beautiful child that her jubilant father sent a score of telegrams to his friends, announcing that "LILLIAN GISH IS IN MOURNING CONSTANCE TALMADGE IS A BACK NUMBER AS SECOND MARY PICKFORD HAS ARRIVED." In reply Mencken, who had once ghosted a book called *What You Ought to Know About Your Baby*, plied him with facetious advice. After suggesting that their little girl should be christened Charlotte in honor of Charles Evans Hughes, Mencken wrote Scott:

> I am delighted to know that your posterity is viable and active. One of my friends here is an eminent pediatrician. He says that babies should never bawl. Simply clout them over the head, and they will cease. No narcotics! Simply scaring them is enough.

But instead of resorting to such drastic measures, Scott averred that he had dazzled his daughter's eyes with gold pieces in hopes that she would marry a millionaire.

One of Fitzgerald's friends reported that not long before Scottie's birth, as they drove past a Catholic church in St. Paul, he had heard Scott muttering to himself, "God damn the Catholic Church, God damn God." Nevertheless, he insisted upon having his daughter baptized in his own faith, with Father Joe Barron acting as godfather. According to Scott, he made his last confession while he was stationed in Montgomery, where he had dated a girl who was also a Catholic. One Friday afternoon as they were walking down Lawrence Street past St. Peter's Church, Scott remembered that he had not yet been to confession there and suggested that this was a good time for him to go. After he had been shriven, he persuaded his date that she, too, should confess. She obediently knelt down in the confession box. "Father, forgive me for I have sinned," she began, "I . . . I . . . I. . . ." Recovering her composure, she listed half a dozen minor transgressions. When she ran out of peccadilloes, she began to stammer again.

"Is that all, my daughter?" the priest asked sternly.

"I . . . I . . . think so."

"Are you sure, my daughter?"

"That's . . . that's . . . all I can remember."

"No, that's not all, my daughter. I fear I shall have to prompt you."

"Why, Father?"

"Because I heard your young man's confession first."

Scott was more irked than amused by the incident, and his attitude towards the Church became increasingly ambivalent. After Father Fay's death, he described himself as a "relapsed Catholic" and a "spoiled priest"; and his story "Absolution," which he originally intended to be a picture of Gatsby's early life, offended many of the "Papists" when Mencken published it in the June 1924 issue of the *Mercury*.

During the winter in St. Paul, Scott did what he considered two good stories, "Tarquin of Cheapside" and "The Popular Girl" and several mediocre ones. Between potboilers he worked on a play called "Gabriel's Trombone," in addition to polishing the proofs of *The Beautiful and Damned*. Zelda not only helped him greatly with the proofs but also suggested another ending for the novel. More than one critic was to say that Anthony and Gloria bore a striking resemblance to Scott and Zelda. The sketches on the dust jacket of the book served to convey the same impression. On it Gloria looked very much like Zelda; and that was all very well, Scott said, but he protested to Perkins that Anthony's picture presented a "debauched" image of him, with short ugly legs that made him appear to be no taller than Gloria—a runt who looked like a young tough in his first dinner jacket.

To his disgust, when the *Metropolitan* magazine began to seri-

alize *The Beautiful and Damned,* he found that the editor had
butchered it by cutting over forty thousand words from it. Nor
was he pleased when Scribner's published the novel on March 3,
1922 without having changed the all-too-revealing jacket. Further,
Zelda's flippant review of the novel did more than suggest that it
was autobiographical:

> To begin with every one must buy this book for the following
> aesthetic reasons: First because I know where there is the cutest
> cloth of gold dress for only $300 in a store on Forty-second Street,
> and also if enough people buy it where there is a platinum ring
> with a complete circlet, and if loads of people buy it my husband
> needs a new winter overcoat, although he has one that has done
> well enough for the last three years. . . .
>
> It seems to me that on one page I recognize a portion of an old
> diary of mine which mysteriously disappeared shortly after my
> marriage, and also scraps of letters, which though considerably
> edited, sound to me vaguely familiar. In fact, Mr. Fitzgerald—I
> believe that is how he spells his name—seems to believe that
> plagiarism begins at home.

Mencken congratulated Scott on striking out in a new direction
in his book rather than having simply rewritten *This Side of
Paradise.* Edmund Wilson, who had read *The Beautiful and
Damned* in manuscript and suggested cutting a few florid passages, now found it better organized and a distinct improvement
on Scott's first book. Most of the other reviews were mixed. The
sales fell short of Fitzgerald's expectations, and those of his *This
Side of Paradise* had leveled off. Meanwhile, Wilson, who had
called Scott's first novel, "an exquisite burlesque of Compton
Mackenzie with a pastiche of Wells thrown in at the end," did an
article on Fitzgerald for the "Literary Spotlight" in *The Bookman*
of March 1922, in which he took Scott to task for overplaying the
tragedy and the "meaninglessness" of life in *The Beautiful and
Damned.* "Hitherto," Wilson said, "he [Scott] had supposed that
the thing to do was to discover a meaning in life; but he now set
bravely about to produce a distressing tragedy which should be
also 100 percent meaningless."

Scott took Wilson's criticism with very little protest, but a mordant review by Frances Newman, an Atlanta librarian and a

friend of Cabell's, drew fire from Fitzgerald. By her own admission, the review was written "with intent to murder." Scott wrote her a caustic letter in which he declared that her contention that he had plagiarized Compton Mackenzie's *Sinister Street* in *This Side of Paradise* was as farfetched as to say that Cabell's *Jurgen* was an imitation of Anatole France's *The Revolt of the Angels.* Miss Newman retorted that she felt as if she had pulled the curls of a small, spoiled boy and made him cry. When Scott ran into her friend Joseph Hergesheimer in the Kilmarnock Book Shop that winter, he was still "sore" from Miss Newman's thrusts at him.

Hergesheimer's fame had crested with his latest novel, *Cytherea*, and he was still glowing with its success when he stopped over in St. Paul on his way back from Hollywood, where he had scored another hit with his scenario for *Tol'able David.* Scott's first impression of him was of an intolerably affluent, complacent Pennsylvania Dutchman, whose cropped poll, thick-lensed glasses, and stocky body contrasted oddly with his flamboyant silk shirt, monogrammed handkerchief, coonskin coat, and gold-tipped cane. But after sipping a few glasses of wine with him before the fire in the back room of the book shop, Scott was surprised to find that despite Hergesheimer's outward stolidity and opulence, he was a highly sensitive man, an innate artist, and a hard-working, conscientious craftsman. Before the afternoon was over, he had invited the novelist to go home with him to dinner and to meet Zelda.

At the table, affecting Nathan's bored, world-weary pose, Scott complained of the vicissitudes of a writer's life. Hergesheimer, who had written for fourteen years without selling a book, listened patiently until Scott declared that in his frustration and despair, he wished that he had been anything but a writer. "Sometimes," he added, "I even wish I'd been a carpenter, don't you, Mr. Hergesheimer?"

"Good God, no!" he exploded. After he had recounted his own hardships as a young writer, living off cornfield peas and hominy in the wilds of the Appalachians, Zelda said, "But, at least, you didn't have to live in St. Paul on the edge of the Arctic Circle." Zelda fascinated him as she did most men, and when she told him how lonely she was and how she longed to get back to New York and "festivity," he promised to give her a party at the Algonquin that would make up for all the bleak months in Minnesota.

Although Scott denounced St. Paul as a "dull hell-hole," he was determined to stay there until he finished his play. Despite Zelda's plaint to Hergesheimer that she was lonely there, Scott's friends swarmed into the house on Goodrich Avenue at all hours of the day and night. For the most part they were Midwesterners with whom she had little in common, and she frequently countermanded Scott's invitations to them. On several occasions when their noisy celebrations waked the baby, she asked them to leave. Consequently, many of them liked her as little as she did them, and they fabricated many of the more shocking stories about her that have come to be accepted as truth instead of fiction. She shuddered at the chores entailed by entertaining them at home and shivered at the heavy snows and biting winds she had to face if she went out with them. As she wrote Ludlow Fowler, "This damned place is 18 below zero and I go around thanking God, anatomically and proverbially speaking, I am safe from the fate of the monkey."

To make her lot in St. Paul more difficult, after Hergesheimer's visit, Scott retired into seclusion and celibacy to work on his play, while Zelda's creative efforts were strangled by a Niagara of domestic trivia. During Scott's hibernation that winter, he was too preoccupied to play the demon lover. The processes of artistic creation and amorous passion never exist simultaneously; the exercise of the one obliterates the other for the time being; and in Scott's periodic absorption in his writing and Zelda's in her painting and dancing lay the cause for their marital difficulties, not, as *A Moveable Feast* asserts, in a matter of mathematical measurements.

In February Scott wrote James Branch Cabell that he had had a protracted amour with a beautiful case of Spanish influenza, and like all such illicit affairs it had left him weak and chastened. Being both physically and financially depleted, he was in low spirits. He had borrowed over fifty-six hundred dollars from Scribner's as advance royalties on *The Beautiful and Damned* before it appeared. But encouraged by Edmund Wilson's verdict that his new play was one of the best American comedies ever written, Scott and Zelda struck out for New York to celebrate and have Nathan read the script. They stayed at the Plaza Hotel, which Zelda described as "an etched hotel, dainty and subdued, with such a handsome head waiter that he never minded lending five dollars or borrowing a Rolls-Royce."

In those days the very air of Manhattan was heady with prosperity. As Zelda said in *Save Me the Waltz*, it was a time when:

> Paul Whiteman played "Two Little Girls in Blue" at the Palais Royal; it was a big expensive number. Girls with piquant profiles were mistaken for Gloria Swanson. New York was more full of reflections than of itself—the only concrete things in town were the abstractions. Everybody wanted to pay the caberet checks.
>
> "We're having some people," everybody said to everybody else, "and we want you to join us," and they said, "We'll telephone."
>
> All over New York people telephoned. They telephoned from one hotel to another to people on other parties that couldn't get there—that they were engaged. It was always tea-time or late at night.
>
> David and Alabama invited their friends to throw oranges into the drum at the Plantation and themselves into the fountain at Union Square. Up they went, humming the New Testament and Our Country's Constitution, riding the tide like triumphant islanders on a surf board. Nobody knew the words to "The Star-Spangled Banner."

The Fitzgeralds' stay there began and ended in an interminable party, during which Scott confessed that he "never once got sober enough to tolerate being sober." John V. A. Weaver took them out on the town one evening to tour the Village night spots; they ended up three days later at a party at Nathan's apartment. Scott enjoyed the fragmentary meetings with Wilson, Peale, and Donald Ogden Stewart and the "bawdy luncheons" with Horace Liveright, a wealthy publisher, noted for his riotous parties. But, on the whole, Scott reported that he had had a poor time.

Perhaps one explanation of why he did not enjoy the trip is that in his Ledger under an entry headed a "Trip to New York" and dated March 1922, where surprisingly enough in view of Scott's Catholic prejudices against birth control, there is a note on Zelda and her abortionist. This was the first of three similar incidents, each of which drove another wedge into their marriage.

Another source of discord sprang from Scott's increasing attentions to other women. Through Horace Liveright, he had met Dorothy Parker. Although she was the most quoted wit among those who gathered at the Algonquin Round Table, she characterized herself as "born Rothschild but not those Rothschilds." She was, she said, "just a little Jewish girl trying to be cute," a mischievous little elf, with very bright dark eyes, deeply set just below the straight bangs of a boyish haircut. She not only tried to be cute but also succeeded so well that she made herself the center of attention at every party. If this did not sit too well with Zelda, who was accustomed to being the star of the evening, Miss Parker's skill at mocking her Southern accent and Scott's infatuation with Miss Parker pleased his wife even less. Dorothy found him to be "attractive and sweet when he wanted to be nice," and even though she said that he had no sense of humor, she professed to like him as a person better than any other serious writer. According to Lillian Hellman, years later, Dorothy confessed to her "that she and Scott had slept together . . . in a casual one or two night affair." If this is true, Scott must have recovered from the chastening effects of his amour with Spanish influenza. In justice to Scott, however, let it be said that there is no mention of that episode or any subsequent one in his records.

When I arrived in New York, on my way to make the grand tour of Europe with Miss Margaret Booth, Lawton Campbell's aunt and principal of the preparatory school from which I had just graduated, we hoped to see Scott and Zelda, but they had gone back to St. Paul. However, Lawton took us for cocktails at the Plaza and amused us with stories of the Fitzgeralds' antics. Scott, he said, claimed that Hearst had a newsman to follow them to report on everything they said and did while they were in New York. Just to be sure that the reporter didn't run out of copy, Scott had dived, fully clothed, into the Pulitzer fountain in front of the Plaza. He had insulted his hosts, as well as those who declined to serve as such, and he had passed out with his head on Zelda's shoulder at a literary tea.

Whether Scott and Zelda did not enjoy their trip to New York that spring or whether they felt that they must get back to the baby, whom they had left with a nurse in St. Paul, they had returned to Goodrich Avenue by the first week in April. While Scott busied himself with *Tales of the Jazz Age*, a collection of his short stories that Scribner's was to publish the next fall, Zelda looked for a place for them to spend the summer. She decided on the Yacht Club at White Bear Lake, where she would be relieved of the domestic chores and Scott of the household clamor. But there, once again, they were merely "fully airing the desire for unadulterated gaiety." Scott toyed with a Midwestern novel involving a Catholic element, but shelved it when two Hollywood scouts approached him with a proposal to make a movie of *This Side of Paradise*, in which he and Zelda were to be starred. Zelda was enthusiastic over the idea, and Scott was all for it until Perkins objected strenuously. Even though Scott promised that it would positively be their first and last appearance, Perkins talked him out of it by telling him that it would end his career as a serious novelist.

Toward the middle of August, Scott wrote Perkins asking him to deposit a thousand dollars to his credit. Arthur Hopkins, he added, now had his "Gabriel's Trombone" (which later became *The Vegetable*). Scott predicted that the play would make him rich and that he would never have to bother Perkins again.

By September they were back at the Plaza. On my return from Europe I had tea with Zelda in the Palm Court there. After the summer at White Bear Lake, she looked fit, tanned, and rested. She and Scott were "theoretically on the water wagon," she announced, so she ordered tea for herself and hot chocolate for me. "You're too young for cocktails," she said. While we were comparing notes on the experiences of innocents abroad, Scott joined us. Before he said a word, he did a happy little jig. He had just been to see Sam Harris about *The Vegetable*; and despite the fact that Arthur Hopkins, Gilbert Miller, George Selwyn, and Jed Harris had turned down the play, Fitzgerald, on the basis of the things Wilson and Nathan had said about it, had continued to have faith in it. And now Sam Harris had agreed to produce it, cast Ernest Truex in the leading role, which Frank Craven had declined, and scheduled the play for a tryout in Atlantic City in November.

"It's going to be a big money-maker," Scott boasted. He was even more excited over it than Zelda was over the curtain for the new Greenwich Follies, on which she was depicted in a favorite pose—diving into a fountain. Fame and fortune were at hand; their financial troubles were over. New York had a million-dollar look to both of them. The skies had never seemed so blue, the clouds so bright, the air of the city so exhilarating as it did that bright autumn day.

A few days later, Scott, who considered John Dos Passos's *Three Soldiers* to be the outstanding book of the previous fall, arranged to meet its author and invited him to lunch at the Plaza, where Dos Passos remembers that the carpets were thick, the perfume from the coiffeur's shop thicker, and the "elevator man's gold buttons flashed like gold sovereigns." Scott met him at the door of the suite and introduced him to Sherwood Anderson, who was then at the zenith of his fame.

After chiding Dos Passos for being late, Scott, who had forgotten about the water wagon, plied him with Bronx cocktails and afterward with champagne. They had lobster croquettes for dinner and creamy sweet butter to spread on crisp French rolls. Meanwhile, Dos Passos reported that Scott and Zelda had begun their usual inquisition:

> Their gambit was to put you in the wrong. You were backward in your ideas. You were inhibited about sex. These things might perfectly well have been true but my attitude was that they were nobody's goddamn business. I held them off as best I could until Sherwood got talking about his writing and I could listen and roam around the room and look out the tall windows into Central Park where the leaves were just beginning to turn and at the skillful elderly waiter and the glittering luncheon table.
>
> Afterwards I used to kid Scott about his silly questions. They were like the true or false lists that psychologists make up. Even that first time I couldn't get mad at him and particularly at Zelda: there was a golden innocence about them and they were both so hopelessly goodlooking.

Sherwood Anderson left them after lunch, and the Fitzgeralds asked Dos Passos to drive out to Great Neck, Long Island, with them to look for a house there because they wanted to escape continuous bacchanalia in New York. They set off in a red touring car with a chauffeur. Scott chaffed Dos Passos about his "social" interests, which were unfashionable at the time, and Dos Passos teased him about his infatuation with the rich. But Dos Passos conceded later that when Scott talked about writing:

> His mind, which seemed to me to be full of preposterous notions about most things, became clear and hard as a diamond. He didn't look at the landscape, he had no taste for food or wine or painting, little ear for music except for the most rudimentary popular songs, but about writing he was a born professional. Everything he said was worth listening to.

They picked up an expansive real estate man in Great Neck, who showed them a number of "gentlemen's estates," but nothing they saw pleased them; and when they wearied of teasing him, they let him out and dropped in to see Ring Lardner, a humorist whom they considered master of the pungent lingo of the sports world—a tall, gaunt man, with hollow cheeks, hollow eyes, high cheekbones, a high-bridged nose, and a long face, dark and solemn as an Indian's. He habitually spoke with extraordinary slowness; but when the Fitzgeralds and Dos Passos arrived, he was too far gone in his cups to speak at all; he simply stood motionless by the fireplace and stared at them. Scott claimed him as his private drunkard. "Everybody should have a private drunkard," he said. After a few drinks with Lardner's wife, they started back to New York. When they passed a carnival, Zelda and Dos Passos insisted on stopping to ride the roller coaster and the rickety Ferris wheel; but Scott refused to join them and sulked in the car with a bottle he had hidden under the seat, mulling over the ideas that germinated in "Winter Dreams," which he called "a sort of first draft" of *The Great Gatsby*.

Dos Passos left them under the gilt marquee of the Plaza feeling that he had been on a lark with a pair of charming, golden-haired children. "They were celebrities in the Sunday supplement sense of the word," he reflected. "They were celebrities and they loved it." Although they did not originate the expression "Do your own thing," they made a habit of it. In the twenties they were always where the action was and the action was always where they were. The "happenings" created by the young people of today, though more violent and destructive, seem stereotyped and unimaginative in comparison with those of Scott and Zelda in the Jazz Age. As Lillian Gish once said, "They didn't make the twenties; they were the twenties."

5. Ash Heaps and Millionaires

WHILE ZELDA went back to St. Paul to fetch Scottie, Fitzgerald resumed the search for a suitable house on Long Island. Before she returned, he had bought a secondhand Rolls-Royce coupe and rented what she described as a "nifty little Babbitt home" at 6 Gateway Drive near Great Neck. If it was not a "gentleman's estate," it impressed Mencken as a "palazzo," and it rented for three hundred dollars a month.

Scott met Zelda and the baby with a new nurse whom he had hired. Zelda promptly fired her and hired another one, who refused to eat with the Swedish couple, who tried to bring order out of the wild confusion on Gateway Drive. In a letter at that time to Cousin Ceci, Scott noted with pleasure that

> Great Neck is a great place for celebrities—it being the habitat of Frank Craven, Herbert Swope, Arthur Hopkins, Jane Cowl. . . . It is most amusing after the dull healthy Middle West. For instance at a party last night where we went were John McCormack, Hugh Walpole, FPA [Franklin P. Adams, the columnist], Neysa McMein, Arthur William Brown, Rudolph Friml and Deems Taylor. They have no mock-modesty and all perform their various stunts upon the slightest request so it's like a sustained concert.

Samuel Goldwyn, General Pershing, Gene Buck, and Ring Lardner lived nearby. To the Oscar Kalmans Zelda described Lardner as a typical newspaper man, adding:

> He is six feet tall and goes on periodical sprees lasting from one to X weeks. He is on one now, which is probably the reason he called on us. He plays the saxophone and takes us to Mr. Gene Buck's house. Mr. Gene Buck originates Ziegfield's [*sic*] Follies and lives in a house designed by Joseph Urban. It looks like a lot of scenery glued together. Mr. Buck says "seen" where he should say "saw" and is probably a millionaire. He discovered Olive Thomas and tells me I look like her. He married a Dulcy-type chorus-girl who has lovely legs and consequently a baby.

Between partying and revising his play, Scott had little time left for his new novel. Since it was only half an hour by train from Great Neck to New York, he commuted during rehearsals. The wastelands along the tracks, the beady-eyed gangsters on the Long Island Express, the extravagant parties and great estates of Long Island made such a deep impression on him that one of the many titles that he contemplated using for *The Great Gatsby* was "Among Ash-Heaps and Millionaires."

Zelda frequently went to New York with him, and they stayed overnight at the Plaza after spending the evening at the Rendez-vous, the Montmartre, the Plantation, the Club Gallant, or at some speakeasy, where Scott made a study of bootleggers, gangsters, and gamblers. Arnold Rothstein, a noted gangster; Edward M. Fuller, a Long Island neighbor who was sentenced to five years in Sing Sing for a series of crimes; and a gentleman bootlegger who lived like a millionaire all furnished part of the material for *The Great Gatsby*.

In November Scott and Zelda went to Princeton for the Yale game. It was the first time that Scott had been back to his alma mater since he was suspended from the Cottage Club. Princeton won the game, which was almost all that he and Zelda remembered about it. Afterward they went around to the clubs, feeling like a pair of Methuselahs. In the course of the evening they picked up a crew of tipsy young friends, took them to eat at the Baltimore Lunch and then to call on Herbert Agar, who had been a fellow student of Scott's at Princeton. The deans and professors gathered at the Agars' looked on stupefied and incredulous while the Fitzgeralds and their troupe sang and danced for them. Scott drove back to New York through a misty evening that smelled of burning leaves, chrysanthemums, and liquor. He was nostalgic and blue because once again his extemporaneous performances had not been appreciated at Princeton.

The Vegetable, with Ernest Truex in the lead, opened on November 20, 1923, at the Apollo Theater in Atlantic City. The first night was a gala affair. The Lardners and a number of friends from Long Island and New York, among them Mayor J. F. Hylan, came down for the opening and a party at Evelyn Nesbitt's café, but the play was such a complete frost that the audience began to walk out after the second act. Scott wanted to close it then and there, though at Sam Harris's request he tried for a week to patch it up, but the play folded before it reached Broadway. Afterward, Zelda wrote Sandy Kalman an account of what she called "the murder":

> [I refer to] "The Vegetable," of course, which brings me to another very different theme, which should be read slowly three or four times to the accompaniment of Massenet's Elegy and the death march from Saul, which is all the music I know. However, I know some things which could be recited during the reading which I won't mention. In brief, the show flopped as flat as one of Aunt Jemima's famous pancakes.
>
> Scott and Truex and Harris were terribly disappointed and so was I as I had already spent the first weeks of the N.Y. royalty for a dress to wear to the opening night that could not be exchanged.
>
> The first act went fine but Ernest says he has *never* had an experience on the stage like the second. . . . People were so obviously bored! and it was all very well done, so there was no use trying to fix it up. The idea was what people didn't like—just hopeless! Scott suggested fixing it by having Ernest's teeth fall out when he heard about the Buzzard Islands, but I don't think anybody liked the suggestion but us—It's too terrible to contemplate.

For the last six months Scott had coasted along on the ten thousand dollars he had received for the sale of the movie rights to *This Side of Paradise*. To his dismay, on his return to Great Neck after the failure of *The Vegetable*, he informed Perkins that he was five thousand dollars in debt and in such dire need of six hundred fifty dollars that he would have to pawn the furniture if he did not get it to the bank by Wednesday morning.

After *Hearst's International* cancelled the option that it had taken on all of his short stories, with the fortitude of which he frequently proved capable in an emergency, Scott hibernated that winter in a chill room over the garage heated only by an oil stove. Sometimes he worked there all night, often turning out a story between dinner and breakfast. By April he had produced eleven stories, which netted him seventeen thousand dollars—enough to pay his debts and allow him to go back to his novel. But his work on it was stymied by a series of parties, which Zelda described as so alcoholic and chaotic that they had never been equaled except in Rome and Nineveh. Heartsick over the deterioration in the quality of his work, he went on a Brobdingnagian binge.

Mencken and Nathan, John Dos Passos, Max Perkins, Ludlow Fowler, and the Kalmans came to visit them. The evening would begin at a speakeasy in New York, followed by a wild ride to Great Neck with Scott singing "Who'll Bite Your Neck When My Teeth Are Gone" and Zelda driving the Rolls-Royce into ponds and over fire plugs because it seemed more fun.

Burton Rascoe remembered one of the Fitzgeralds' parties at which Scott had entertained the guests with some card tricks that Edmund Wilson had taught him, told them the plot of the great American novel that he was writing, after first having made them promise not to give the plot away, outlined a number of scenarios that he had been mulling over, gave one of his extempore orations, and concluded the performance with a song of his own composition, "Dog, Dog, Dog." Mencken irked him by insisting upon calling him Mr. Fitzheimer, and Nathan galled him by teasing him about the plots he had disclosed. It was not one of the better parties at Gateway Drive.

Zelda proved to be more inventive than Scott in devising amusements during their parties. She concocted a summer cooler composed of three parts gin, one part water, and the juice of a lemon, which she said she should patent and offer to Ed Wynn; she introduced the literati to "soul" food, as a recipe for corn pone in her cookbook is there to prove. To rouse a dull New Year's party, she made a game of tossing the guests' hats into the bowl of the chandelier; and by way of making a graceful exit after a riotous evening, she rode out of the Kalmans' room in a laundry cart. Although her antics were never vicious, she atoned for them by going about in sackcloth and ashes for days afterward, particularly after Rosalind, her favorite sister, arrived in Great Neck to find a "happening" in progress, comparable to the one that greeted Judge and Mrs. Sayre at Westport, and began to remonstrate with Zelda about the way she and Scott were living.

Eleanor Browder and the Lloyd Hoopers, who also visited the Fitzgeralds at Gateway Drive, were almost equally dismayed to find that the "nifty little Babbitt home" there was run like a deluxe country club with a set of house rules that made conversation as far south as Montgomery: "Visitors are requested not to break down doors in search of liquor, even when authorized to do so by the host and hostess," and "Week-end guests are respectfully notified that invitations to stay over Monday, issued by the host and hostess during the small hours of Sunday morning, must not be taken seriously."

While Livye Hart's mother was on a shopping trip to New York, she asked Scott and Zelda to have tea with her one afternoon at the Astor Hotel. To her surprise, Zelda arrived alone and insisted that they wait in the lobby for Scott. Although Scott and Zelda passed each other several times, "in their slightly *tipsy* condition," as Livye's mother charitably put it, they failed to recognize each other. After they finally located Scott in the main dining room, he could not get a word in edgewise because Zelda "for a full hour expatiated, declaring with force and sincerity her undying friendship and loyalty" to Livye. Despite Zelda's best speeches, when Livye received a most cordial invitation to visit the Fitzgeralds, her mother refused to let her go.

Zelda, Livye said, "was undoubtedly the personification of the 'Roaring Twenties'. . . . One of her main characteristics was her apparent delight in shocking people. And that is what she almost invariably did. All the time reveling in it." Zelda, she added, also had an elastic sense of humor. Just after Livye's first son was born, Zelda combined shock value with humor by sending him a beautiful blue Angora wool snow suit, which was ridiculous because it rarely snows in Montgomery and startling in that the suit, made for a four-year-old child, swallowed Livye's nine-pound boy. Zelda, however, made up for her joke the next day by sending him a lovely satin-tufted comforter for his crib.

Zelda's articles in the *Metropolitan* and Scott's stories in the *Post* kept them in the public eye; and if their escapades dismayed their families and friends, they delighted the gossips. When Joseph Conrad visited his publisher, Nelson Doubleday, on his estate at Oyster Bay, Scott and Ring Lardner honored him with a bacchic dance on the lawn there until they were forcibly removed by the gardeners. At a dinner they gave for Rebecca West, the honorée failed to appear. In revenge, Fitzgerald painted a face on a pillow, stuck a ridiculous hat on it, gave it Miss West's place at the table, and enlivened the meal by making scathing remarks to it about the Englishwoman's life, works, and love affairs. After he socked a detective who called Zelda down at a dance, the episode was headlined, "Fitzgerald Knocks Officer This Side of Paradise."

A violent, destructive note had crept into Scott's binges. Anita Loos braved current stories of his strange behavior to have dinner with the Fitzgeralds at Gateway Drive. Before going to the table, she and Zelda waited for Scott until almost time for the servants to leave. Just as the roast was brought on, Scott staggered in. "You didn't wait for me!" he shouted. "Why didn't you?"

"Because we were hungry," Zelda replied calmly.

Scott seized a candelabrum from the table and raised it to strike them. "I'll kill you both," he shouted. The butler sprang forward and caught his arm. With his free hand, Scott snatched the cloth from the table, dumping the dishes, glasses, silver, and dinner on the floor. While the butler restrained Fitzgerald, Zelda and Anita, in fear of their lives, fled to take refuge with the Lardners, who lived across the drive.

Lardner persuaded Scott that he needed to get away from the ash heaps and millionaires and finish his novel about them. Although he had not even completed a first draft of it, he had accumulated a surplus of seven thousand dollars. So, having decided that they could live more cheaply on the Riviera, they sailed for Europe aboard the S. S. *Minnewaska* on May 3, 1924.

Two years before in Paris I had first seen the man who was to become Scott's idol and Zelda's evil genius. The seacoasts of Bo-

hemia along the *carrefour* at the intersection of the Boulevard
Raspail and the Boulevard Montparnasse were out of bounds at
that time for young ladies on the grand tour; but one afternoon
while Miss Booth and her charges were having tea at Rumple-
meyer's, I persuaded a young newspaperman I knew to take me
to the Rotonde. The terrace was so crowded with brass-bound,
marble-topped tables that the Algerian rug peddlers and the
purveyors of pornographic postcards had to walk in the gutter.
Waiters in black coats and white aprons darted in and out like so
many busy penguins among the noisy, bizarre-looking crowd of
students, artists, models, and tourists. While we waited for one of
them to find a seat for us, my friend nodded to a young man
sitting alone reading a racing sheet in a corner against the parti-
tion that separated the Rotonde from the next café. "There's a
chap that may do something someday," my friend said, pulling a
clipping from his pocket. "He stayed with me at the Hotel Jacob
when he first came here. A smart boy but a bit of a rough cus-
tomer or we'd go sit with him."

The clipping he handed me was a feature story from the *Toronto Star Weekly*, "American Bohemians in Paris a Weird Lot,"
written, my friend told me, by the young man immersed in the
racing sheet. It was a good description of the "strange-acting and
strange-looking breed that crowd the tables of the Café Rotonde.
They have all striven so hard," it continued, "for a careless indi-
viduality of clothing that they have achieved a sort of uniformity
of eccentricity." And, may I add, certainly few had been so
successful in their endeavor as the author of the story. Even
among the broad black hats and the flowing ties, the paint-
smeared smocks and mandarin coats jammed together at the sidewalk tables, his clothes were conspicuously sloppy. He wore a
dirty singlet, a pair of old corduroy trousers, grimy sneakers, and
no hat. He was tall and well built but thin, almost gangling. His
face was round, with high cheekbones, dimples, flat planes, and a
deeply cleft chin. Had his skin not been so pale one might have
suspected that he had Comanche blood. As it was, his sullen
features, his dark hair, dark eyes, and long, dark sideburns made
him look more like a Latin than an Indian.

"If he had a cap pulled down over his eye and a cigarette

drooping from his lip, he could pass for an Apache anywhere in Paris," I said.

"Well, he does live in a garret off the Quarter," my companion laughed. "A horrible place on the third floor over a *bal musette* in rue Cardinal Lemoine, next to the Apache hangouts in the Place Contrescarpe—no hot water, no bathroom, no bed. He and his wife sleep on a mattress on the floor. But he doesn't seem to mind."

"If, as he says in his article, 'the artists of Paris who are turning out creditable work resent and loathe the Rotonde Crowd,' why does he come here?"

"To get away from the dump he lives in, I suppose. He gets his mail here, reads all the papers on the café rack, writes his stories at the table there—all for the price of a few demi bocks."

"Quite a few." I nodded to the pile of saucers racked up in front of the racing sheet. "He'll soon need guy wires to hold that stack up. Where'd he come from, Greenwich Village or the Barbary Coast?"

"On the contrary, from a bourgeois suburb in the Middle West, Oak Park, Illinois. His father's a doctor there. Ernest joined the American Field Service, drove an ambulance in Italy, and came home quite a hero—wounded and decorated and all that—but he couldn't wait to get back to Europe. So he got a job with the *Toronto Star* at space rates—a cent a word—married and came to Paris to try to write. And unlike most of the literary crowd that hang out here, Hemingway's serious about it. Damn serious. I guess he has to be, though his wife has an income of her own. He showed me a story once that he'd rewritten eleven times and still hadn't finished it."

As we sat there drinking our coffee, with the sunlight falling through the broad leaves of the plane trees and dappling the sidewalk tables, casting strange lights and shadows over "the weird lot" jammed in around them, I finished reading the article in the *Toronto Star*. And I wondered whether, "since the good old days when Charles Baudelaire led a purple lobster on a leash through the same old Latin Quarter," any more trenchant piece ever had been written about it than the one in my hand by the morose young man in the corner. Even so, as we watched him scowl over the francs and centimes marked on the saucers before him as he totted up the bill, neither one of us would have believed it had we been told that he would someday be world famous, win the Nobel Prize, and die a millionaire.

Hemingway had arrived in Paris about six months before with a letter from Sherwood Anderson to Gertrude Stein. He sat at her feet in her apartment in the rue de Fleurus and absorbed her theories. Through Sylvia Beach, the daughter of a Princeton clergyman, who ran a bookshop called Shakespeare & Co. in the rue de l'Odéon, he met James Joyce and Ezra Pound. At first Hemingway was wary of Joyce's erudition and Pound's flowing ties and oversize velvet berets, but their conversation and kindness to him soon won him over. Pound sent some of Hemingway's poems to the *Dial* and was responsible for having some of his paragraph-length stories published in the *Little Review*. In 1923 Robert McAlmon brought out a slim volume by Hemingway, entitled *Three Stories and Ten Poems*.

By the time Fitzgerald arrived in Paris in May 1924, Hemingway had made little reputation for himself and less money. Scott liked the stories of Hemingway's that had appeared in the *transatlantic review*; and in October, about six months before he met Hemingway, Scott wrote Maxwell Perkins, his editor at Scribner's, advising him that the young man from Oak Park had a brilliant future and suggesting that Perkins should "look him up right away."

Hemingway never forgave his early literary sponsors for having helped him. Only Ezra Pound, who shared his treacherous streak, escaped his malice. When Hemingway came to pay the others off, with unparalleled ingratitude he satirized Sherwood Anderson in *The Torrents of Spring* and painted pathological portraits of Gertrude Stein, Alice Toklas, Wyndham Lewis, Ford Madox Ford, and Scott Fitzgerald in *A Moveable Feast*. Scott had made Hemingway's first really lucrative contract for him in the publishing world through Max Perkins; therefore, Scott caught the brunt of his venom with what his daughter Scottie has called "Mr. Hemingway's piercing jabs at that prone body."

Hemingway's bitterness toward Scott and Zelda was partially rooted in the difference between his crushing poverty and their relative affluence during their early days. In 1922 Scott had earned more than twenty-five thousand dollars and in the next year more than twenty-eight thousand. During their first year in Great Neck, they had spent thirty-six thousand. They were accustomed to high living now. When they returned to Europe in the spring of 1924, they were well heeled, well dressed, and well publicized.

At the Hôtel des Deux Mondes in Paris, they bathed the baby in the bidet by mistake. After little Scottie drank a gin fizz instead of lemonade while they were lunching in the Bois, Zelda and Scott hired an English nanny for her, who accompanied them to the Riviera. In *Save Me the Waltz* Zelda later remembered:

> The train bore them down through the pink carnival of Normandy, past the delicate tracery of Paris and the high terraces of Lyon, the belfries of Dijon and the white romance of Avignon into the scent of lemon, the rustle of black foliage, clouds of moths whipping the violet dusk—into Provence, where people do not need to see unless they are looking for the nightingale.

After a brief stay at Grimm's Park Hotel in Hyères, disgusted by the goat's meat served to them and bored by the complaints of the invalids there, they moved on to the Ruhl in Nice. Stars fell in their plates as they dined on the terrace "alone with the deep blue grandeur and the *filet de sole Ruhl* and the second bottle of champagne." In Monte Carlo, the Hôtel de Paris reminded them of a palace in a detective story. Since the Murphys were in Antibes, where they were building their Villa America and removing the flotsam and jetsam from its little Plage de la Garoupe, Scott and Zelda lingered at the Continental in St. Raphaël to be near them. Charmed by the gay little town, with its groves of eucalyptus, lemon, and olive trees, its red-roofed houses that seemed to tumble down to the sea in an avalanche of tile, and its sun-drenched beaches, in June the Fitzgeralds settled down there for the summer in the Villa Marie. Surrounded by terraced gardens that rose like steps from the sea and protected from the sun by plane trees and parasol pines, the villa appealed to them as an ideal retreat. In her novel, Zelda described the setting:

> The deep Greek of the Mediterranean licked its chops over the edges of our febrile civilization. Keeps crumbled on the gray hill-

sides and sowed the dust of their battlements beneath the olives and cactus. Ancient moats slept bound in tangled honeysuckle; fragile poppies bled the causeways; vineyards caught on the jagged rocks like bits of worn carpet. The baritone of tired mediæval bells proclaimed disinterestedly a holiday from time. Lavender bloomed silently over the rocks. It was hard to see in the vibrancy of the sun.

Zelda loved it at St. Raphaël. She swam, tanned herself to a biscuit brown on the Moorish balconies of the villa, and played with Scottie. To amuse her and her playmates, Zelda built an elaborate little cardboard castle, complete with battlements, towers, and a moat. Scott staffed it with lead soldiers and delighted the children by showing them how it would have been besieged in the Middle Ages. In the evenings, Zelda read Henry James while Scott read Byron and Shelley and began *War and Peace.* Living "in a sort of idyllic state among everything lovely imaginable in the way of Mediterranean delights" was more conducive to dreaming than writing his novel. However, he worked continuously, if slowly, with only two major interruptions. The first one, to judge from an entry in Scott's Ledger, came in June 1924, when the name of Edouard Josanne, a French naval aviator, appears.

Scott misspelled Jozan's name and misinterpreted the young aviator's attentions to Zelda. Born at Nîmes as the son of a French army officer, Jozan had inherited an aristocratic tradition and, with it, a chivalrous attitude toward women. After he was graduated from the naval college at Brest, he entered upon a career as a naval aviator, which left him with little time or inclination for serious love affairs. He and his fellow officers flirted as insouciantly with the young women that they met in their ports of call as Zelda did with the young men she encountered on her travels. Like Jozan and his friends among the aviators who were stationed with him at Fréjus, Zelda was looking for some momentary diversion rather than for a passionate attachment. However, Jozan was undeniably attracted to Zelda, and she to him. While Scott toiled away at *The Great Gatsby,* Zelda danced, played tennis, swam, and sat in the sun on the terrace of a café with the young officers, sipping a porto while she bantered with them. Jozan spoke English well enough to pay her charming compliments, and she amused him with her pungent comments on French customs. He and his fellow officers found her to be a vivacious, witty companion as well as a lovely young woman, all the more fascinating for being a bit strange, for saying and doing unexpected things.

When I met Jozan in Paris last spring, almost half a century after Zelda's flirtation with him, it was not hard to understand her attraction to him. For he is still an unusually charming and handsome gentleman. Tall, trim, and erect, except for the sprinkling of silver at his temples, he shows few traces of his years or of the rigors of his long and distinguished career in the French navy. In his youth he served for many years in Indochina. After the outbreak of World War II, he was put in command of a flotilla at Dunkirk. Subsequently, he was captured by the Germans and interned in a prison camp. As soon as he was released, he returned to the service. He became vice-admiral of the French fleet in 1952 and later returned to the Far East as commander of France's naval forces there. Ten years ago, he retired as a full admiral and returned to Paris, where he now lives.

Even before he became a decorated hero, as a young lieutenant who had yet to be awarded the Croix de Guerre, The Grand Croix du Mérite de l'Ordre de Malte, and the Grand-Croix de la Legion d'Honneur, Jozan doubtless bore the cachet of a distinction that Zelda sensed in him. He was a born leader, with a tradition of honor, bravery, and nobility. Further, he was healthy, athletic, and vigorous, assured, and obviously destined for a successful career in the service. In short, Jozan had all the qualities that Scott would have liked to have; and, inevitably, Fitzgerald became violently and irrationally jealous of him. On the other hand, Jozan found Scott brilliant, sophisticated, and "a bit of an *intellectuel*," who, despite his talent and imagination, appeared to be more concerned with commercial than artistic success—a proud, domineering man, who was sometimes tender and sometimes cruel.

Jozan thought that Zelda was merely flirting with him to make Scott jealous. Although she seemed to Jozan to be "a little abnormal" at times, he said that some of the letters about her that he has received in recent years were so full of "wild ideas" in regard to her that the authors of them seemed to him to be "raving mad." Zelda's account of her affair with him in *Save Me the Waltz*, he added, is almost an exact report of what happened at St. Raphaël. Hence, on the face of it, the story that a "young French aviator" committed suicide after his tragic romance with Zelda appears to be an absurd invention. Likewise, almost equally incredible is the story of Scott's going from St. Raphaël to the Hôtel du Cap in Antibes—a distance of fifty-two kilometers—at three or four o'clock in the morning, to get help from the Murphys because Zelda had taken an overdose of sleeping pills during the "Big Crisis." For, by Jozan's account, as well as by Zelda's, in *Save Me the Waltz*, their "affair" was nothing more than a summer flirtation, romantic, decorous, and slightly comic.

In Zelda's novel, in which Jozan appears thinly disguised as Lieutenant Jacques Chevre-Feuille [Honeysuckle], she records that she was introduced to him and five of his fellow officers by the proprietor of Jean's plage, who invited her and her husband to have a cocktail at his café after a swim. The scimitars, the brass trays on African drumheads, the small tables inlaid with mother-of-pearl, the grilled red lamps, the Algerian rugs, the smell of brine and incense made the place seem like a pirates' cave or an opium den. Feeling slightly guilty but very "fresh and slick and salty," she looked about for some way to fix her hair. With Latin gallantry, the lieutenant offered her his own small red comb. When she hesitated, doubtful as to whether she should take it, he protested that he was not a "germe." Although it was hardly a romantic introduction, she noted that he had curly blond hair, the head of a gold "Christmas coin," strong bronze hands, and broad convex shoulders emphasized by the tunic of his white duck uniform. She told her husband that Chevre-Feuille looked like him, "except that he is full of the sun, whereas you are a moon person." After explaining that he had no money, the aviator asked them to have a simple porto, and they invited him to dinner.

Late that evening he buzzed their villa in his plane and dropped a note written in blue pencil, "*Toutes mes amitiés du haut de mon avion.* Jacques Chevre-Feuille." Annoyed because she could not read it, at her husband's suggestion she bought a French dictionary and a copy of *Le Bal du Comte d'Orgel* to learn the language. In quoting what he says is a "piece of journal-

ism" written by Scott at this time, Andrew Turnbull confuses
Jacques with his fellow officer Bobbé: "in half an hour René and
Bobbé [Edouard Josanne], officers of aviation, are coming to
dinner in their white ducks. . . . Afterwards, in the garden, their
white uniforms will grow dimmer as the more liquid dark comes
down, until they, like the heavy roses and nightingales in the
pines, will seem to take an essential and indivisible part in the
beauty of this proud gay land." The bracketed interpolation is
Turnbull's. He is also mistaken about the seriousness of Zelda's
involvement. She and Scott drank Cinzano and champagne at the
Café de la Flotte with the French flyers; Zelda danced with
Jozan, confessed that she was attracted by him to a degree that
kissing him would be "like embracing a lost religious rite," and
promptly forgot about him. Unfortunately, Scott's memory of the
affair never dimmed; he brooded over it, dramatized it, and distorted it into a threat to his marriage. According to Zelda, he even
resorted to the medieval stratagem of locking her in the Villa
Marie for a month to prevent her from seeing Jozan. For, as usual,
Scott inclined to take the men who fell in love with Zelda much
more seriously than she did. He threatened to "wring the aviator's
neck"; but being the younger and stronger, Jozan refused to fight
with him. When Scott announced that he would leave Zelda if she
saw the aviator again, Jozan asked to be transferred to another
station. After he left for Provence, he never saw or heard from
her again. She tore up the letter and the photograph he sent her
with the philosophical reflection that "You took what you wanted
from life, if you could get it, and you did without the rest."

Scott went back to work on *The Great Gatsby*. Zelda whiled
away the time by reading Dickens and helping Fitzgerald revise
his novel. Toward the end of August he wrote Perkins that it
would be finished in about a week but that he and Zelda wanted
to take a complete rest before going back over it. Meanwhile,
however, there came a second interruption—in the person of Ring
Lardner. He and his wife came to St. Raphaël in September to
see the Fitzgeralds. In Zelda's scrapbook there is a long poem that
Lardner had sent her, in which he complained that Scott had
been tactless in sending him biographies of Wilde and Crane,
who like Lardner "had battled with consumption." The poem to
Zelda concluded:

So, dearie, when your tender heart
Of all his coarseness tires,
Just cable me and I will start
Immediately for Hyères

To hell with Scott Fitzgerald then!
To hell with Scott, his daughter!
It's you and I back home again,
To Great Neck, where men are men
And the booze is ¾ water.

When Lardner arrived in St. Raphaël, he was off the wagon and depressed because the doctors had confirmed his own diagnosis of the pain in his lungs as "consumption." Ring was dying of alcoholism and tuberculosis—two diseases which Fitzgerald feared that he himself might develop. Consequently, he was in no mood to carouse with his "private drunkard"; nor did he relish the idea of entertaining another of his wife's admirers. Lardner lay all day in a bathrobe on a Louis XV sofa at the Hôtel Beau Rivage with a bottle beside him, directing wry remarks at Scott and paying Zelda tipsy compliments. After he left, Scott marked down that September of 1924 in his Notebooks as a time when "I knew something had happened that could never be repaired."

Ten days later, he felt that things between Zelda and himself had begun to clear up again, and he set to work on the revisions of his novel. On October 27 he wrote Perkins from the Villa Marie that he was sending him the manuscript of *The Great Gatsby* and would not get a good night's sleep until he heard from him about it. Just before Scott left St. Raphaël, he wrote Perkins that he had been considering other titles for the novel, "Gold-hatted Gatsby," "The High-bouncing Lover," "Trimalchio," and "On the Road to West Egg"—but had decided to stick to his first choice, "Trimalchio in West Egg."

Despite the fact that Scott found the sunshine and salt air so wonderful that he no longer coughed, itched, and tossed from one side of the bed to the other at night, he decided to leave St. Raphaël as soon as he finished the short story he was writing. He and Zelda had been there over five months; they were both restless. Zelda used to say, "I hate a room without an open suitcase in it—it seems so permanent." Inspired by reading *Roderick Hud-*

son, she persuaded Scott that they should spend the rest of the winter in Rome before going to Capri, where he wanted to see Compton Mackenzie, who had a villa on the island.

They drove south the first week in November, stopping first at Genoa and then at Pisa. It was so dark when they arrived there that they could not find the Leaning Tower. But the next morning on their way to Rome, they passed it accidentally, standing "stark in a field by itself." Their comments on the Eternal City were as ingenuous as they were original. The Quirinal Hotel was stuffy and depressing. Marion Crawford's mother had died there. "All the chamber-maids remember it and tell visitors about how they spread the room with newspapers afterwards. The sitting-rooms are hermetically sealed and palms conceal the way to open the windows. Middle-aged English doze in the stale air and nibble stale salted peanuts with the hotel's famous coffee. . . ."

They soon found smaller, less fashionable, less expensive lodgings at the Hôtel des Princes in the Piazza di Spagna. Their bill there was only five hundred twenty-five dollars a month, including tips and meals. They "lived on Bel Paese cheese and Corvo wine and made friends with a delicate spinster who intended to stop there until she finished a three-volume history of the Borgias." For all that, Rome did not particularly interest them:

> The sheets were damp and the walls were perforated by the snores of the people next door, but we didn't mind because we could always come home down the stairs to the Via Sistina, and there were jonquils and beggars along that way. We were too superior at that time to use the guide books and wanted to discover the ruins for ourselves, which we did when we had exhausted the night-life and the market places and the campagna.

During their exploration of the night life, a humiliating experience occurred that impressed Scott so deeply that it was to crop out not only in his unfinished "Our Type" but also in *Tender Is the Night*. On their way back to the hotel late one night, enraged by the extortionate charges of a group of taxi drivers who asked a hundred lira to take them to the Piazza di Spagna, Scott struck out at them. They returned his blows, and when a plain-clothes officer tried to intervene in the melee, Scott knocked him down.

Bruised and battered, he was hustled off to jail by two *carabini-eri*. Zelda managed to free him the next day with the help of the United States consulate and a hundred dollars, not liras.

It is probable, to judge from one of Scott's after-dinner stories, that another tragicomic incident, which also appears in a slightly altered form in *Tender Is the Night*, was based on an actual event. In the novel the Divers and their children go to Boyen for a fortnight's visit with the widow of a friend, now remarried to the Conte di Minghetti, an Asiatic "not quite light enough to travel in a Pullman south of Mason-Dixon," who has acquired a fortune and a papal title. They are met at the station by their hosts, a retinue of turbaned retainers, and two half-veiled women who walk behind the new contessa, a girl risen from a room over the shop of a paperhanger in Newark to a princely chateau in Italy. Her household there seems to be run by the two veiled women. They also care for two of the conte's "very tan children by another marriage." That evening Dick Diver has too many highballs to listen to what his hostess is saying. Consequently, the next day, on finding that his son has been bathed in the same water from which one of the conte's sons—said to be afflicted with an Asiatic skin disease—has just emerged, Diver orders one of the veiled women to clean the tub. The woman bursts into tears and rushes from the room. The contessa informs him that the woman is not a servant but her husband's sister, who serves as one of her ladies-in-waiting. Since Diver has insulted her, the conte's honor requires that he and his family cannot remain under the same roof that shelters Diver. Dick trades insults with his hostess, and she leaves her major-domo to arrange for the Divers' departure.

Scott soon developed an aversion for everything Italian from its *pasta* to its *carabinieri*. His distaste for the Eternal City increased as an unusually damp, cold winter set in. His ill humor flared into a murderous rage when the maître d'hôtel ordered him to yield his table in the dining room to a Roman aristocrat. Nevertheless, he was so fascinated by the film company that was making *Ben Hur*, and particularly by Carmel Myers, who was starring in it, that he lingered on to study the technique of movie making, feeling that it was to open a new and lucrative field to him.

Despite the plaid shawl that Miss Myers gave the Fitzgeralds to keep them warm while they watched the filming "in bigger and grander papier-maché arenas than the real ones," Scott developed influenza; and Zelda, colitis, the fashionable disease of that year.

In search of sunshine they drove south in January, stopping first in Naples, where they visited Pompeii and bought a phallic figurine from an archeologist. Then they went on to Sorrento to see a real tarantella. By the time they reached Capri, Scott by his own admission was so drunk that he had to be told where he was. They put up at the Tiberio, "a high white hotel scalloped about the base by the rounded roofs of Capri, cupped to catch rain which never fell." While Scott worked on a short story, Zelda began to paint. When the cocktail hour came, they strolled over to the piazza to sit in front of a café. Norman Douglas was not in Capri then, but Scott looked up his old idol, Compton Mackenzie, who appealed to him as attractive, cordial, and urbane. Mackenzie seemed unaware that the quality of his work had fallen off and that the war had shattered him as it had so many of his generation. Scott spent half the night talking to him but remembered only that "strange birds protested their sleepiness beneath the overwhelming cypress while Compton Mackenzie told us why he lived in Capri: Englishmen must have an island."

Scott and Zelda shipped their car from Naples to Marseilles. From Marseilles they drove to Lyon, where they stayed in a hotel that had an obsolete air and where no one had ever heard of lyonnaise potatoes. Zelda suffered another attack of colitis. Both she and Scott became so discouraged with touring that they left their car in Lyon and took the train for Paris, where their Right Bank hotel proved to be even more depressing than Italy.

6. The World's Fair

IN MAY 1925 Scott and Zelda moved into a walk-up apartment on the Right Bank at 14 rue de Tilsitt in a fashionable neighborhood near the Étoile. After arranging with Max Perkins to publish another collection of short stories to be entitled *All The Sad Young Men*, Scott dug in to work on "The World's Fair," a novel about the expatriates in Europe, which was to occupy him for the next three years.

Meanwhile, on April 10 *The Great Gatsby* had appeared. The first words of praise came from Mencken, who found Fitzgerald's writing beautiful and charming. Although in a review in *The Dial* of August 1925 Gilbert Seldes called it "one of the finest of contemporary novels," and Stephen Vincent Benét lauded its "almost magic craftsmanship" in *The Saturday Review of Literature*, Scott complained of the critics' reception of the book. So far, he noted on May 1, Laurence Stallings had written the only intelligent review of it. He received approving letters about it from Edmund Wilson, Gertrude Stein, Edith Wharton, and T. S. Eliot, and the laudatory reviews continued. But Scott could not forget that the novel would have to sell twenty thousand copies to pay his debt to Scribner's. If it failed to sell, he wrote Perkins, the unimpressive title and the fact that the book contained no important woman character would be responsible.

In June the sale of the dramatic rights to *Gatsby* alleviated Scott's financial difficulties for the time being and mitigated his disappointment over the initial reception of the book. The taste of success was once more sweet on his lips, even though the chores that his new-found fame entailed soon became irksome. He was besieged by visitors, by requests for information about his life and works, for advice on how to write short stories, and for autographs. But from the verses with which he replied from Paris on June 26 to a letter from Silas M. Hanson, an autograph collector in Chicago, it is evident that Scott had regained some of his usual good humor and playfulness:

> Of wonders is Silas M. Hanson the champ
> He asked for an aut'graph and sent me a stamp
> But none of his pleadings would go on the shelf
> If he'd added an envelope 'dressed to himself.

A reunion with Donald Ogden Stewart had cheered both of the Fitzgeralds. Stewart had turned up in Paris, where he was then riding the crest of the wave. For his success with the antics of *Mr. and Mrs. Haddock Abroad* had liberated him from the grind of selling bonds in New York. His humor appealed to Zelda, and his gift of making friends among the noted expatriates, to Scott. In fact, it was Stewart who had first introduced him to Sara and Gerald Murphy, wealthy socialites and bons vivants, who were then living in Paris. Gerald was studying painting under Fernand Léger and Sara was making a name for herself as a charming and imaginative hostess. Like Stewart, Gerald had made Skull and Bones at Yale, an achievement that always attracted Scott. Tall, slender, and redhaired, Gerald affected long sideburns, wide-brimmed white hats, a cane, and the impeccable clothes of a Parisian dandy. His family were lace-curtain Irish from South Boston; but eventually his father moved the Mark Cross leather store to New York, where he made money enough to allow Gerald to follow a career in art. Sara's talent for food, wine, and people made their apartment—on the top floor of an ancient house on the corner of rue Gît-le-Coeur close by Notre Dame—a gathering place for the artists and writers of the Left Bank. Through the Murphys, Scott and Zelda met most of the "people who mattered" there, including Lubov Egorova, the Princess Troubetskoy, who was to become Zelda's ballet teacher.

After her retirement from the Russian Imperial ballet, Egorova had come to Paris. At the instance of Diaghilev, a great friend of hers and of the Murphys, she opened a studio in 1923 and began giving ballet lessons. Honoria, the Murphys' little daughter, had been taking lessons from Egorova, and Zelda was as eager to meet the princess and Diaghilev as Scott was to be introduced to Ernest Hemingway, whose writing appealed to Fitzgerald as being "the real thing."

In May 1925 Don Stewart arranged a meeting between Scott and Hemingway at the Dingo Bar in the rue Delambre, a bistro behind the Rotonde, frequented by the sporting set that sparred and exercised in a nearby Montparnasse gym. While the Fitzgeralds had been on the Riviera, living "in a sort of idyllic state" and touring Italy with an English nurse for their daughter, Hemingway and his wife, Hadley, were living very frugally in a sparsely furnished apartment over a sawmill off the Latin Quarter at 113 rue Notre-Dame-des-Champs. There, despite her private income of two thousand dollars a year, Hadley did the cooking, and Ernest fixed the bottles for Bumby, his infant son. The Fitzgeralds went for cocktails at the George the Fifth or the Ritz, dined on *pâté aux truffles* at Maxim's, and pressed duck at the Tour d'Argent. The Hemingways drank at the zinc bars in the Latin Quarter and thought they were lucky when they could borrow money enough from Sylvia Beach to eat at the Brasserie Lipp. Zelda's clothes came from Chanel and Patou; Hadley's from Au Bon Marché. Neither Hadley nor Ernest owned anything approaching evening clothes. When the Fitzgeralds went out with them after dinner they either had to go to a *bal musette* to dance or to the Cirque d'Hiver to see a boxing match. And in the differences in their circumstances was rooted Hemingway's bitterness, which came to its full pathological flower forty years later in *A Moveable Feast.*

Shortly after they met, Scott asked the Hemingways to lunch with him and Zelda at their apartment. All that Zelda could remember about the meal was that there was a Lalique turtle filled with white violets on the table; Ernest recalled only that the first time he saw her he "thought she was crazy." Zelda and Hadley had nothing in common; Scott and Ernest, little beyond their literary ambition, their Midwestern origins, and a taste for the bottle. Hemingway had a Gargantuan capacity for alcohol. He could drink all day and half the night and still work the next morning. But if Scott took more than three cocktails, he was off on a spree that left him shot for a week. Later, when Scott's writing began to suffer from his drinking, Zelda blamed it on Hemingway's influence; Hemingway, on Zelda's. The truth was that Scott began drinking too heavily at Princeton, long before he met either of them.

In the course of their first strained luncheon together, Scott asked Hemingway to go to Lyon with him to bring back his Renault, which he and Zelda had abandoned there when she became ill. By Hemingway's account of the trip in *A Moveable Feast*, it was a distressing fiasco. He depicts Fitzgerald as a drunk, a hypochondriac, a literary imbecile, a ninny, and a virgin before his marriage to a wife who was subtly undermining him by taunting him with his sexual deficiencies. Granted that Scott was an alcoholic and a psychoneurotic, he was as far from being a literary imbecile and a ninny as he was from being a virgin before he married Zelda. It is highly improbable that Scott ever made any such claim as Hemingway attributed to him; if he did, he flatly contradicted it in *The Crack-Up*, when he said of his failure to become a big shot at Princeton, "There were to be no badges of pride, no medals, after all. It seemed on a March afternoon that I had lost every single thing I wanted—and that night was the first time that I hunted down the spectre of womanhood that, for a little while, makes everything else seem unimportant."

There is also a curious contravention of Hemingway's story of the trip to Lyon in a letter from Scott to Gertrude Stein, written immediately after their return, in which he told her, "Hemingway and I went to Lyon shortly after to get my car and had a slick drive through Burgundy. He's a peach of a fellow and absolutely first-rate."

Hemingway had taken Scott to see Miss Stein and the fabulous collection of Picassos, Utrillos, and Braques in her studio in rue de Fleurus near the Luxembourg Gardens. Her paintings had not impressed Scott, who knew little about the graphic arts and cared less, but he was intrigued by her theories on writing and pleased with her reception of him. He flattered her and played up to her; and she, in turn, found that Scott had "certain syrup" but, unlike Glenway Wescott's, it poured. Fitzgerald's "flame," she predicted, would be remembered when those of others around him were forgotten.

Her dictum vexed Hemingway as deeply as that of Sara and Gerald Murphy did Scott. The Murphys, whom Scott revered as the arbiters of art, letters, and fashion, regarded Hemingway as a better writer than Fitzgerald. On the other hand, Zelda shared the Murphys' interest in French poetry, abstract painting, and the Russian ballet and preferred spending her evenings with them at one of Étienne de Beaumont's "Soirees de Paris" or a Diaghilev première than watching a boxing match or touring the "gay" bars of the rue du Lappe with the Hemingways. In the spring of 1925, at the instance of Scott, who thought that Zelda needed something to do, Gerald Murphy arranged for her to take ballet lessons from Egorova, who at one time had also worked with Diaghilev's troupe, for which Gerald and Sara had helped to paint the scenery. Thus the seeds of the Fitzgerald's discord over Egorova and Hemingway were sown before Scott and Zelda left to visit the Murphys in Antibes that summer.

When I arrived in Paris in the spring of 1926, the lindens in the Luxembourg were green again and the horse chestnuts along the Champs Élysées were in bloom. In the mornings I audited lectures at the Sorbonne and in the afternoons pursued the higher learning in the Bois de Boulogne, the Jockey Club, the Ritz bar, the Closerie des Lilas, or Aux Deux Magots. Scott and Zelda had gone to take a cure at Salies de Béarn in the Basses-Pyrénées. Finding only two goats and a paralytic there for company, they had fled to the Riviera and rented a villa at Juan-les-Pins. Consequently, I did not see them until early in the summer. But on my way from the rue d'Assas, where I was living, to the Sorbonne, I frequently passed Ernest Hemingway as I cut through the Luxembourg Gardens. He had put on flesh, grown a little moustache, and acquired a purplish scar on his forehead. His baggy tweed suit was patched at the elbows, and the pocket of his coat was torn from the notebooks jammed into it. With Bumby astride his hip and Hadley following him as silently as an Indian squaw, he strode along, his head down, kicking at the gravel with his sneakers.

In Our Time had been published; and frequently while I was browsing in Shakespeare & Co., Hemingway came in to pick up his mail and ask how his book was selling. Sylvia Beach, with her brown hair, brown eyes, and brown-velvet jacket, was an arresting figure, a colorful and kindly woman, who had taken Hemingway under her wing. She lent him books and money, fed him tea and brioches in the back room of the bookshop, and criticized his stories. In talking to her, now and then, he would break into a boyish grin, surprisingly pleasant with its strong, white teeth in the face of a scowling, sulky young man. With the other Americans who frequented Shakespeare & Co., he was remote, self-absorbed, and abrupt in his replies to their questions about his work. I often saw him there, strolling along the quais, or sitting alone at a table in one of the cafés of the Latin Quarter; but beyond *"Bonjour"* he never exchanged a word with me, nor I with him. He was not a man who made friends easily nor one with whom one bantered freely.

Scott once told me that Hemingway hated his first name, but it fitted him like a glove. Ernest was not only earnest, he was a deadly serious and an angry young man. When his friends tried to joke with him, he was apt as not to ask them to come outside and settle it. But people who criticized him for being surly and ill-tempered in those days have never tried to support themselves by writing for a paper at space rates and contributing to the little magazines. One of the most admirable facets of Scott's character was his wholehearted devotion to Hemingway and the unstinted help and encouragement that he gave him during the lean years of his apprenticeship.

One afternoon that summer, Scott Fitzgerald shepherded two Westport girls and a half a dozen Princeton boys into the ladies' bar of the Ritz in Paris, where we were having cocktails with René Herrera, son of the Spanish ambassador to the United States. René had brought along Michael Arlen, an elegant young man with a British accent and a Mayfair manner, whom Nancy

Cunard had introduced in Paris as the only Armenian that had never been massacred. After his novel *The Green Hat* created a sensation, Arlen was very much in vogue among the literati, and when Scott saw him, he left his companions to join us at our table.

Urbane and debonaire, Scott led off by telling Arlen how much he liked *The Green Hat*. Since it was now outselling *The Great Gatsby*, Fitzgerald's latest novel, he added that he thought Arlen would probably be his successor as the most popular fiction writer of the day. Arlen winced at the backhanded compliment, but expressed his appreciation of Scott's talent—if in measured terms. Although Arlen was polite about *The Great Gatsby*, he was patently not enthusiastic about it or about Ernest Hemingway's *In Our Time*. His conversation with Fitzgerald was amiable enough, however, until Scott took issue with him over Hemingway's work.

To Fitzgerald, the hothouse product of St. Paul soirées, Princeton clubs, and New York cocktail parties, Hemingway appeared as a Byronic hero—for he had been decorated for bravery during the Italian campaign in World War I, while Scott, to his regret, had not even been sent overseas. He was impressed by Hemingway's war experiences and the terse, muscular prose with which he had reported them as well as by his prowess as an athlete and sportsman who hunted, fished, skied, fenced, and boxed with the skill of a professional. On the other hand, to Arlen, a lion of Parisian salons, Hemingway was a struggling journalist, clumsy on the tennis court, boorish in his manner, and something of a roughneck. His criticisms of Scott's current hero nettled Fitzgerald, who retorted that Arlen was "a finished second-rater that's jealous of a coming first-rater."

René intervened diplomatically by suggesting that it was time we were going. But Scott insisted that I leave Herrera and Arlen and go with him to see Zelda, who was in the American Hospital at Neuilly, "having her appendix removed," according to Scott's euphemistic description of the operation. He argued that it would cheer her up to see someone from home, so I went along with him. In those days Scott fancied himself a social impresario, possessed of the "extraordinary virtuosity with people" that he later attributed to Dick Diver in *Tender is the Night*. Once he took your life in hand, you either had to humor him or cross him—and crossing him when he was drinking was an invitation to trouble.

Rather than have a scene there in the Ritz, I made my excuses to my friends and went with Scott to rejoin the Princeton boys and Westport girls. When they had finished their sidecars, he invited us all to dine with him at the Vert Galant before he and I went to Neuilly. First, however, he had to stop by Harry's New York Bar to see one of the foreign correspondents who hung out there. His real motive, as we discovered, was to find out whether or not Hemingway, who had gone with Sara and Gerald Murphy to the fiesta at Pamplona—"the world's series of bullfighting"— had yet returned to Paris.

A few weeks before, an article on Hemingway by Scott had appeared in *The Bookman*. When the newsman began to rag Scott about his efforts to promote Hemingway, Scott flared up and asked him whether he wanted to make something out of it. Realizing that Fitzgerald was half seas over and spoiling for a fight, the newsman made a quick exit, leaving Scott flushed and furious, but victor in the verbal sparring match.

After that the party gathered momentum. It was already late before we started out for the Vert Galant. There was not a cab in sight so Scott set out to find a fiacre. Half an hour later he returned with a bottle of *fine*, a hearse he had commandeered, and two *poules de luxe* left over from the funeral. Despite our protests, he herded us into the hearse—an open French affair with black plumes and somber ebony draperies of carved wood. Climbing in after us, he ordered the driver to go to 14 rue de Tilsitt, where he had left some books that he wanted to take to Zelda. What he described as "a swell apartment" turned out to be a depressing flat over a brasserie at the corner of rue de Tilsitt and Avenue de Wagram, a fifth-floor walk-up, with strange purple-and-gold wallpaper. Louis Bromfield said that it reminded him of a window of a furniture shop. "It smelled," Zelda observed, "like a church chancery and was furnished with genuine Louis XV from the Galeries Lafayette."

By the time Scott had unearthed the books, he was drunk and quarreling with the *poules*. After he called them by their proper names, they walked out on the party, and the Princeton boys finally steered him back to the hearse. "Scott, will you kindly get something to eat and stop acting like one of the characters in your novels. It's too late to go see Zelda," I protested. "It'll only upset her to barge in on her at this time of night."

"Maybe you're right," he agreed, after some argument. "I'll tell her you're coming to Juan-les-Pins as soon as we get back, and she can see you there."

It was also too late to go to the Vert Galant; and since I was then living nearby on the Avenue Hoche, I asked him to let me out at the Étoile. Instead, he poked the driver with his cane and shouted, "*Plus vite, plus vite,* you son of a bitch."

"*Mais où? Mais où, m'sieu?*" the driver demanded, as the hearse careened down the Champs Élysées.

Scott was all for going, but he had no vague idea where. Finally, an inspiration struck him, and he ordered the driver to take us to Les Halles, the old market behind the Louvre. "We'll see the flower stalls and have some onion soup," he announced. And off we went down the rue St. Honoré in the hearse. To make the midnight expedition more macabre, Scott, with his elegant gray fedora askew and his cane for a baton, led the Princetonians in a maudlin chant:

> The worms crawl in and the worms crawl out,
> The worms crawl over your chin and mouth.

We careened along the *quais,* threading our way in and out among the high-wheeled carts clip-clopping along the cobblestones, loaded with produce for the market stalls—crates of eggs, coops of fowls, trusses of chickens, guineas, and pheasants; dressed beeves, rabbits, lambs, and pigs with gules of blood dripping from their noses; garlands of leeks, chives, onions, and garlic; piles of strong cheeses that gave off a ripe smell, which contrasted strangely with the fragrance from the trays of herbs and flowers; baskets of crisp, green celery and lettuce, of the ubiquitous *haricots verts,* of white butter beans, whiter cauliflowers, and bunches of earth-stained carrots.

Between the Louvre and St. Eustache, there were a number of eating places that stayed open all night for the benefit of the farmers, restaurateurs, and greengrocers. Many of these bistros, particularly the Grand Comptoir and Au Chat Qui Fume, were frequented by the expatriates of the Latin Quarter because the food was good, the white wine and Calvados were cheap, and the music of the accordions and guitars was lively. Scott opted for Au Chat Qui Fume because he liked the rich, dark onion soup there. But before we could get enough soup and coffee down him, he had passed out. The Princeton boys piled him in the hearse, left him as a hostage to the driver for the bill, and took us home in a taxi. And that was *that* night in Paris.

Toward the end of the summer, while I was at the Hôtel du Cap in Antibes, Scott and Zelda drove over to take me to Juan-les-Pins, where they had first leased the Villa Paquita, then the Villa St. Louis. Set among a grove of oranges and lemons, the Villa St. Louis had a garden overgrown with pink oleanders, purple clematis, and scarlet bougainvilleas. A path shaded with lemon and orange trees led down to a little beach, a narrow scimitar of sand along the jade and amethyst shallows of the Golfe Juan. The Hemingways, Zelda told me, had rented a smaller villa nearby; but they gave it up because of their domestic difficulties, and they had left before I arrived. Hemingway had brought his novel, *The Sun Also Rises*, with him, which both Scott and Zelda had read in manuscript.

When I asked what his novel was about, Zelda said, "Bullfighting, bullslinging, and bull. . . ."

"Zelda!" Scott cut her description short. "Don't say things like that."

"Why shouldn't I? When you've been scrawling four-letter words all over the walls." Scott and Charlie MacArthur, Helen Hayes's husband, had, it appeared, written a scenario about the wickedest woman in Europe, which they were filming, enlivened by obscene titles, chalked up on Grace Moore's garden wall to be photographed.

"Say anything you please," Scott growled, "but lay off Ernest."

"Try and make me!" she retorted. "He's a pain in the neck—talking about me and borrowing money from you while he does it. He's phony as a rubber check and you know it."

Hemingway claimed that his wife, Hadley, had lost a suitcase full of his manuscripts, carbons and all. Things had never been the same between them since. To widen the breach, a friend of Hadley's, Pauline Pfeiffer, who was to replace her as Mrs. Hemingway the next year, had gone with them to Pamplona. Hadley did not care for the idea of a *ménage à trois*. Nor did Zelda— when Hemingway began to spend all of his time at the Villa St. Louis. The trouble, as Hemingway unconsciously revealed years later, in saying of Zelda in *A Moveable Feast*, "Hawks do not share," was that he was jealous of her and irritated by Scott's habit of referring everything to her. Beneath Hemingway's honesty and integrity as a writer, there was a base metal in the man that never rang true to Zelda. Under his objective, robust interest in war, sports, and tippling, there was a morbid preoccupation with offbeat sex and the sadism and necrophilia that go with it that was repugnant to her. Further, she thought it was shameful of him to join the Catholic Church in order to have his marriage to Hadley annulled and marry Pauline Pfeiffer.

The first twelve months of his friendship with the Fitzgeralds must have been, as he said, "the one year that everybody drank so much and nobody was nasty." For the last six months, I gathered, everyone had been very nasty indeed. At first, Hemingway had been enchanted with Zelda, and his early letters to Scott are filled with affectionate messages to her. But after Zelda began to object to Scott's constant loans to him and to their drinking bouts, Ernest's attitude toward her abruptly changed. Zelda blamed Hemingway for Scott's sprees in Paris as well as for interrupting his work in Juan-les-Pins.

During the last year, Scott had sold only five stories and made little progress on his novel. As Joseph Hergesheimer once remarked, "Scott could write and didn't; couldn't drink and did." The frenetic days and hectic nights of his life abroad had begun to leave their mark on Scott. His hair was still yellow as a jonquil, but he had lost the fresh-scrubbed look of an Arrow collar advertisement. His hands were stained with nicotine, and he was constantly drumming a tattoo with them or wiping the perspiration from them with a damp handkerchief. Under his sunburn, his skin had a greenish tinge; there were purple circles under his eyes; and he had developed what he called "a pot."

Zelda had kept her lithe, lovely figure. Her features retained their classic beauty. But her hair, once golden blond, had darkened and lost its luster; her blue eyes, their sparkle. For all her vivacity, she was no longer relaxed and gay as she had been when I saw her in New York just before she and Scott sailed. In unguarded moments, her nervousness was apparent in the way she twisted her hands together and chewed at the corner of her mouth; but, as far as I could see, there was no evidence of what Scott alleged to be a "hysteria which is only to be relieved by a doctor bearing morphine." In fact, he appeared to be much more edgy and overwrought than she did; and one of the first things he said to me while we were having a gin fizz at the casino was "I can only have one drink; I'm an alcoholic now, you know."

For all the outward opulence of their life in Juan-les-Pins, it was apparent that they were both fast drifting into the emotional slum in which all too many expatriates ended up abroad—working too little, drinking too much, having transient love affairs, quarreling with their friends, roaming aimlessly about Europe in search of some romantic paradise, lost with the first flush of their youth. Scott had written to Edmund Wilson that "Zelda and I think we're pretty good, as usual, only more so," and to John Peale Bishop, "Zelda and I sometimes indulge in terrible four-day rows that always start with a drinking party but we're still enormously in love and about the only truly happily married people I know." Despite his complacency, however, under the bright, brittle surface of their marriage the relentless feud between them already had begun to smoulder. Zelda, Scott complained, took no interest in his friends. During Hemingway's visits, she either snubbed Ernest or sniped at him. She had refused point-blank to go with Scott when they were invited to have tea with Edith Wharton at the Pavillon Colombe because she did not want any such *grande dame* looking at her over her lorgnette and making her feel provincial.

"That was better than going and making an ass of yourself as you did, telling her we lived in a brothel in Paris when all we did was to go to The House of All Nations one night," she retorted. To make matters worse, she added, when Mrs. Wharton had politely asked what they did in the bordello, Scott had behaved like a flustered adolescent and had come home to pound on the table and cry, "She beat me! She beat me!"

Zelda pointed out that she certainly shared Scott's attachment to Sara and Gerald Murphy, who were now living nearby in the Villa America at Antibes. Both of the Murphys returned Zelda's affection to a degree that irked Scott and led him to ask them frequently whether or not they "liked Zelda better than me." Gerald Murphy frankly admitted, "I don't think we could have taken Scott alone." Zelda had a flair for carrying off her pranks in a gay, insouciant way that made them charming rather than offensive, as Scott's often were. If her wit was sometimes barbed, it derived from the surprise of incongruity and from searching, humorous observation. "She hardly ever said anything that wasn't personal," Sara Murphy remarked. "And the strange thing was that no matter what she did—even the wildest, most terrifying things—she always managed to maintain her dignity. She was a good woman, and I've never thought she was bad for Scott, as other people have said."

Scott's high jinks all too often displayed a latent hostility toward those whom he regarded as his superiors and an arrogant contempt toward his inferiors. Upon one occasion, according to John Dos Passos, coming out of a bistro where he had been drinking too much, Scott saw an old woman at the door selling candy and cigarettes. In reply to her "*Voulez-vous achetez, m'sieu?*" he kicked her tray out of her hand—a heartless act for which Gerald Murphy made amends with a fifty-franc note. Upon another occasion, Scott and Charlie MacArthur kidnapped the *patron* and the waiters from a café in Cannes, roped them together, dragged them to the edge of a cliff, and terrorized them by threatening to throw them over. Again, they frightened the wits out of a bartender by stretching him across two chairs with the avowed intention of sawing him in two to see what was inside of him, until they were deterred by Zelda, who insisted that he was only stuffed with shards of broken saucers, shreds of menus, stubs of pencils, and the like.

On the other hand, Zelda's antics were ominously self-destructive. She was given to diving from dangerous heights into shallow waters on rocky shores. One evening coming home from Monte

Carlo, she threatened to drive the car off the cliffs of the Grande Corniche and came perilously near doing so. Early one morning after a party, she threw herself down in front of their car and dared Scott to drive over her. On their way home from Vence, after having dinner and a few drinks with the Murphys at a restaurant there, she and Scott drove their Renault out on a streetcar trestle. They both fell asleep and were pulled off by a peasant in the nick of time to escape the first morning trolley.

When we went to the Plage de la Garoupe to swim, Scott, who had forgotten that he was an alcoholic and could have only one drink, left us ostensibly to go get his swimming trunks, but in reality to fetch a bottle of gin that he had left in the car. "Two drinks put him in a manic state," Zelda said, patently frightened. "Absolutely manic—he wants to fight everybody, including me. He's drinking himself to death."

"He's committing suicide on the installment plan," I had to agree, for I had not seen him really sober since he was in the army. More than any man I ever knew, Scott wanted to be good, kind, noble, and lovable; and when he was not drinking, he came very close to being all these things, but when he was drunk, he was sometimes the antithesis of them.

Zelda eyed him with pity and contempt as he returned with his bottle in hand. His bathing trunks accentuated his long trunk, short legs, growing "pot." He swayed a little as he stood over us, digging his feet in the sand, for he still had that strange "Freudean complex" about them. "I wish I had been born a Catholic," Zelda said. It was apparently an irrelevant remark, but there was no mistaking the look of revulsion that accompanied it, which made all too plain what was happening to the "romance of the century." Scott's latent Catholicism was still strong enough to make him want his daughter to be brought up in the Church, to feel the sting of the charges that "Absolution" was a sacrilegious story, and to object to birth control; yet he never seemed to share Zelda's sense of guilt about her operations.

He flung himself down on the sand beside us, turned up the bottle and took a drink of raw gin. For a little while under its stimulus, something of his old gaiety returned, and he began to tell us the latest gossip about the "New York courtesy celebrities" whom we both knew. But as the lift of the drink wore off, he lapsed into a bitter mood and began to carp at Zelda again. "She thinks I'm in love with every woman that I shake up a cocktail for," he grumbled, "and carried away with every man whose work I praise. Yet she flirts openly with George Jean Nathan, René Silvé, Edouard Jozan, or anyone else she chooses, and I'm supposed to get a kick out of watching her."

René Silvé's and Edouard Jozan's infatuation with Zelda at St. Raphaël two years before had infected Scott with the germs of a bitterness that still festered. Yet never once during their quarrels did I ever hear Scott imply that Zelda had been overtly unfaithful to him, that the young French aviator had killed himself, or that Zelda had taken an overdose of sleeping pills as a result of their "tragic romance." What Scott did say was that she had "gone Southern on him and made eyes at" Jozan and his friends in a deliberate attempt to make him jealous. At the thought that she had even attempted to learn French in order to banter with the "flamboyantly brilliant" aviator, Fitzgerald's face flushed and his eyes flashed. In his indignation he forgot his own flirtations with *poules de luxe* and stars of the screen and stage. Only recently, when he and Zelda had gone with the Murphys to dinner at a restaurant in St.-Paul-de-Vence, he had spent the evening paying court to Isadora Duncan, who stroked his hair while he knelt at her feet and called him her "centurion." However, according to the Murphys, when Miss Duncan had indicated to Scott that he might visit her later on that night, Zelda had showed no resentment toward her or toward Scott. Instead, she watched them silently for a while, then she suddenly rose and flung herself down a flight of stone steps and lay there until the Murphys rescued her. If Zelda's eyes wandered, Scott's pride prompted him to attack her and the man to whom she was attracted; but if Zelda's *amour propre* was wounded by Scott's attentions to other women, she wanted only to destroy herself.

With his growing capacity for self-pity, Scott imagined himself to be an injured husband. Although Zelda was staunchly loyal to him in public—and continued to be until the end of her life—she now realized clearly that her marriage was headed for the rocks. Further, she was plainly tired of being a successful novelist's wife, who provided the copy for his stories and books. She, too, was intelligent and artistic; she wanted to make a life of her own, to achieve, at least, a modicum of intellectual and financial independence. When Scott became so jealous of the stories to which she signed his name and of the articles that she published under her own that she either had to leave him or turn her talents to a less competitive field, she went back to painting. In this she was inspired by Gerald Murphy, whose "Boatdeck" had created a stir in Paris when it had been exhibited at the Salon des Indépendants two years before.

Scott was not only contemptuous of both her writing and her pictures but he was also truculent and insulting to her after two drinks. In one of his drunken rages, he struck her, and defended himself later by demanding of a group of friends, "Is there any man present who can honestly say he has never hit his wife in anger?" She was physically afraid of him in his manic states and obviously beginning to suffer psychologically from having his vices projected on her and having his ego continually whetted against hers.

Zelda and Scott were still sniping at each other when I left them the next afternoon, and I heard no more of them until I was back in Baltimore the next spring. Sara Haardt, who had just returned from Hollywood, regaled us of an evening with the wild tales that she had brought back from the Coast. The most startling of the stories, both to Mencken and to me, were those about the Fitzgeralds.

About six months before Sara Haardt went to Hollywood as a scenario writer for Famous Players, Scott, who had returned from Europe with the intention of settling down in Montgomery, was summoned to the West Coast by United Artists. They offered him twelve thousand dollars to do a flapper story for Constance Talmadge. He and Zelda took an apartment in one of the luxurious bungalows of the Ambassador Hotel, where John Barrymore and Carl Van Vechten were also staying, and embarked upon a party that lasted three months. At a luncheon given for them at Pickfair by Douglas Fairbanks and Mary Pickford, Scott met Lois Moran, who became the Rosemary Hoyt of *Tender Is the Night*. He was fascinated with her and she with him. Within a week's time she had persuaded him to have a screen test taken, with the intention of having him as her leading man in her next picture. But when Famous Players had wanted to do *This Side of Paradise* with Scott cast as Amory and Zelda as Rosalind, on the advice of Maxwell Perkins Scott had vetoed the idea on the ground that it would injure him as a writer. Zelda was furious and understandably so. In reprisal for Scott's attentions to Lois Moran, Zelda began to take Black Bottom lessons and look about for a movie role for herself.

Scott had to be the center of attention at a party or he was unhappy. When he found that Zelda's songs and dances were drawing more admirers than his banter, he began to make himself conspicuous, even in Hollywood, by his sophomoric pranks. At a cocktail party given by Lois Moran, he played the zany by collecting the guests' rings, bracelets, and watches and boiling them in tomato soup. On a visit to William Randolph Hearst at San Simeon, he made fun of his host for having catsup bottles on the table in his baronial refectory and shocked him by borrowing one of Zelda's brassieres to clothe one of the nude statues in the garden there.

After Scott's story for Constance Talmadge was rejected, he piled all the furniture in the bungalow into a pyramid in the middle of the floor, stuck his unpaid bills on top of it, and he and Zelda departed for the East. With his ever-increasing tendency to project, Scott announced that he disliked movie people because of their "almost hysterical egotism and excitability hidden under an extremely thin veil of elaborate good-fellowship."

Early in March, en route to Washington, Scott stopped over in Baltimore to tout Hemingway to Mencken. The editor of the *Mercury* took him to lunch and listened politely. But Scott did not score a hit with him, either for himself or for Hemingway, by telling Mencken that Ernest longed to beat the Sage up. Nor did Scott endear himself to Sara Haardt and me by his scathing remarks about Zelda. Shortly afterward, Carl Van Vechten reported to Mencken that the Fitzgeralds were "keeping a very wet house in Delaware." A letter from Zelda to Van Vechten, written from Ellerslie, a neo-Colonial mansion in Edgemoor, Delaware, near Wilmington, which she and Scott had leased, is indicative of the effect the life into which Scott had led her was having upon her:

> From the depths of my polluted soul, I am sorry that the week-end was such a mess. Do forgive my iniquities and my putrid drunkness. This *was* such a nice place, and it should have been a nice party if I had not explored my abyss in public. Anyhow, please realize that I am sorry and contrite and thoroughly misera-ble with the knowledge that it would be just the same again if I got so drunk.

In Hollywood, when a scenario writer had criticized Scott's manners at a party at which he had insulted his hostess and then sulked by lying face down on the floor, Sara Haardt had pro-tested, "Scott's one person when he's drinking and another when he's sober."

"But he's never sober," the writer said.

"Oh, yes, he is," she insisted. "Fundamentally, he's really a very sweet, thoughtful person."

"That may be true. But to all outward appearances, he's a consummate snob—and one who couldn't tell a parvenu from an aristocrat with a microscope—just a suck for the rich. He may be as fine a writer as he says he is, but that doesn't entitle him to be so arrogant and so rude to other people."

"It's a kind of defense mechanism with him," Sara explained. "He's trying to cover up a feeling of social inferiority he's always had. Underneath it, he's a nice, sensitive boy who's pathetically eager to have people like him."

"Underneath it," the scenario writer retorted, "as you and I both know, Scott's a so and so."

Mencken was inclined to be more charitable. "Scott," he said, "has gone Hollywood, which is to say, he's gone *mashuggah*."

7. The Drunkard's Holiday

FROM the Ambassador Hotel in Los Angeles Scott wrote his Cousin Ceci that movieland impressed him as a hard-working, tragic place, so full of beautiful girls that he never wanted to see another one. Yet, despite the disillusionment with Hollywood that followed the rejection of "Lipstick," his story for Constance Talmadge, not all his memories of California were unhappy ones, nor were all the impressions that he and Zelda left behind them befogged with an alcoholic haze. In "Show Mr. and Mrs. F. to Number——" they remembered with nostalgia that

> White roses swung luminous in the mist from a trellis outside the Ambassador windows; a bright exaggerated parrot droned incomprehensible shouts in an aquamarine pool—of course everybody interpreted them to be obscenities; geraniums underscored the discipline of the California flora. We paid homage to the pale aloof concision of Diana Manners' primitive beauty and dined at Pickfair to marvel at Mary Pickford's dynamic subjugation of life. A thoughtful limousine carried us for California hours to be properly moved by the fragility of Lillian Gish, too aspiring for life, clinging vine-like to occultisms.

Long afterward, in *The Movies, Mr. Griffith and Me*, Lillian Gish recalled that meeting with the Fitzgeralds. At the time Miss

Gish was making *La Bohème* and living with her mother in Mrs. Pickford's beach house in Santa Monica. Because it was Sunday afternoon, Miss Gish's secretary, Phyllis, answered Scott's knock at the door:

> "I am a fan of Miss Gish's," he said. "I've come all the way from Milwaukee [*sic*] to see her."
> "Oh, I know you," Phyllis said, "you're Scott Fitzgerald."
> "Yes," he admitted. Zelda was in the car, and he asked whether he might bring her in. They were the most beautiful couple Phyllis had ever seen.
> They had come to the beach, they explained, to ride the roller coaster at the amusement park at Santa Monica.

At that time, Miss Gish says, they drank their whiskey "as if it were water with seemingly no effect." In a letter to Arthur Mizener, Lois Moran contended that although the Fitzgeralds did get tight and pull a lot of sophomoric pranks, they "never were mean, cruel, or unkind."

However that may be, they left a trail of fantastic stories behind them from coast to coast. After Mencken visited Montgomery on his way to California in 1926, he wrote Scott that while he was in Zelda's ancient stronghold he was shown the place where she had jumped a horse over haywagons and the grave of the colored clergyman on which she landed. Livye Hart once remarked that she never knew Zelda to deny any story about herself, no matter how absurd it was; nor, to the best of my knowledge, did she ever deny that one of Mencken's.

Hoping that the old mansion on the Delaware, with its gracious portico, square, high-ceilinged rooms, and somber horse-chestnut trees might bring them a "judicious tranquility," Scott and Zelda settled down at Ellerslie, determined to rusticate. Zelda, who had written little or nothing since "What Became of Our Flappers and Sheiks?" published by *McCall's* in October 1925, began to turn out articles again. One of them, "The Changing Beauty of Park Avenue," appeared in *Harper's Bazaar* in January 1928; two others, "Looking Back Eight Years" and "Who can Fall in Love After Thirty?" were published in *College Humor* in June and October 1928. Like the article in *McCall's*, they were signed F. Scott and

Zelda Fitzgerald, though Scott credited them chiefly to Zelda. For his own part, Scott felt stymied and unable to get along with his writing. He was still very much in vogue, and his work was constantly interrupted by interviewers, invitations, and guests.

One of the first visitors to Ellerslie was Lois Moran, whom Scott had invited to come and see them while he was in Hollywood. Zelda obviously did not enjoy the weekend that Miss Moran spent with them, but she played the gracious hostess and arranged a cocktail party and a picnic on the Delaware River for the actress's amusement. Scott had also asked his parents to visit them. Shortly after their arrival a stream of weekend guests from New York and Philadelphia began to descend on Ellerslie and turn the old mansion into a country club, another Gateway Drive. After the departure of Scott's parents, John Dos Passos arrived to find a continual houseparty in progress—and one so "deliriously" wild that although the drinks flowed freely, the guests frequently had to drive to Wilmington to get a sandwich.

Zelda issued invitations as recklessly as Scott did. In urging Carl Van Vechten to visit them, she promised to "have the Coolidges and the Indian guide from the Stillman case and the bathtub girl from Earl Carroll's chorus and the Sistine Madonna and John Charles Thomas—Good simple people and all intimate friends—" Among those that she *did* have were Edmund Wilson; Richard Knight, a lawyer from New York, whom Scott disliked; another lawyer, John Biggs, Scott's former classmate at Princeton, who was then practicing law in Wilmington; Thornton Wilder; Joseph Hergesheimer; and Emily Clark Balch, the former editor of *The Reviewer*. Scott invited Cecelia Taylor, a young cousin from Norfolk, to come for a weekend and entertained her with a dinner dance and a polo match, staged with croquet mallets and plow horses for mounts. The Fitzgeralds' revels dismayed the young girl, and, despite Scott's efforts to amuse her, her visit to Ellerslie proved to be more frightening than pleasurable. In February Rosalind and Newman Smith came for a weekend that turned out to be even more disastrous than Rosalind's trip to Gateway Drive. For Scott came home from a jaunt to Princeton, where he had been carousing at the Cottage Club with the undergraduates. He was still very drunk and during the row with Zelda that ensued, he struck her and made her nose bleed. Before Rosalind left early the next morning, she again reproached Zelda for her way of living and advised her to leave Scott.

Reports of what Zelda termed "the mess" of their lives at Ellerslie continued to reach Mencken's ears. Sara Haardt, who was doing a series of articles on the wives of famous men, had asked me to drive her to Ellerslie to write a story on Zelda, which she had arranged to do while the Fitzgeralds were in Baltimore. But alarmed by Van Vechten's reports of the high jinks in progress there, Mencken advised us to abandon the trip and declined their invitation to him on the grounds that his sister-in-law was coming to Baltimore for surgery.

Scott was too restless to make any progress on "The World's Fair." He and Zelda went to Long Island to visit Tommy Hitchcock, the polo star and World War I ace; to upstate New York to visit Teddy Chanler and his mother; to Princeton to gather material on Scott's alma mater for an article for *College Humor*; and to Virginia Beach to rest and swim. "Next time we went, lost and driven now like the rest, it was a free trip north to Quebec. They thought maybe we'd write about it. The Château Frontenac was built of toy stone arches, a tin soldier's castle."

In an effort to stabilize her life and find some way of passing the time while Scott worked, Zelda began to take ballet lessons under Catherine Littlefield, a former student of Lubov Egorova's. On one of Zelda's trips to Philadelphia, she bought an enormous Victorian mirror in an ornate gilt frame—"a regular whorehouse mirror," Scott called it—which Zelda installed in the drawing room, with a ballet bar in front of it. There she and Scottie, who was also taking ballet lessons from Catherine Littlefield, practiced their routines. In an attempt to drive himself to work on his novel, Scott was drinking heavily. But he spent more time in the speakeasies in Wilmington and New York than at his desk. Left alone with Scottie for much of the day, Zelda amused the child by building an elaborate dollhouse for her, papered, painted, and furnished with miniature period pieces. When the possibilities of the dollhouse were exhausted, Zelda decorated a series of lampshades for Scottie with scenes of the places they had lived here and abroad.

On February 25, 1928, Edmund Wilson attended a house party given by Scott and Zelda, which Wilson described in "A Weekend at Ellerslie" and which put a period to further work on "The World's Fair." Since Wilmington had now turned out to be a veritable "black hole of Calcutta," and Zelda had begun to yearn for Chablis, curry, and *fraises des bois* with peaches in champagne, Scott put aside his novel and began trying to bridge the Atlantic with *Saturday Evening Post* stories. In May, equipped with letters from Gilbert Seldes to Tristan Tzara and Jean Cocteau, introducing Scott as the most gifted novelist in America and Zelda as possessed of a very extraordinary talent, the Fitzgeralds sailed for France to spend the summer.

The Murphys had taken an apartment in Paris on rue Guynemer, facing the Luxembourg Gardens. In order for Scottie to be able to play there with the Murphy children, Scott and Zelda rented a dismal furnished flat, which they called Hôtel de la Morgue, at the intersection of rue de Vaugirard and rue Guynemer, overlooking a corner of the Luxembourg Gardens.

From Paris Scott wrote Max Perkins that he and Zelda were hiding out there, that he was working on the novel and nothing but the novel, and that he would "come back with it or on it in August." His letters to Perkins during that summer are sadly at variance with the terse account in Scott's Ledger: "Drinking and general unpleasantness. First trip to jail. C—R—and dive in Lido, second trip to jail. General carelessness and boredom." After the Murphys left for Antibes, Scott and Zelda both felt lonely. On Sundays they sat in front of "the Deux Magots and watched the people enter old doors or else watched the French read newspapers." Their weekdays were almost equally dull; and when I ran into them one afternoon at the Guaranty Trust in Paris, it was obvious that neither one of them had enjoyed the summer.

"Hello. What are you doing here?" Scott asked somewhat foggily. His eyes were bloodshot, and his hand shook as he ripped open a bill.

"I'm on my way to the Riviera with my brother. And you?"

"We're spending the summer here—of all places," Zelda grumbled.

"It was your idea," Scott snapped. Zelda, he went on to tell me, had been studying ballet in Philadelphia while they were at Ellerslie and had decided that she wanted to continue under Egorova in Paris. "Too bad she didn't make up her mind that's what she wanted to do twenty years ago," he added.

"But she did, Scott," I protested. "I can't remember the time that Zelda didn't want to be a dancer." When she was a child, the Montgomery *Advertiser* had predicted that she might someday "dance like Pavlova if her nimble feet were not so busy keeping up with the pace a string of young but ardent admirers set for her."

"Never argue with a woman—much less two of them. Let's go get a drink." Scott took us down the Boulevard des Italiens and steered us across the Place de l'Opera.

Zelda balked as Scott pulled out two rattan chairs for us under the sycamores in front of the Café de la Paix. "Not here, Scott. I hate this place and the way it smells—gasoline fumes, Chypre, and too many kinds of drinks on too many people."

"Paris," Gertrude Stein had said, "is where the twentieth century is." And the Café de la Paix was at the crossroads of its world. In the hum around its sidewalk tables and above the twang of American tourists, one could hear German, Italian, Spanish, Greek, and now and then even a French conversation going on. On its menu there was something for everybody; sauerbraten for the Germans; wiener schnitzel for Austrians; ravioli and scallopini for the Italians; mixed grill and Brussels sprouts for the English; hotcakes and fried chicken for the Americans; potage St. Germain and bouillabaisse for the natives who occasionally dropped in.

"*Garçon!*" Ignoring Zelda's protest, Scott snapped his fingers at a waiter and ordered a round of martinis for them and a beer for me. "Excuse me," he called over his shoulder, as he rushed over to join some old Princeton friends at another table.

"That's the reason I don't like this place," Zelda fumed. "It's always like old home week at Nassau Inn here. God, I'm glad to see somebody that doesn't get het up about Hobey Baker's touchdowns. What's going on at home? Tell me about John Sellers."

"I married him—in the time of my innocence," I said, "and divorced him when I came of age."

"What happened to him?"

"Too many parties, too many hangovers, too much money."

"You can't have too much money. I believe in money and lots of it. I have to believe in it—because after all there's nothing else to believe in nowadays. Nothing!" she repeated.

"Believe in yourself."

"I want to but Scott won't let me. He doesn't want me to believe in anything but him. I try to, but I can't—not here. Paris is haunted. I think maybe it's the Russians; there's nobody here in summer but ex-Czarists and tourists. I want to go home."

"You can't."

"Why?"

"Because home isn't home any more. The order we were born into is going, going, gone. Its creeds are dead, its rites are dead, and its old houses have been taken over by morticians and insurance agents."

"By the way, what happened to Peyton Mathis and Sara Haardt?"

"Peyton wired Sara that he was coming to Baltimore to marry her. He took a few drinks on the train and ended up in Charleston, South Carolina, married to another girl."

"Marriage and drinking don't mix." Zelda grimaced at her martini. "Look at Scott and me. We've had everything—love, money, and a big time—everything but happiness." Just then Scott came back to the table, and she abruptly changed the subject. "Tell Scott about Sara Haardt," she said.

"Is she living with Mencken?" he asked.

"Good grief, no! She's living on one side of town, he on the other."

"Do you think they'll ever get married?" he demanded.

"Probably—if she ever gets well."

"What's wrong with her?"

"She had TB."

"I've had it twice," Scott said, as if it were an achievement. "Have another drink."

"No, thanks. I have to go back to the hotel and pack."

"Where're you going?"

"Cap Ferrat."

"Why there?"

"Somerset Maugham asked us to come see his new house there, and my brother wanted to go."

"Are you coming back to Paris?"

"Not until the end of the summer. The *Herald Tribune* wants me to go back to North Africa."

"Let us know when you come back," he said. "We're living at 58 rue de Vaugirard, just across from the Luxembourg Gardens."

"Let's go to North Africa, too," Zelda began. "I've always wanted to go there."

"We can't go anywhere until I finish my novel," he growled.

"You'll never finish it as long as you spend all day hanging around a gymnasium and all night in a bistro," she retorted.

"Well, what am I supposed to do while you wear yourself out practicing *entrechats* and *pas-de-bourrées*? And don't pretend that I haven't been working. I've had five stories in the *Post* in the last six months."

Although he regarded writing for the *Post* as a form of prostitution, one of Scott's favorite boasts was of the prices it paid him. "Here's a last flicker of the old cheap pride," he told Hemingway. "The *Post* now pays the old whore four thousand dollars a screw. But now it's because she's mastered the forty positions—in her youth one was enough."

At the rates paid by the *Post*, he should have earned twenty thousand dollars since the first of the year. But when Zelda renewed her pleas to go to Algiers, or even Cap Ferrat, he told her that he was not only broke but also still in debt. He had always cherished the notion that all big men spent money freely. Where Scott's went, he never knew. On the Riviera it was reported that he used to chew up hundred-franc notes and spit them in the waiters' faces. Again, the Fitzgeralds themselves recorded:

> We went to the Perroquet with friends, one of us wearing a blue hyacinth and the other an ill temper, which made him buy a wagon full of roasted chestnuts and immediately scatter their warm burnt odor like largesse over the cold spring night.

Expensive pastimes but, even so, not ones that would account for how he could run through thirty-six thousand dollars a year with little or nothing to show for it. He never owned a house, a boat, a new car, a horse, or any security other than his "bond," an elaborately engraved piece of paper with no cash value.

Scott's attitude toward wealth was strangely ambivalent. His awe of and admiration for the "very rich" in his sober moods led him to cotton to them to a degree that often was highly embarrassing; in his cups, he showed a hostility to them that manifested itself in crude and outrageous ways. His behavior at Antibes and Juan-les-Pins during the summer of 1926 had alienated and alarmed his friends. If a chic, opulent couple arrived at the Casino, he would turn and try to stare them out of countenance. Failing that, he would skip an ashtray across their table or throw salt cellars at the windows behind them.

Irked by the idea of a champagne and caviar party that the Murphys were giving at the Villa America, to which they had invited the Princess de Poix and the Princess Caraman-Chimay, Scott deliberately set out to disrupt it. He started the ball rolling by putting two questions that he liked to ask whenever the conversation struck him as dull (i.e., whenever it veered away from him or his work). They were strange questions that irritated his friends and revealed a great deal about his own emotional problems: "Are you a homosexual?" and "Did you sleep with your husband before you married him?" When he found himself ignored—a thing which was intolerable to him—he picked up a ripe fig and threw it at the Princess de Poix. She started and froze for a second as the cold, wet fruit struck her bare shoulder, and then she calmly resumed her conversation. Indignant that she failed to notice him, he was preparing to plump another fig at her when Archibald MacLeish called him off and told him to behave himself. Without a word, he wheeled on MacLeish and swung a haymaker at the poet. The momentary ripple of excitement made him once more the cynosure of all eyes. Then the party went on as gaily and heedlessly as if he had never existed. Determined to influence people, if not to win friends, he began to hurl the Murphys' Venetian wine glasses over the garden wall in a last bid for attention. That was too much for his hosts; the Murphys banished him from the Villa America for three weeks.

Zelda, too, had made history and conversation at parties on the

Côte d'Azur. One of Grace Moore's best stories was of a dinner given on the terrace at Eden Roc in honor of her fiancé, Chato Elizaga, and Alexander Woollcott, the drama critic. Scott and Zelda arrived, she said, looking as if they had walked straight out of *The Beautiful and Damned.* Zelda sat aloof and remote, immured in a world of her own, from which she emerged only to make polite replies to the questions addressed to her until the toasts had been drunk. Then, with a sudden gesture she rose and ripped off her black lace step-ins. "I have been deeply touched by all these kind words," she began with a flourish of Southern oratory. "But what are words? Nobody has offered our departing heroes any gifts to take with them. I'll start off." With that, she tossed her step-ins to Woollcott and Elizaga. In the scramble over them, Elizaga won. A gallant act worthy of the lady's favor was called for; waving the black lace panties above him, Elizaga plunged from the rocks into the Mediterranean, followed by the portly Woollcott. Moments later, Alexander Anadyomene rose from the sea, stark naked. Without a word, he clapped on his straw boater, lighted a cigarette, and with more dignity than any rotund nude ever assumed before or since, stalked into the lobby of his hotel, picked up his key at the desk, and took the elevator up to his room.

At the end of the summer I returned from Morocco and put up at a small hotel, the Auberge aux Navigateurs. Coming back from the office of the *Paris Herald,* I frequently idled along the quais in the late sunshine, watching the boats lower their stacks as they passed under the Pont Neuf, the fishermen casting their lines from the abutments of the bridge, and the artists at their easels painting the narrow streets of the Ile de la Cité, which looked as if they might have been stage sets done by Utrillo. One afternoon I was rifling through some prints in a book stall on the Quai de l'Horloge when a small voice behind me said, *"Bonjour, mam'selle."* I looked over my shoulder to see a chubby, rose-cheeked little girl, with a face as round as the hoop she was rolling, break away from her blue-veiled French *nou nou* and plant herself beside me, waiting to be recognized.

"Scottie, *c'est toi! Et tes parents, où sont-ils?"*

"Ici, chez nous. Vous venez nous voir?"

"Bien sûr. J'enverrai une pneumatique à ta mère ce soir."

Two days later I met Zelda for lunch at Prunier's. She arrived looking very chic and svelte in a Patou tailleur of horizon blue and a navy cloche. She had lost weight since I saw her last, and the classic bone structure of her face was accentuated in a way that made it look sharper, more mature. The sparkle had gone out of her as it does out of champagne that has been swizzled too often. She gulped down one martini after another, but refused to eat anything except shrimp and salade niçoise.

"Remember the shrimp cocktails at the Pickwick at home?" she asked. "Even Scott says they're the best in the world."

"How's Scott's new book coming on?"

"It's not coming. It'll be a breech presentation—if it ever arrives. It's been a rough summer all the way around—rough and foggy." She was discouraged about her own work as well as Scott's. "All I do is dance and sweat—and drink to keep from getting dehydrated." She pulled a mirror out of her purse and studied the puffiness under her eyes. "God! I'm twenty-eight years old, and I've already got sweetbreads under my eyes and calipers around my mouth. Look at me!"

"You look very *femme du monde*," I assured her.

"Don't try to be so damn tactful. I look like hell, feel like hell, and act like hell. Scott and I had a row last week, and I haven't spoken to him since—not even at the table to say, 'Pass the butter, please.' When we meet in the hall, we walk around each other like a pair of stiff-legged terriers spoiling for a fight. He hates Egorova and he thinks she's working me to death at the studio."

Zelda's admiration for Egorova had deepened into the classical attachment of pupil to teacher. Every day on her way to her ballet lesson, Zelda stopped by the flower stalls near the Madeleine and bought flowers to take her—"gardenias like white kid gloves," jonquils, poppies, narcissus, ragged robins, "yellow roses like Empire satin brocade," "white lilacs and pink tulips, moulded like confectioner's frosting," "lemon yellow carnations perfumed with the taste of hard candy," "deep-red roses like a Villon poem," and "garden roses purple as raspberry puddings." Scott regarded the flowers as an uncalled for extravagance in view of the expensive ballet lessons. He complained bitterly when Zelda left him alone to take the Troubetskoys to tea at Rumpelmeyer's or to a concert at Pleyel. On one occasion, he went to dinner with Zelda at Madam's and passed out; on another, when the Fitzgeralds took Egorova to dine at Hotel George V, Scott tried to flirt with the ballerina in a bibulous fashion.

Determined to be another Pavlova or else, Zelda attended her ballet classes in the morning, took private lessons in the afternoon, and practiced for four hours a day at home. Consequently, she was too tired to go out with Scott in the evening. His drunken lovemaking revolted her and left her unresponsive and irritable. Her growing indifference hurt and angered him, and he blamed it on Egorova's influence.

"It's no fun here any more," Zelda said; "if we go out at night Scott gets pie-eyed; and if we stay at home we have a row."

Little by little Zelda told me about "that summer in Paris." Scott had done nothing but tour the bistros in Montparnasse and the *boîtes de nuit* in Montmartre with a crew of questionable characters. She had worked herself to a frazzle with Egorova, hoping to get a role in Diaghilev's Ballet Russe and ended up with an offer to do the shimmy in the Folies Bergère. It was a long, sad story, and afterward I wrote Sara Haardt:

> Scott apparently spent the summer trying to make a name for himself as toper laureate of Montmartre, attempting to outdrink Hemingway and Co., and ending up in jail, declaring that he was going to write the great American novel, "The Drunkard's Holiday," and wanted to collect source material for it. He's undoubtedly on the skids and dragging Zelda down with him—into a state which Scott's egotistical delirium seems to have driven her—a terpsichorean passion, comparable only to the dancing mania that swept Europe in the 16th Century, which Scott blames on Egorova and is taking Zelda back to the States. They were to have sailed last month; and, since they have not been seen lately, I suppose they did.

The Fitzgeralds sailed for New York in September. After a rough crossing, Scott landed, three sheets in the wind, with a couple of hundred dollars worth of unpaid bar checks, and less than a hundred pages done on his novel—"Our Type," revamped as "The World's Fair," and revised as "The Drunkard's Holiday"

—on which he already had drawn eight thousand dollars in advances from Scribner's. He promised Perkins faithfully that he would finish it by spring. He and Zelda settled down at Ellerslie again. Scott went on the water wagon for three months and smoked only Sanos, a brand of denicotinized cigarettes, instead of his usual Chesterfields. With all the concentrated intensity of her nature, Zelda threw herself into painting and practicing her ballet routines. Scott let his novel slide in order to boil the pot with a series of Basil Duke Lee stories, based on his youthful escapades in St. Paul. When he found Zelda too preoccupied with her own concerns to go out on the town with him in the evenings, he took along Phillipe, a French pugilist whom he had picked up in Paris at the gymnasium where he and Hemingway boxed and had brought home as a chauffeur. Their excursions into Wilmington's tenderloin frequently ended up in brawls that had to be explained to a magistrate.

To add to Zelda's troubles, the Hemingways arrived for a visit. Ernest was immensely pleased by his title for his new book, *Men without Women*, because he thought it would sell well to the "gay" boys and the old Vassar girls. His jokes with Scott about pederasty, anal eroticism, and other forms of perversion annoyed and frightened Zelda. And to judge from Ernest's unpublished letters to Scott, she had reason to be alarmed. Fitzgerald and Hemingway went on a bender, got in a fight, and landed in jail. Zelda was further outraged when she learned that Ernest had borrowed a hundred dollars from Scott before he left.

After the Hemingways' visit to Ellerslie, during which Scott confessed to being intermittently unconscious, he gave up all pretense of being on the wagon. Once more, he said, the stomach pumps were being polished up and made ready for use; once more he was apologizing for his rough language and his talk about "fairies." Scott had a growing tendency to turn every party into a group therapy session, at which his Freudian know-it-all offended his friends. He could not, Sara Murphy protested, expect people to like his continual sessions of analysis and subanalysis. On the whole, she added, his psychoanalytic evenings were unfriendly and quite unpleasant.

To Zelda's embarrassment, Scott liked to bring out the pictures of himself made up as a soubrette to prove that he had been "considered Triangle Club's Most Beautiful Show Girl." Although his grades had barred him from appearing in his feminine finery in the Triangle musical, *The Evil Eye*, he had set the University of Minnesota on its ear by donning it and going to a Psi U dance, escorted by his friend Gus Schurmeier. While he was in the army, he sent Edmund Wilson two photographs of himself in a letter, saying that he enclosed two pictures for Wilson to give to some poor, motherless poilu fairy who had no dream. In 1924, from St. Raphaël, he told Wilson that he had just been reading the advertisements of the brothels in the French magazines and seethed with passion for a bain-massage, with *volupté*, oriental delights in a Hotel Particular, or else he longed to go with a young man *affectueux* for a paid amorous weekend on the coast. It was, he added, deep calling to deep. Ironically enough, just as it was chiefly Zelda's stories about herself that made tongues wag, it was Scott's own off-color jokes about himself that touched off the gossip, the charges and countercharges, that drove the final wedge between him and Zelda, broke up their marriage, and were eventually at least partially responsible for her breakdown.

When their two-year lease on Ellerslie expired in the spring of 1929, the Fitzgeralds decided that they were not cut out for rusticating. In March, after an attack of influenza, Scott excused himself to Perkins for sneaking off without sending him the chapters of the novel that he had promised to complete, and he and Zelda sailed for Genoa. It was good, Zelda said, to find themselves foreigners again. But she had begun to realize the futility of their shuttling back and forth across the Atlantic, exiling themselves from first one paradise and then another, in an effort to outdistance their private devils.

At Bertolini's they found a green-tile bath, an attentive *valet de chambre*, and a brass bed that served admirably as a bar for practicing ballet. They spent the rest of March on the Riviera at Cannes and at Nice, taking in the cheap ballets at the Casino and driving to Villefranche for bouillabaisse flavored with saffron. But it was still cold in Nice and the ice-edged mistral that swept down on the Promenade des Anglais made them hurry on to Paris.

After a year of graduate work at the University of London, I flew to Paris to get some new clothes before I returned to the States. On the merry-go-round of couturiers that ring the Place Vendôme, I ran into two friends of the Fitzgeralds who had been to Ciro's with them the night before and were frank to say that if you got involved with them these days you did so at your own peril. Scott had ended the evening by taking a baker boy's tricycle and pedaling up and down the Champs Élysées, thwacking with a long loaf of bread the gold-braided Russian doormen in front of the night clubs, and shouting, "*Vive la révolution! À bas le corps des pages!*"

That spring there were strange stories going around the Latin Quarter about Scott. One credited him with shouting from the balcony *à tout Paris*, "Behold! I am Voltaire! I am Rousseau! I am Victor Hugo!" By another story, when Sylvia Beach, through whose bookshop, Shakespeare & Co., James Joyce's *Ulysses* had been published, invited the Fitzgeralds to dinner with him, Scott offered to jump out the window by way of paying honor to the Dubliner's genius. Joyce restrained him and remarked afterwards, "That young man must surely be mad. If he's not watched, he will certainly do himself some injury."

Hemingway, too, was back in Paris. I seldom passed St. Germain-des-Prés that I did not see him either at the Café de Flore or Aux Deux Magots. Usually he was alone, bent over his notebook, writing slowly, as if he weighed every word, cutting his sentences sharply, as he chiseled his gem-hard prose. One had only to watch him take out a conical pencil sharpener, fit it carefully over his pencil, turn it slowly and methodically, and sweep the cedar shavings into his palm to know that he was a man intent on method and process whether in tying a trout fly, loading a gun, or even sharpening a pencil. He was a journalist who would not only always tell when, where, who, what, and why, but how—an artist with words of one syllable and four letters, economical rather than discriminating with his materials. He had long since forgotten Gertrude Stein's warning, "Hemingway, remarks are not literature."

Although he still went without a hat or tie, his linen was clean, his shoes polished, his clothes well cut. He looked robust, prosperous, successful—a young man upon whom assurance sat like a horsehair plume upon the casque of a Garde Républicaine. Now and then Robert McAlmon, one of the most active of the expatriate editors and whose Contact Press had published Hemingway's first book, *Three Stories and Ten Poems*, would be at the table with him or Ford Madox Ford, a rotund English novelist and a professional gourmet and connoisseur of wines, who edited the *transatlantic review*, to which both Hemingway and Joyce contributed.

In *A Moveable Feast* Hemingway paid his venomous respects to Ford, as well as to another of his early literary sponsors, Wyndham Lewis, a critic, essayist, and painter—leader of the Vorticist movement. Lewis had bushy brows, a chubby face, and a mouth enclosed by deep parentheses. With his horn-rimmed glasses, briar pipe, and broad black hat, he looked much more like something out of *Trilby* than the vagabond that Hemingway described as having "the eyes of an unsuccessful rapist." Hemingway evidently thought that Lewis had it coming to him, for Lewis, with his deadly gift for satire, had said, "The expression of the soul of the dumb ox could have a penetrating beauty of its own if it was uttered with genius—with bovine genius (and in the case of Hemingway this is what happened)." Hemingway never forgave him for that; nor did he ever forgive the Fitzgeralds for the cracks they took at him, which, like Lewis's, were made while Hemingway was living and could have retaliated. Instead, he waited to take a cowardly and ignominious revenge after their deaths.

Even during her lifetime Gertrude Stein was not safe from Hemingway's grudge against his benefactors. Although he had often acknowledged how much she had taught him about writing, he reported that if he could resign himself to not making sense, he could work ten or twelve hours a day, as Scott claimed to do, and be as perfectly happy as Gertrude Stein, who had never known a moment's unhappiness in her work since she gave up making sense some eighteen years ago.

Alice B. Toklas once observed that Scott himself was not averse to giving Hemingway "a little dig." And, undoubtedly, Fitzgerald nettled him by referring to him as "Hemophile, the Bleeding Boy." But it was Zelda who infuriated him by calling him "bogus," "a phony," and "a sort of materialist mystic." Hemingway was a genuine war hero, a first-rate reporter, and a conscientious craftsman of mosaic prose. It is true that he was not a gentleman in the sense that Zelda understood the term, but then he never professed to be. In fact, he disliked the breed; his way of commending one friend to another was to announce, "You'll like him—he's tough." Polite conversation he derided as "damn women's talk." He went to great lengths to show the world that he was a man's man. Refinement in the male of the species smelt suspiciously like degeneracy to him, and he devoted a great deal of time in trying to camouflage his own decadence.

During the last year, while Zelda slaved away at the ballet bar in Madam Egorova's studio over the Olympia Music Hall, Scott had spent his time hanging around a gymnasium in rue de Vaugirard run by a doubtful character named Georges, where Hemingway boxed with Ezra Pound, Robert McAlmon, and Morley Callaghan, a Canadian newspaperman. Fitzgerald, who was no pugilist, acted as timekeeper in the matches. Upon one unfortunate occasion he became so absorbed in watching Callaghan punish Hemingway in the ring that he forgot to call time at the end of the round. Hemingway got the worst of the match; and to top it off, the newspapers reported that Callaghan had knocked Hemingway out. This, it seems, was a false report; but, even so, it was intolerable to a competitive man who had never learned to lose gracefully. The Lucretian pleasure that Scott had taken in seeing Callaghan slug him infuriated Hemingway almost as much as the trouncing he had taken, and he accused Scott of letting the round run overtime on purpose. A few weeks later, in the course of a drunken quarrel with Hemingway, Fitzgerald confessed to a secret longing to beat him up. In 1963 Callaghan included the whole controversial episode in his book *That Summer in Paris.*

At the time I had a beau on the *Paris Herald* who was helping a friend of his write a book on Paris restaurants, and we went every evening to a different place to try the vintages and the *spécialités de la maison.* As far as I know, philosophers have never decided what the *summum bonum* of life is; but Zelda and I once agreed that we would settle for being young and in love in Paris in the springtime.

I saw little of the Fitzgeralds that year, for I was dancing at Les Acacias—watching the sunset from the Pont des Arts and the rosy flares of the street lights bloom along the river—strolling along the quais in the twilight with the stark outline of the Conciergerie softened by the violet mists rising from the Seine, where the port and starboard lights of the barges dragged their red and green banners over the ripples left by the wakes of the *bateaux mouches*. We dined at Lapérouse on *gratin des langoustines* and Pouilly Fuissé—sampled the rare old Armagnac at Taillevent. Then we rode home in a fiacre in a mauve-and-gray dawn after an evening in a Russian *boîte de nuit* on the Champs Élysées, where the hat-check girl was a former countess and the son of a grand duke served *shashlik* on a flaming sword to the music of gypsy violins.

All that was a long, long way from the hell-raising and home-wrecking brawls between the expatriates who hung out at the Dingo Bar. Consequently, all I know about the charges they were flinging at each other was what Zelda told me and what I heard at the *Herald* office and in the Left Bank Cafés.

The day before I flew back to England I went to meet some of my friends at Deux Magots. The first person I saw was Zelda, sitting at a table in the corner, looking like a Fra Angelico angel on the morning after the night before. She was with Scott and some people I did not know. I caught her eye and beckoned her to join me. As she embraced me, she said, "God, you smell expensive! What's that perfume?"

"One Mahomet Enfer concocted for me in Tunis last summer."

She sat down and sniffed at her wrist. "L'Origan, stale bath powder, and gin—horrible *mélange*," she decided, wrinkling up her nose. "We've been on a party. Nobody knows where it started, when it'll end, or whose party it is. All of the people were white, I think. But one of the women had slept with a Negro, a six-day bicycle racer, and a prizefighter that sniffs cocaine. Mere peccadilloes, *ma chérie*. Another one says she sleeps with men for money and women for fun. And she looked like such a nice, simple, home-loving type. Just some of the swell friends Scott's picked up at the Dingo Bar. All they talk about is sex—sex plain, striped, mixed, and fancy. Nice life, sitting in a café all day and a *bal musette* all night. You have to drink yourself blotto to keep from being bored to death. I'm thinking of going into a nunnery on the Peloponnesus. Or maybe I'll be a lady lama. Either way, I'd have to shave my head. So that's out. How do you like my hair?"

She paused long enough to fluff out her tousled bob. "Something new—the peony cut—Antoine styled it for me. I love peonies—my favorite flowers. Violets and *muguets* and lilacs are so tame and self-satisfied, don't you think? Or what *do* you think? You're too damn polite to say. But I know. You think I'm off my kazip, don't you?"

"Off the wagon would be more like it," I said.

Zelda's chatter always had run along like the man who leaped on horseback and rode off in all directions; her *non sequiturs* were famous—an integral part of her wit and a reflection of her quicksilver moods. It was not what she said but the way she looked that worried me. There were triangular hollows under her cheek bones, and she was thin as a rail. "You're off your feed, too, aren't you?" I asked.

"No, I eat everything in sight. But I work it off at the studio, straining and stretching and ending in nothing. Look at my stomach; it's so flat it'll soon come out at the back. And then I'll have to begin life all over again, hindpart before. I wish I could. Really I do. I'd try so hard. Scott and I had it all—youth, love, money—and look how we've ended up, sitting around cafés, drinking and talking and quarreling with each other."

Her eyes darkened and clouded with something fey—something, as she once said, so like "a soul lost in the mist on a moor," that a chill ran through me. For a moment Paris lost its April charm. The lushes, *poules*, and male prostitutes among the students, professors, and spade-bearded deputies reading *Le Monde* were thrown into high relief. The smoke of their *"Bleus"* and *"Jaunes"* hung in a gray cloud over the *terrasse* and mingled, brassy and acrid, with the fumes of petrol and the ammoniac stench of the *pissoirs* along the boulevard. Suddenly the *citron pressé* I was drinking tasted like diluted sulphuric acid. Whether it was that or the sour note in Zelda's account of herself, my teeth were on edge before Scott lurched over and fell into a chair beside me. It is not a pleasant experience to see people you are fond of wreck their lives when there is nothing you can do about it but sit on your hands and bite your tongue.

I soon learned from him that not only were he and Hemingway quarreling like a pair of jealous prima donnas but also they both had fallen out with Robert McAlmon, whose unsavory talk about them had gone so far abroad that Fitzgerald wrote Maxwell Perkins:

> By the way, McAlmon is a bitter rat and I'm not surprised at anything he does or says. He's failed as a writer and tries to fortify himself by tying up to the big boys like Joyce and Stern and despising everything else. Part of his quarrel with Ernest some years ago was because he assured Ernest that I was a fairy—God knows he shows more creative imagination in his malice than in his work. Next he told Callaghan that Ernest was a fairy. He's a pretty good person to avoid.

Zelda, I gathered, wished that Scott would avoid all of them. In fact, she did not like any of the friends he had picked up in France. None of them had any principles, she said, and their wit, if they ever had any, had long since been pickled in alcohol. There was no use wasting your personality on people like that. They weren't amusing; they weren't even funny.

"What about Alec Woollcott?" Scott demanded, downing his *fine*.

"Well, what if he is witty? I can't see that it gives him a license to walk around the terrace at Eden Roc, stark naked, like a fat Buddha in a straw hat."

"You started the strip tease, throwing your pants at him, didn't you?"

"Yes, but I had on lots of other things."

"*Parbleu!* So what?"

"Dialogue by Ernest Hemingway. Come on, let's hear some more of his bright remarks," she jeered.

" 'Yes, we have no bananas,' " Scott grinned.

"The master's favorite cliché."

"You don't like Ernest," he complained.

"All right, I don't like him. But who does?" Further, she added,

she didn't think much of him for parodying Sherwood Anderson
—whose disciple he had been—in *The Torrents of Spring* and
boasting that it had made a bum out of an ace novelist and best
seller. "Ernest quarrels with his friends faster than he makes
them."

"That's no reason for you to insult him."

"I didn't insult him. I just said he was a phony."

"A phony?" I repeated incredulously. "What makes you say
that?"

"She's jealous," Scott said.

"Of what? A rugged adventurer, big-game hunter, sportsman,
and professional he man, a pansy with hair on his chest?" Zelda
laughed.

Scott's face went scarlet and his eyes bulged. "Zelda! Don't ever
say that again!"

"Well, he is, and you know it," she persisted. "He thinks I'm
crazy and says so. Why shouldn't I say anything I choose to about
him?"

"Because you *are* crazy when you say things like that about my
friends. Besides, it's slanderous."

"Then why didn't he sue McAlmon? He started the story; I
didn't. And after all he's in a position to know."

"Just because you hate Ernest, you don't . . . ," he began furiously.

"Yes, I hate him," she broke in. "And I hate your drinking with
him. If he goes to North Africa with you, I'm not going."

"All right, I'll leave you here with Egorova."

"Don't start on Madame!"

"Damn Russian bitch! She was going to put you in Diaghilev's
ballet, was she?"

"Give her time."

"God, she's had time—and money, too! And where's it gotten
you? An offer from the Folies Bergère to do the shimmy for them!
It's like somebody who wanted to lead the Philadelphia Symphony being asked to act as assistant conductor of Ben Bernie's
band."

"You don't understand about ballet. Madame. . . ."

"To hell with Madame!" He simmered down and turned to me

apologetically. "If Zelda gets started on ballet, we'll never hear the end of it. God, it's driving me wild."

Just then my friends arrived and extricated me from the fracas. As I rose to go, Scott said, "Listen, we're back at 58 rue de Vaugirard, Hôtel de la Morgue, but if you don't mind the depressing atmosphere, come have an early lunch with us before Zelda goes to her lesson. I'm at a loose end. . . ."

"Loose ends are what men hang themselves with," Zélda said, her voice flat and toneless as if her anger had burned the timbre out of it as fire does the temper out of steel. "Do come for lunch. Scott gets so lonely while I'm at the studio."

"Give me a rain check. I'm going back to London tomorrow."

The Fitzgeralds—and I use the plural because it remains for some brave scholar to dissect the corpus of their work and assess exactly how much Zelda *did* contribute to it—certainly interpreted the Jazz Age more vividly and accurately than anyone else ever has or will. Moreover, they were the living incarnation of the Lost Generation. They seemed to have a talent for synchronizing the events of their lives so as to dramatize the *Zeitgeist* of each of the successive periods through which they lived: the Gilded Twenties, the Dark Thirties, the Tragic Forties.

I left them at the Deux Magots, with the rift between them widening into the chill shadows of the crevasse that was to engulf them just as the boom of the twenties burst. They were both, even then, overshadowed by the penumbra of the dark night of the soul ahead. The avalanche of troubles that were to crack them both up began with the quarrels with and over Hemingway that spring. In a curious entry in his Notebook, Scott said, "I really loved him, but of course it wore out like a love affair. The fairies have spoiled all that." When they started to drive south that summer, he and Zelda had an argument over where they were to stay in Beaune. Scott insisted on stopping at a hotel where Hemingway had liked the trout. Zelda balked, and they drove all night.

They had set out on a sentimental journey to recapture the magic of other summers on the Riviera. But they found that "it is sadder to find the past again and find it inadequate to the present than it is to have it elude you and remain forever a harmonious conception of memory." They took the Villa Fleur des Bois at Cannes, where Zelda had an engagement to dance in a ballet. Dorothy Parker, whose story "Big Blonde" had won the O'Henry prize, was staying nearby at the Hôtel Beau Rivage in Antibes. But Scott did not see as much of her as he would have liked because she was working on a book, which with characteristic kindness he recommended to Max Perkins. Things were gay in Antibes, as usual, but the Fitzgeralds' arrival at the Murphys' parties brought tension and confusion to the Villa America. Sara and Gerald Murphy were fond of both of them and fond of Hemingway, whom they had visited at a ranch in Montana the previous fall. To add to the strain that the Hemingway imbroglios had put upon the friendship between the Fitzgeralds and the Murphys, Scott began to study them to use as source material for *Tender Is the Night*. He questioned them constantly in a most irritating way, Gerald Murphy reported. He kept asking Murphy what his income was, how he got into Skull and Bones, and whether he and Sara had lived together before they were married. His questions annoyed the Murphys a great deal, although they could not seriously believe that he intended to put them in his novel. In fact, they had begun to doubt it would ever be finished. Scott himself was so vulnerable on that score that when Robert Penn Warren asked him how it was coming along, Scott growled, "You mention that book again and I'll slug you."

Neither Scott's questions nor his answers that summer were of a kind to endear him to his friends. In August, he wrote Hemingway from Cannes, "It's been gay here but we are, thank God, desperately unpopular and not invited anywhere. See the Murphys once a week or so—Gerald is older, less gay, more social, but not so changed in five years as most people." The next month, he added in another letter to Hemingway, ". . . I haven't a friend in the world and likewise care for nobody, generally including Zelda and often implying present company . . ." At this time Frank Scully remembers Scott as frequently subject to black moods, during which he used to pace up and down the beach, brooding on using the tideless blue sea as an emergency exit. To add to his isolation and depression, he learned that Edmund Wilson, who had been his "intellectual conscience" ever since they were at Princeton together, had suffered a nervous break-down and that Ring Lardner, one of his best friends and drinking companions, from whom he was drawing Abe North in his new novel, was dying of alcoholism, complicated by tuberculosis.

The signs on the road that Scott was traveling were written large and plain. But like *"Candide, chassé du paradis terrestre, marcha longtemps sans savoir où,"* he and Zelda left Cannes as soon as the swimming was over and headed north. The night of the stock market crash found them hung over, desperate, and "horribly in debt" at the Beau Rivage in St. Raphaël in the same room that Ring Lardner had occupied in a happier year. They left as soon as they could and returned to Paris via Arles, Vichy, and Tours. In the nameless hotel in the rue du Bac, where they stayed until they could find an apartment, the potted palms withered in the dank lobby and the thin partitions made them privy to the natural and unnatural functions of their neighbors. The mind finds only what it looks for. And Scott and Zelda noted such signs of decay in the City of Light as the mold on the columns on the Odéon and the gangrene on the statue of Catherine de Medici behind the fence of the Luxembourg Gardens.

8. One Trip Abroad

WITH HIS infallible instinct for sensing the trend of the times, Scott foresaw the tragic end of "the most expensive orgy in history." The Jazz Age was over before he and Zelda had sailed for Europe the previous spring, hoping to escape from the hangovers that a high-living, hard-drinking, hedonistic decade had left behind it in the United States. In "Echoes of the Jazz Age" he said:

> By this time contemporaries of mine had begun to disappear into the dark maw of violence. A classmate killed himself and his wife on Long Island, another tumbled "accidentally" from a skyscraper in Philadelphia, another purposely from a skyscraper in New York. One was killed in a speak-easy in New York and crawled home to the Princeton Club to die; still another had his skull crushed by a maniac's axe in an insane asylum where he was confined. These are not catastrophes that I went out of my way to look for—these were my friends; moreover, these things happened not during the depression but during the boom.

Nor were he and Zelda the only Americans who were wandering over the earth, trying to forget the staleness, the frustration, the violence at home. Their "friends seemed eternally bound for Russia, Persia, Abyssinia and Central Africa. And by 1928 Paris had grown suffocating. With each new shipment of Americans spewed up by the boom the quality fell off, until toward the end there was something sinister about the crazy boatloads."

The Fitzgeralds spent a lonely, trying winter there in an *appartement meublée* at 10 rue Pergolèse, a narrow, winding, somewhat sinister street, just off the Avenue de la Grande Armée, the continuation of the Champs Élysées west of the Étoile. Like their flat in the rue de Tilsitt it was a dark, depressing place in an expensive neighborhood inhabited largely by rich wastelanders. They had only moved from one side of the Étoile to the other. Their life went around in the same vicious circle that it had the year before. Scott drank like a seasoned toper; Zelda danced as if she were possessed. Although they were unhurt by the Wall Street crash of 1929—for Scott's bond had no value in the best of times—they had a depression of their own to cope with in the rue Pergolèse.

Scott's debts kept him so busy turning out potboilers that he made no progress on his novel. Zelda was writing fast and furiously to pay for her ballet lessons. Five of her pieces appeared in *College Humor*. One of her stories, "Our Own Movie Queen," signed by Scott, brought a thousand dollars from *The Chicago Tribune*; the *Post* paid four thousand for "The Millionaire's Girl," written chiefly by Zelda and published under Scott's name.

In *A Moveable Feast* Hemingway paid Zelda off—discreetly after her death—for the cracks she had taken at him by charging that she made Scott jealous by running around Paris with women. As one of Zelda's life-long friends in Montgomery remarked, aptly if inelegantly, on reading his canard, "Zelda had no more use for women than a pig has for a sidesaddle." And if she had any intimate women friends beyond those she grew up with in Alabama, I never heard of them. She was typically and wholly a man's woman. Women and their concerns, as she was frank to say, "bored the tar" out of her. With the exception of Sara Murphy and Sandy Kalman, the only woman that she saw frequently in Paris was Egorova. Scott had no reason to be jealous of Sara Murphy or Sandy Kalman; nor was he, as far as I ever knew. And his jealousy of Egorova grew out of the amount of time and money Zelda spent in her studio rather than any personal attachment of hers to the elderly ballerina. Zelda's writing brought in money; her dancing lessons brought little or nothing in the way of financial returns. In her absence Scott's own writing suffered and his output dwindled, for Zelda was more than his Egeria, more the mainspring of his work than its inspiration. He had published nothing commercially before he met her and very little after he left her—a hard fact for Fitzgerald's biographers to admit—and one that has been sedulously avoided by them—but common knowledge among his friends.

It was a cold, hard-bitten winter. Zelda had hoped to go to Montgomery for Christmas, but Scott vetoed the idea because of the expense of the trip and the interruption of his work. His optimistic reports of his progress are belied by the entries in his Ledger recording the sprees, the rows, and the troubles with friends. With the exception of a dinner with John Peale Bishop and his wife and the annual dinner of the Princeton Club of Paris, the Fitzgeralds found little of interest to record. To pass the time away, Zelda practiced her ballet routines while Scott took Scottie to the Palais de Glace to skate.

All the amusing people that Scott and Zelda knew had left. Paris was not only depressing but dull. Neither of them had ever troubled to learn more than a few words of French; consequently, their friends were, by and large, expatriates, and many of them had been forced to return to the States by the Depression. In February, "to forget the bad times," the Fitzgeralds went to Algiers. Their impressions of North Africa were vivid, typical, and revealing. In "Show Mr. and Mrs. F. to Number ——" they said:

> The Hôtel de l'Oasis was laced together by Moorish grills; and the bar was an outpost of civilization with people accentuating their eccentricities. Beggars in white sheets were propped against the walls, and the dash of colonial uniforms gave the cafés a desperate swashbuckling air. Berbers have plaintive trusting eyes but it is really Fate they trust.
>
> In Bou Saada, the scent of amber was swept along the streets by wide desert cloaks. We watched the moon stumble over the sand hillocks in a dead white glow and believed the guide as he told us of a priest he knew who could wreck railroad trains by wishing.

The Ouled Naïles were very brown and clean-cut girls, impersonal as they turned themselves into fitting instruments for sex by the ritual of their dance, jangling their gold to the tune of savage fidelities hid in the distant hills.

The world crumbled to pieces in Biskra; the streets crept through the town like streams of white hot lava. Arabs sold nougat and cakes of poisonous pink under the flare of open gas jets. Since *The Garden of Allah* and *The Sheik* the town has been filled with frustrated women.

It was in Biskra, Zelda told me afterwards, that she first realized the depths into which Scott's drinking had plunged him. They had a violent quarrel, in which she threw the stories of his depravity up to him, and he threw a vase at her. She threatened to leave him and air her complaints in the divorce court. It was then and there that Scott realized that she had to be silenced. Hemingway already had indicated how it could be done.

In "One Trip Abroad," which appeared six months later in the *Post*, under the guise of fiction, Scott recalled the scenes that led to what he euphemistically described as "emotional bankruptcy" on his part and exaggerated into madness on Zelda's. She returned to Paris tense and frightened by Scott's behavior in Biskra, only to have Powell Fowler, Ludlow's brother, arrive in Paris with his bridal party, which called for ten days of wild celebration. In one transparent sentence, Scott reported to Max Perkins a carefully censored account of what had happened: ". . . I got unfortunately involved in dinners and night clubs and drinking; then Zelda got a sort of nervous breakdown from overwork and I haven't done a line of work or written a letter for twenty-one days."

The commonly accepted story of Zelda's collapse is that Scott had invited Sandra and Oscar Kalman to lunch at the apartment in the rue Pergolèse. The guests lingered until Zelda was afraid that she would miss her ballet lesson. The Kalmans noted that she was nervous and overwrought. And no wonder! Life with Scott during the last two years was enough to have driven a far more stable person than Zelda off the deep end. In her despair, she, too, began trying to find solace in the bottom of a bottle. "The world's in chaos," she said, "and when I drink I'm chaotic." This was a mild term for the state of any woman faced with the failure of her marriage, the inability to create an independent life for herself, the constant anxiety and embarrassment over her husband's escapades, exacerbated by the irritability and despair of his hangovers. The rigorous discipline of the ballet was her one avenue of escape, and she threw herself into it in the vain hope of exorcising the devils that were driving her.

Seeing that the fear of being late to her lesson was making Zelda more and more fidgety, Oscar Kalman called a cab and took her to the studio. She changed into her ballet skirt and shoes in the taxi. When it was caught in a traffic jam on the Boulevard des Batignolles, Zelda jumped out and ran all the way to Egorova's studio. Convinced that she was in no state to get home alone, Kalman called Scott.

Zelda was obviously run down and physically ill. A short time before, she had returned to the apartment to find Scott drinking with Michael Arlen. She made herself agreeable to Arlen, but she was very cross with Scott, who obviously preferred the Armenian's company to hers. In explaining her irritation to Arlen, she excused herself by telling him that she had been ill. He advised her to go to a clinic for treatment. Egorova recommended La Sanitarium de la Malmaison, and Zelda entered it voluntarily on April 23, 1930.

The sanitarium was located about ten kilometers from Paris in the little town where Napoleon had once installed Josephine. The spacious buildings of the hospital were guarded by iron gates and surrounded by a beautiful park, planted with geometrical beds of tulips, iris, roses, and pansies. In taking her there, Scott hoped that the enforced rest amid the luxurious surroundings would soon restore her. He told the doctors there that she had worn herself out in attempting to compete with professional ballerinas, driven herself with stimulants until she had to take drugs to relax, become hysterical and taxed him with the canards about his friendship with Hemingway. Although the charges that he and Ernest were "fairies" had originated with McAlmon, not Zelda, Scott insisted that they were hallucinations on her part and indicative of mental illness.

In his biography of Scott, Andrew Turnbull quotes the doctor's report as saying that when Zelda arrived at Malmaison, she was "slightly tipsy" and "in a state of acute anxiety, unable to stay put, repeating continuously, 'It's frightful, it's horrible, what's going to become of me, I must work and I no longer can, I must die and yet I have to work. I'll never be cured, let me go, I have to see Madame [Egorova], she has given me the greatest joy in the world, it's comparable to sunlight falling on a block of crystal, to a symphony of perfumes, to the most perfect strains of the masters of music.'" How Turnbull came by his information I do not know, for he cites no source for his quotation, and he is now dead.

The buildings on the Place Bir-Hacheim that were occupied by the sanitarium when Zelda was a patient there were taken over by the French army after the outbreak of World War II and were subsequently seized by the Germans. The director of the *maison de santé* who treated Zelda there has been dead for many years, his records have been lost, and the new Centre Psychothérapique at Malmaison was not opened until 1965. The directress of the Centre, Mme. Kalmanovitch, tells me that there is no connection between the old and the new institutions. Both she and the mayor and archivist of Malmaison, M. Pourtout, assure me that it is highly unlikely that records of the old hospital would have been shown to a layman. If Turnbull nevertheless did have access to them it may be that in the translation into French and from French back into English, Zelda's idiom was lost, for the quotations do not ring true.

After a week at Malmaison—an apt name for the place according to Zelda—she became restless. The doctors interested themselves in her problems; but instead of discussing her difficulties with them, she became evasive, flirted with them, and tried to charm them into releasing her. When she failed to do so, she fled precipitately and returned to Paris and her ballet routines.

Scott had been partying with the Murphys, who had taken a house at St. Cloud, partying with the Fowlers, with John Peale Bishop, and with Don Stewart. The protracted binges left him irritable and depressed. On Zelda's return from Malmaison, Scott found that her health had improved, but she was still nervous, distrait, preoccupied, and resentful of his efforts to control her. They wrangled continually. Scott complained of their dreary apartment, of their incompetent servants, of Zelda's laissez-faire management of the household, of the noise that Scottie made, and of the smell of her nurse. Zelda retorted that if he would devote his time to writing short stories instead of touring the bars of Montparnasse with Hemingway, he could rent a more cheerful apartment, hire more efficient servants, and employ a nurse who did not reek of perspiration and cheap perfume. But underneath their constant bickering with each other, the crux of their estrangement lay in the fact that Scott was jealous of Zelda's devotion to Egorova, and Zelda was jealous of Scott's attachment to Hemingway.

From the charges that they hurled at each other in their quarrels, and which became part of Zelda's case record, their biographers have probably drawn doubtful inferences; certainly, they have used the wrong terminology. For by no stretch of the imagination could either Scott or Zelda be called "homosexual" in the exact meaning of the word; nor is "bisexual" the correct description of either one of them, except that in the medical sense of the word, all normal human beings are bisexual in that both sexes secrete male and female hormones, which govern their masculine and feminine characteristics.

There are so many conflicting versions of Zelda's hospitalization that, having heard hers, Scott's, Rosalind's, Scottie's, and Oscar Forel's—and read a dozen others—it is impossible for me to reach even a tentative conclusion as to what actually happened. Of only this much am I certain: when I saw the Fitzgeralds in the spring of 1929 and in Montgomery in the fall of 1931, Zelda appeared to be saner, soberer, and more responsible than Scott.

Alarmed by Scott's reports, Colonel and Mrs. Newman Smith, who had been living in Brussels ever since their return from Turkey, arrived in Paris to see about Zelda. Rosalind found her sister's mental and nervous condition to be better than Scott's. Nor had Rosalind noted anything strange in Zelda's conduct during her recent visit to the Smiths in Brussels. Their impression— and mine—was that Zelda's frantic efforts to make a career for herself as a writer or a professional dancer were not motivated by an obsessive illness but by a clear-eyed realization of the financial uncertainties of her life with Scott and, perhaps, also by her unhappiness over their marital difficulties. However, she put up a brave front and refused to admit to her family that there was trouble between her and Scott. Far from being jealous of his literary achievements, she was loyal to him beyond reason. She had brilliant gifts, an unconquerable urge to express herself, and a very sensible desire to earn a living for herself. Unfortunately, according to Rosalind, Scott refused to see it that way. He wanted her to continue to be dependent upon him, and he insisted upon treating her like a wayward child.

On May 22, three weeks after Zelda's return from Malmaison, Scott took her to Switzerland, where he had her put under observation in the Valmont Clinic. The doctors there reported that there was nothing organically wrong with her and that she had no neurological disorder. Zelda protested that she was not sick, did not want to be hospitalized and had been brought there under duress. Scott insisted on Hemingway's diagnosis: Zelda, he told the doctors, was mentally ill. At their suggestion, since the Valmont Clinic specialized in gastrointestinal disorders, not psychiatric ones, Scott called in Dr. Oscar Forel, who had recently opened a sanitarium, Les Rives de Prangins, for the treatment of mental illness.

Scott was immediately impressed by Dr. Forel's competence and knowledge. As the son of Auguste Forel, an internationally known naturalist, neurologist, and psychiatrist, Dr. Forel had an impeccable scientific background. After having taken his degree at the University of Berne and served in the first World War, he studied under his father and eventually went into practice with him. Like his father, he was a man of wide interests and many hobbies—painting, photography, music, and horticulture interested him particularly. He was well versed not only in the sciences but in literature, history, and philosophy. During his first consultation with Zelda, he seems to have won her confidence by telling Scott that she could not be treated at Prangins unless she agreed to come there willingly.

Presumably, Zelda at first agreed to enter Prangins; but after a violent scene with Scott in Lausanne, in which she charged that he had abused, humiliated, and broken her, she changed her mind. Scott then sent for Newman Smith, who arrived the next day and helped to quiet her and persuade her to put herself under Forel's care. Though Zelda said that "Scott lied in his teeth" about her conduct, she now realized that she was ill and in need of treatment. On June 5 she voluntarily entered Prangins. Obviously, she was still angry with Scott, for she refused to see him or answer his letters. She described the luxurious sanitarium as a "nut farm," and wanted to leave immediately.

Les Rives des Prangins, which was more like an elegant country club than a mental hospital, stood in the midst of a hundred-acre park on the shore of Lake Geneva, two and a half kilometers from Nyon, a small town between Geneva and Lausanne. Its baronial château, which served as the main building, had once belonged to Joseph Bonaparte. Surrounding it were seven cottages, three of which were occupied by the staff and four by the "guests," as the patients were called. Extensive facilities for diverting the patients as well as for treating them made Prangins seem more like an expensive resort than a clinic. There were music rooms, billiard rooms, winter gardens, hothouses, riding stables, a bathing beach, and ateliers for occupational therapy. The patients could play tennis on the courts there, or golf in Lausanne and Geneva, or ski at St.-Cergue. If the "guests" desired it, a *dame de compagnie* would share their games or sports.

For weeks Zelda took no part in the activities provided for her and avoided all possible contacts with the other patients. Forel noted that she eventually did develop an emotional attachment for some of the nurses and for another woman "guest." Zelda, he told me, proved to be a very difficult patient—changeable, moody, and impulsive. While her prismatic moods appealed to him as an intrinsic part of her charm, she never reacted in the way that one expected her to do.

When Forel declined to diagnose Zelda's illness as schizophrenia, he gave as one of his reasons the fact that she did not manifest the stereotyped thoughts and actions that are symptomatic of that form of mental illness. Another reason for his decision was that there was no history of schizophrenia in her family; nor did he think her illness was due to any family or educational difficulties or to her romance with Jozan. She appealed to him as hypersensitive, original, undisciplined, proud, ambitious, and self-centered. Forel could not decide whether her hysterical symptoms indicated a neurosis or a psychosis. He considered her emotionally unbalanced and to some extent the victim of the undisciplined life that she had led with Scott. But he pointed out a very important fact, which has usually been overlooked in judging the Fitzgeralds' conduct: they had lived in the turbulent, unbalanced period to which the norms of today cannot be applied. The Jazz Age had been a wild, crazy time, which was, at least, in some measure to blame for Scott's and Zelda's aberrations.

Forel advised Scott to give up drinking because his sprees were partially responsible for Zelda's anxiety and hysteria, but Fitzgerald told him that he considered wine as one of the rights of man, and he would no more agree to give it up than he would to give up sex. One of the puzzling aspects of the case to the psychiatrist was that Zelda showed no erotic feeling for her husband and refused to have sexual relations with him. Fitzgerald once said that he must have written Forel over forty thousand words in an effort to straighten things out. When Scott finally was allowed to visit Zelda, she literally broke out in a rash, an eczematous eruption on her neck and shoulders that made her feel as if she were in the grip of a medieval instrument of torture. But despite her mental anguish and physical suffering, she continued to work. While she was at Prangins, she wrote the libretto for a ballet and three short stories, "A Workman," "The Drought and the Flood," and "The House."

Alarmed and repentant, though unable to face his responsibility for the state into which Zelda had lapsed, Scott wrote Maxwell Perkins a letter in which his praise of her writing is noteworthy in view of his comment in his Notebook: "Zelda's style formed on her letters to her mother—an attempt to make visual, etc." He said:

> I'm asking Harold Ober to offer you these three stories which Zelda wrote in the dark middle of her nervous breakdown. I think you'll see that apart from the beauty and richness of the writing they have a strange haunting, evocative quality that is absolutely new. I think too that there is a certain unity apparent in them— their actual unity is a fact because each of them is the story of her

life when things for a while seemed to have brought her to the edge of madness and despair. In my opinion they are literature tho I may in this case read so much between the lines that my opinion is valueless.

In a subsequent letter to Perkins, written about two weeks later, after Ober had refused to make an advance to Scott on his own work, Fitzgerald's unprecedented appreciation of Zelda's literary talent became understandable:

> Zelda is sick as hell, and the psychiatrist who is devoting almost his entire time to her is an expensive proposition. I was so upset in June when hopes for her recovery were black that I could practically do no work and got behind.

Dan Piper, one of the best of Fitzgerald's critics, notes that after Zelda's collapse, the quality of his stories deteriorated sharply. Occasionally, however, he turned out a remarkable piece like "Babylon Revisited" or "Crazy Sunday," which he sold to the *Mercury* for two hundred dollars after it had been rejected by the *Saturday Evening Post, Cosmopolitan,* and *Redbook.* Scott had hardly touched his novel for a year and a half, and it is certainly questionable whether his concern for Zelda, either before, after, or during her breakdown was responsible for his literary paralysis. At all events his anxiety did not prevent him from beauing Emily Vanderbilt around Paris, leaving Scottie alone with a governess in Paris to go on a trip to Munich with Gerald Murphy, or taking off for Switzerland with Tom Wolfe, who had replaced Hemingway as Scott's literary hero.

Obscurely, Scott recognized that Hemingway had deliberately tried to alienate him from Zelda and break up his marriage. For all his vagaries Scott had an almost Puritanical conscience where sex was concerned, while Hemingway, so Zelda said, had none. Scott's romantic ideals about love and marriage frankly irritated Hemingway. Indeed, Ernest frequently laughed at him about them. "I wonder what your idea of heaven would be," Hemingway said to him after they returned from Lyon, where Scott had annoyed him by his long-distance calls to Zelda, "a beautiful vacuum filled with wealthy monogamists all powerful and members of the best families all drinking themselves to death."

When Scott came back to Paris in 1929, Hemingway had tried to avoid him, and Scott had complained of Ernest's "coldness." Now that Hemingway's *A Farewell to Arms* had sold twice as well in its first year as *The Great Gatsby* had, his manner toward Fitzgerald was not only chill but also condescending. In his Notebooks, Scott remembered "Ernest—before he began to walk over me with cleats."

Wolfe's garrulous good nature was a relief from Hemingway's terse jibes and moody silences. Fitzgerald had met Wolfe first in Paris during the dark days in June, in which Zelda's resentment against Scott was at its height. He and Wolfe had spent a cheerful day, talking and drinking in first one bar and then another. They met again later in the summer in Switzerland, where Wolfe delighted Scott by antics as sophomoric and outrageous as his own. Some of their experiences, Scott wrote him long afterwards, had become legendary. One of Scott's favorite stories, whether "a lie or a truth," was of the night that the Antaean Tarheel flung up his arm, inadvertently knocked down a power line, and put out the lights around Lake Geneva with a Gargantuan gesture. Afterward, he and Scott had only escaped the police by a flight across the border. Scott "liked him enormously." In his enthusiasm, he wrote from Geneva to Max Perkins, who had published Wolfe's *Look Homeward, Angel*:

> Tom Wolfe is the only man I've met here who isn't sick or hasn't sickness to deal with. You have a great find in him—what he'll do is incalculable. He has a deeper culture than Ernest and more vitality, if he is slightly less of a poet that goes with the immense surface he wants to cover. Also he lacks Ernest's quality of a stick hardened in the fire—he is more susceptible to the world.

Perkins turned down the three stories of Zelda's that Scott had sent him, but in November he bought a story of hers, "Miss Ella," which was published by *Scribner's Magazine* in December 1931. She was writing at Prangins with the same intensity that she had danced in Egorova's studio, but Scott did not object to that, though he continued to try to put an end to her terpsichorean "madness." He persuaded Forel that she would never be cured of it until she gave up her ambition to become a professional ballerina. At Zelda's request, Scott wrote Egorova asking her to give him her opinion of his wife's potentialities as a dancer. Forel suggested that Scott tell Egorova to word her reply in a way that would discourage Zelda from resuming her lessons. But this Fitzgerald refused to do. In the end, Egorova's letter disappointed both the Fitzgeralds. For she said frankly that although Zelda was no longer young enough to be turned into a *prima ballerina*, she definitely had talent, and, in time, would be capable of dancing a supporting role in a metropolitan ballet.

Zelda continued to plead with Scott to let her leave Prangins. Since she had not been legally committed, theoretically she was free to leave at any time. But when she tried to run away from the *"dame de compagnie"* who had escorted her on a walk, she was brought back by three nurses, and transferred to the Villa Eglantine, which was reserved for disturbed patients. There, her condition deteriorated rapidly. Her eyes troubled her, she complained of optical illusions, and the eczema became so much worse that she lay swathed in bandages for a month.

When the rash failed to respond to medication, Forel decided that it was a psychosomatic condition, which he described as nervous eczema. In September he decided to try treating it by suggestion. He put Zelda under deep hypnosis, with results that he described as the most spectacular he had ever seen. For when she awoke the next day, the eczema had almost entirely disappeared. In her trance, she seemed to have realized the connection between the outbreaks of the rash and her marital difficulties. Later in the fall, when the eczema returned after the renewal of her conflicts with Scott, he appealed to Forel for help in dealing with her. Forel moved her back to the Villa Eglantine. When she failed to improve there, he advised Fitzgerald to call in Dr. Paul Eugen Bleuler, an authority on the diagnosis of certain types of psychoses.

Dr. Bleuler's fee was five hundred dollars, which Scott could not afford, but he nonetheless enlisted Bleuler's aid. After a long consultation with Zelda, Bleuler diagnosed her illness as schizophrenia, advised prolonging her treatment at the clinic, and warned against the resumption of her ballet lessons or her return to the United States. Zelda thought Dr. Bleuler was exceedingly stupid and refused to accept his recommendations.

In addition to her sometimes erratic behavior, there were other reasons why Forel and Bleuler, as well as the other European psychiatrists who treated her, found her a difficult patient and formed an unfavorable opinion of her condition. For one thing, they spoke little English and she spoke little French. Her Southern dialect, her original turns of phrasing, and her personal idiom, with its swift shifts of thought, its *non sequiturs,* and its hyperbole made the language barrier almost insuperable for the French and Swiss doctors. Further, she was reticent about her family and her personal affairs. If they read her letters to Scott, which they probably did, since it is customary for the doctors in psychiatric hospitals to read the patients' letters, they would have been doubly baffled. For Zelda's moods colored her letters; sometimes they were filled with anguish, bitterness, and recriminations; sometimes, with gaiety, love, and longing.

After the consultation with Dr. Bleuler, Scott wrote to Judge and Mrs. Sayre to tell them the results. Despite the fact that Newman Smith had accompanied the Fitzgeralds to Prangins and Rosalind had been in correspondence with Dr. Forel for some time, Marjorie once told me that after Zelda's weekly letters to her parents stopped, they did not know where she was for months. However, since neither Marjorie nor Judge Sayre had been well, Scott and the Smiths may have decided that it was best to keep the news of Zelda's illness and hospitalization from them.

On Bleuler's advice, Scott moved to Lausanne and began to see Zelda every two weeks. She protested that he should not have left Scottie alone in Paris, with only a nurse to look after her. His reply was that he had entered Scottie in the Cours Dieterlen, where she had won a first prize, and since she was doing so well, he felt that it would be unwise to interrupt her schooling there. Besides, he intended to go to Paris every month to make her a little visit.

Another source of discord between Scott and Zelda arose because he had broken his promise to Forel to drink nothing but wine. He contended that he needed strong drink to ease the strain that her illness imposed upon him. Scott wrote Max Perkins that in upholding him in ruling that Zelda must be cured of her balletomania, they had also said that "she can never drink again (not that drink in any way contributed to her collapse), and that I must not drink anything, not even wine, for a year, because drinking in the past was one of the things that haunted her delirium." Did the psychiatrists really imagine that Scott's sprees were merely hallucinations on Zelda's part? Or was it simply another of the clumsy stories with which Scott appealed for sympathy? In his letter he added that Zelda's illness—and the "advice" at Prangins, which presumably "cured" it—had cost him a fortune. "The biggest man in Switzerland gave all his time to her —and saved her reason by a split second," he concluded.

If Scott intended to deceive Perkins, he failed to do so. For shortly after he received the letter, I stopped by Scribner's one morning to show Mr. Perkins some Civil War documents I had unearthed in the South. He was a tall, personable New Englander with a courtly manner strangely at variance with his habit of keeping his hat on in the office. In the course of the conversation he asked me when I had last seen Zelda. After I told him he lapsed into a long silence. When he finally spoke again, it was to tell me of Zelda's illness. To judge by the questions he asked me, he must have had his doubts about what had happened. Then, as if to reassure himself, he added, "But the doctors have agreed on a diagnosis of schizophrenia."

"Zelda . . . in Prangins?" I left his office feeling as if I'd suddenly been shot down a cold, dark elevator shaft. "Schizophrenia? A psychotic split in her personality?" Certainly, there were two Zeldas: Zelda Sayre, well born, well bred, if sometimes indiscreet by ultraconservative Montgomery standards, warm, gay, charming, spontaneously witty and mischievous; and Zelda Fitzgerald, cool, aloof, fey, trapped in the maelstrom of literary cocktail parties and café society into which Scott had plunged her, and where she frequently appeared to be bored, sophisticated, bitter and mordant in her observations. A friend of mine, a psychiatrist, once said in discussing schizophrenes, "All of us have dual personalities to a certain extent; and at what point the ambivalence between them becomes psychotic and the split in personality schizophrenia, it is difficult to say. When it exceeds the norm, psychiatry maintains." But what was the norm for Zelda? When she was drinking she *was* "chaotic" and often distraught; when she was sober, she was calm, contained, coherent, and brilliant. A number of her close friends have told me that they had never seen her when she did not know exactly what she was saying and doing, nor had I.

The morning after I talked to Max Perkins, I went to the Algonquin to have breakfast with Sara Haardt and Henry Mencken, who had been married a few weeks before and were on their way back to Baltimore from their wedding trip to Canada. "Have you heard about Zelda?" I asked.

"Nathan said she's had a breakdown," Sara replied. "Where is she now?"

"In Prangins, a plush sanitarium near Geneva."

"What happened to her?" Mencken looked up from his coffee cup, his eyes bulging with surprise. When I'd repeated what Perkins had reported, he said, "And Scott's still at large? I told you and Sara he was *mashuggah* when he came back from Hollywood. Where is *he* now?"

"Traipsing around Switzerland with Tom Wolfe, I gathered from Max Perkins. He said Scott had informed him that Wolfe is a better writer than Hemingway."

"Well, he is," Sara assured me. "But I'm surprised Scott admits it. Have Scott and Hemingway had a quarrel?"

"I suppose so. I wish it had happened before Hemingway convinced Scott that Zelda was mad as a March hare."

Sara cut a sharp eye at me. "Is she?"

"At least, she wasn't the last time I saw her. She was far saner and soberer than Scott."

Scott came home when his father died in January 1931. After the funeral, he went to Montgomery to explain to Zelda's family what had happened. He said that at first he had not written them how serious her illness was because he did not want to worry them. They were frankly indignant with him, both for taking Zelda to Prangins and leaving Scottie alone with her nurse in Paris. Zelda had improved greatly in the sanitarium, he protested, and he had not wanted to take Scottie out of school. He went to Paris frequently to see her. At Christmas he had taken her to Geneva for a visit with Zelda, but it had been very trying for all of them. Judge Sayre listened with cold courtesy. He always had thought that Scott was too irresponsible to take care of Zelda.

Now he was sure of it. Zelda's family did not think that Scottie should be left in Scott's charge and told him so. Rosalind had already suggested that he let the child live with her, but he declined to do so. Haunted by the fear of a custody suit, he tried to exculpate himself in "Babylon Revisited," a story published in the *Post*. Before it appeared on February 21, 1931, he sent a typescript of it to Rosalind, telling her that it had been inspired by her feeling that Scottie "should be in better hands" and by her suggestion that he let the child live with her.

While Scott was away, Zelda showed marked improvement: her skin cleared up; she ate and slept well, enjoyed the winter sports at St.-Cergue, and began to contemplate translating Arthur Rimbaud's *Une Saison En Enfer*. Forel now allowed her to go to Lausanne or Geneva accompanied only by another patient; yet he insisted on her remaining at Prangins for six months more. The expense of keeping her there forced Scott to go back to work on his return from the United States. Although he could not concentrate for long enough to get on with his novel, he turned out enough stories to bring in almost forty thousand dollars in 1931, the largest sum he ever earned in a single year. He worried because he had not published a novel since *The Great Gatsby* had appeared in 1925. He felt that his work was out of date and that people were forgetting him. The *Post* complained of the quality of his hastily written stories. Admittedly, he was spreading his talent thin, but at least he was slowly getting out of debt; and expensive as keeping Zelda at Prangins was, she was slowly recovering there.

At one point she had told him to begin proceedings for a divorce; there was no use to try to make a life together again; and even if there were, she had not the slightest desire to attempt it. The only trait that he possessed on which to base a relationship to him, she added, was his good looks, and even the headwaiter at the Ritz and her coiffeur had that. But during Scott's absence she had realized how dependent on him she was. The only way out of Prangins was through a reconciliation with Scott; for she was convinced that the psychiatrists would keep her at the "nut farm" as long as he paid them. Because her letters were censored, she had no way of appealing to her family and friends; even if she could run away, she had no money and no means of earning any.

The tone of her letters became more loving, and she showed more affection for him when they were together.

For his part, Fitzgerald had gradually recognized that his conduct had been partially responsible for her illness. In a contrite mood, he tried to make up for the suffering he had caused her by sending her books and flowers, treating her to lunch in Geneva or a weekend in Lausanne. As the conflicts between them were forgotten, the eczema which had caused her such mental and physical anguish vanished completely. In June she was well enough for him to take her on a long trip.

They stayed for two weeks in Annecy at the Beau-Rivage, a hotel garlanded with rambler roses and overlooking the lake. The fortnight they spent there with Scottie was so perfect that they decided they would never go there again because no other time could ever match it. Then they moved across the lake to Mentone, where the water was greener and the shadows long and cool. They played tennis on the baked clay courts of the Hôtel Palace or swam and water-skied while the resin of the white-pine bathhouses seethed in the sun. "It was," they said, "like the good gone times when we still believed in summer hotels and the philosophies of popular songs." They danced a Wiener waltz, "and just simply swep' around."

When Gerald Murphy had visited Zelda some time before, he had told her that he and Sara were taking a chalet in the Tyrol. After Forel suggested that the Fitzgeralds take another trip, Scott, Zelda, and Scottie set out for Austria to see the Murphys.

In Munich, the Regina-Palast was empty, so they were given "a suite where princes stayed in the days when royalty traveled." That time had passed, and now, "The young Germans stalking the ill-lit streets wore a sinister air—the talk that underscored the beer-garden waltzes was of war and hard times." Thornton Wilder, whose novels Scott admired, took them to a famous rathskeller, where the beer was worthy of the silver mugs in which it was served. Under its influence Scott wryly confessed to Wilder that he had bogged down on his novel because Hemingway seemed to have made his writing "unnecessary."

The Bristol Hotel in Vienna was glad to have them because it, too, was empty. Their windows there looked out on "the mouldy baroque of the Opera over the tops of sorrowing elms." They ate at the Widow Sacher's, where one of the Rothschilds dined behind a leather screen. "Over the oak paneling hung a print of Franz Joseph going some happier place in a coach many years ago." The faces of the people about them impressed them as being "harassed and defensive."

From Vienna, they went on to the Tyrol. The Murphys, who had been wary of a visit from the Fitzgeralds, concealed their anxiety and received them graciously. Zelda made herself charming and agreeable, but Scott created a scene over a trivial incident, which is believed to have provided the basis for the story of Dick Diver's run-in with his host, Conte di Minghetti, in *Tender Is the Night*. After the nurse had bathed the three Murphy children, she drew a tub for Scottie and used a kind of bath salts to soften the water that made it appear cloudy. It looked dirty to Scottie, who complained to her parents that the nurse wanted her to bathe in the same water that had been used by the Murphy children. Zelda kept her poise and laughed off Scottie's report, but Scott relayed it to the Murphys, who were hurt that he should believe that such a thing could happen in their house.

Embarrassed as Zelda must have been by Scott's conduct, she made light of the whole affair in a way that convinced him that she had regained her equilibrium. Shortly after their return to Nyon, on September 15, 1931, fifteen months after she entered Prangins, Forel discharged her from the clinic, telling Scott that her prognosis would continue to be favorable as long as conflicts between them could be avoided.

On their way back to France, they stopped for a few days at the Vevey Palace on Lake Geneva. In Paris they found themselves installed amid the faded grandeurs of the Hôtel Majestic. But they lingered there only long enough to book passage back home on the *Aquitania*.

Ten days later they walked off the gangplank in New York, which to them was a lost city in an impossible world, whose shining towers and gilded spires no longer pointed to triumphs ahead and no longer beckoned to them with promises "of fantastic success and eternal youth."

9. Save Me the Waltz

IN NEW YORK, since they were once more short of funds, instead of going to the Plaza as usual, the Fitzgeralds stayed at the New Yorker "because the advertisements said it was cheap." Heretofore, Scott had always gone to the roof of the Plaza to take leave of Manhattan; this time, however, he climbed the Empire State Building to say farewell to it. Below him the jagged steel and concrete canyons that stretched away into the blue mists on the horizon were no longer the gleaming edifices of his imagination but the gray walls of an impossible city. The bright bubbles of the Jazz Age boom had burst in 1929. His barber, who had made half a million dollars in the bull market, had gone back to work. Once more the headwaiters bowed people to their tables, if there were people there to be bowed. His brief meetings with Ernest Hemingway and Edmund Wilson left him depressed. Hemingway still held the Callaghan affair against him. Wilson, who had espoused communism, fretted about the wrongs of Southern mill workers and Western farmers whose plaints fifteen years before would not have penetrated the walls of his ivory tower.

When Scott and Zelda arrived in Montgomery toward the middle of September, they found that despite the changes I had pointed out to Zelda, things there appeared to be much the same at first. Hot and still, the old town drowsed away in the midst of the ribbed cottonfields which fanned out toward the distant blue hills that scalloped the horizon. Lazy Lawrence danced up in waves from the melting asphalt in front of the railroad station, a gabled red-brick monstrosity of the 1880s. The giant Alabama Power Company sign between the station and the wharves, "Montgomery The Key to Your Opportunity," winked off and on as if unwilling to commit itself as to whether travelers were lucky to be arriving or leaving.

As the Fitzgeralds came out of the depot, Scottie was startled by the Negro porters dozing on their baggage trucks, their red caps over their eyes like wax seals askew on bottles of Medoc.

"Will they bother me?" the child asked.

"Of course not. You're safer here than you've ever been in your life," Zelda replied, speaking from the depth of her own experience.

But to Scott, Montgomery revisited after "Babylon Revisited" held the danger of unpleasantness with Zelda's family. Judge Sayre had been ill ever since he had suffered an attack of influenza in April, so Scott made the excuse that the atmosphere in the Sayres' house would be depressing to Scottie and insisted upon taking a suite first at the Greystone Hotel, then at the newer, more elaborate Jefferson Davis—"three rooms and four baths for nine dollars a day." They used one room as a sitting room so the bellboys would have some place to sleep when they rang for them.

Many of the old mansions around the hotel were overgrown and dilapidated, tenanted now by undertakers, fortunetellers, and streetwalkers. An eruption of bungalows had broken out in the suburbs. Traffic lights had been installed downtown, and strange names instead of familiar ones appeared on the store fronts along Dexter Avenue. A white-porticoed country club had replaced the old brown-shingled one.

Scott and Zelda played tennis and golf, swam, and danced. Zelda improved rapidly and began to recover some of her old zest for living. Her prismatic moods, her soft laughter, her wit, and what Livye Hart describes as "her gift for living" still fascinated her old friends and attracted new ones. "She seemed to love everybody and they loved her right back," Livye added.

Although Zelda wrote, painted, and sculpted, it was the poetry of motion in swimming and dancing that captivated her. She never wanted to leave when the band played "Home Sweet Home." Hobart Fulton still remembers an evening at the Country Club when she tipped the orchestra generously to play on so that the two of them could dance while Scott discussed politics with Montgomery's distinguished mayor, William A. Gunter.

So many of Scott's friends in the East—Edmund Wilson and John Dos Passos—had been attracted by Marxism that Fitzgerald had developed an interest in economics and politics. When Walling Keith of the Montgomery *Advertiser* interviewed him shortly after Scott returned from Europe, Keith reported that Fitzgerald discussed the Depression, Prohibition, national politics, communism, current writers, the South, and baseball. Scott announced that he was delighted to find that Montgomery showed less signs of the Depression than any American city that he had recently visited. "The people here don't seem to recognize the existence of a depression. In the East, even at places where people seek recreation and at parties where one goes to forget the day's work, it seemed that I hardly became acquainted with members of the party before they were talking of the depression. I'm going to like it here in Montgomery, I know. It's a relief to spend a few hours in a city where I'm not met with talk of depression."

The Prohibition law, Scott declared, was not only a foolish one, but it was also a hindrance to the machinery of government. "Understand me, I'm purely a fiction writer and do not profess to be an earnest student of government," he explained, "but I believe that such a law as the one prohibiting liquor is foolish, and all the writers, keenly interested in human welfare, whom I know, laugh at the prohibition law."

He was, he continued, amazed to find in Montgomery "a seeming lack of fear of communist activity or thought here. It seems foolish for an American to be afraid of any communistic revolution in this country right now, but I heard so many conjectures of possible reactions here, while in Eastern cities, that at times I felt myself becoming concerned about the question."

Despite the fact that he declared himself to be a Jeffersonian Democrat at heart, he confessed, "In ideals I am somewhat of a Communist. That is, as much as other persons who belong to what we call 'the arts group'; but communism as I see it has no place in the United States and the American people will not stand for its teachings." In conclusion, he mentioned that Ernest Hemingway was finishing a new novel, spoke of his regret at the serious illness of Ring Lardner, and expressed his interest in Southern writers.

With his customary kindness to aspiring authors, whenever any of the local tyros came into his orbit, he lent them books, read and criticized their stories, and advised them how to market them. One of Zelda's friends, Mrs. George Mark Wood, said, "Scott read things I wrote and sent some to Harold Ober. 'You are tender in writing,' Scott told me. 'I am not, therefore my success.'" Forgetting his early struggles and the frieze of rejection slips pinned up around his dreary room on Claremont Avenue in Morningside Heights, when she asked him whether he had ever had a disappointment about the publication of his work, he replied, "No, because I write for publication. I would not send off anything that I thought would not be accepted."

Later, quoting William James, he pointed out there are two kinds of minds, tough and tender. His mind was tough, he said, while hers was sensitive and easily beguiled by illusions. "You can't get away with being sentimental in this age," he warned her; "if you use sentiment, you must do so in an ironical, cynical way." His method of writing a story, he continued, was to do it like a play; think of it in three acts, with the real clash coming at the end of the second act. After he had developed his theories on point of view in writing, he observed, "A man has an easier time in keeping to one point of view because to a man there is just one woman [at a time]: his mother, his wife, his last sweetheart. Each love is the one woman. But a woman is polygamous [*sic*] because each love is separate to her."

The first time that Mrs. Wood met Scott, she salvaged a document that is probably unique in Fitzgeraldiana. They had gone to a party given by Mary McCall Henderson, the wife of a wealthy lumberman, who was then living in what was called the "Alaga

Palace," an ornate Italian villa on Perry Street, the home of one of
Zelda's former beaux, Louis Broughton Whitfield, vice-president
of the Alabama-Georgia Syrup Company and of the W. and W.
Pickle and Canning Company, both of which were owned by his
family. In sending the document to me, Mrs. Wood said that Mrs.
Henderson asked Scott to write something for her. He took a
pencil from his pocket and scrawled off the following sketch.
Then he crumpled it up and threw it in the wastebasket, from
which Mrs. Wood rescued it and kept it, "Because" she said, "it's
a perfect characterization of him every time I saw him."

SKOT FISGUREL
by Merry Mac-caul

I have never scene Skot Fisgurel sobre but he is a grate freind of
mine. He has offen toled me about his methods. He begins in the
mawning with 3 (three) strong whiskeys and from then on for
years and years he seldem stops. I myself am a danscer and kan
skarcely write my own name.

After the first bacchic festivals in celebration of their return,
Scott and Zelda settled down to the business of house-hunting.
Scott wanted to find a quiet place in the suburbs, where he could
get back to work on his novel, which he had scarcely touched for
a year and a half. Zelda would have preferred to be near her
family in the old part of town, where nothing much had happened since World War I. The streets there were still remote and
sleepy. Under the Gothic arches of their oaks, the green flanks of
the front yards rose steeply on either side of the pavement. The
lazy Indian summer air was heavy with the familiar perfume of
magnolias and tea olives. Nothing stirred except the tops of the
pecan trees swaying drowsily in a spent breeze from the Gulf.
Four-o'clocks, metallic zinnias, and dusty cannas still bloomed in
the flower beds. As she stopped the car in front of Judge Sayre's
house, Zelda remembered how many nights after dances she had
coasted to that walk to keep the grind of brakes from waking him.
"The friendly windows shone in the just benediction of her father's spirit, the door opened to the just decency of his will." For
thirty years he had lived in this house, spotless and bright with its

ruffled curtains and chintz slipcovers. In his garden there, he had seen the jonquils bloom in the spring and the moonflowers in the fall, snipped the blighted leaves from his roses, and admired Miss Minnie's ferns.

A walk paved with octagonal blocks of blue and white, caulked with dry bermuda grass, led up to a steep flight of steps between the high concrete slabs where Zelda used to sit to turn the hose on the lawn or wait for Blind Bob, the Confederate veteran who still wore his gray uniform with its bronze cross. He heralded his arrival with the taffy candy which he made and sold, by blasts of the brass bugle that he had blown in the Civil War.

Although Judge Sayre had been confined to his bed since August, Zelda found him still intrenched in an unassailable integrity, immured behind the immutable bastions of the law and the inapproachability, which in *Save Me the Waltz* she called "the flaw in his brilliance." Her father had always seemed to her to be a living fortress, infallible and invulnerable. Without him, "the world would be without its last resource." Now it wrung her heart to see him lying there, thin, listless, and gray, with "the noble completeness of his life slowly withering away," and she was tortured by her inability to stop the useless waste, the inevitable ravages of his illness.

He was a wise and honest man; there were so many things Zelda wanted to ask him as she sat beside his bed—the baffling hows and whys of human life and whether or not "our bodies are given to us as counterirritants to the soul. I thought you'd know," she said. "Why when our bodies ought to bring surcease from our tortured minds, they fail and collapse; and why, when we are tormented in our bodies, does our soul desert us as a refuge?"

Her father lay silent.

"Why do we spend years using up our bodies to nurture our minds with experience and find our minds turning then to our exhausted bodies for solace? Why, Daddy?"

"Ask me something easy," he replied, his voice faint and far away.

Miss Minnie, who had inherited a Spartan courage, concealed her anxiety about the judge's illness from her daughters. Pale and reticent, her white hair wound around her head like the halo of a

Florentine saint, she sat beside his bed night and day. Zelda came every afternoon to take her out for a drive and bring the judge the little things that he liked to eat and the yellow flowers that he loved. He frequently asked to see Scottie. At ten years of age, she was shy yet poised, a charming child, who spoke a patois all her own, composed of French, Yankee, and Confederate. Judge Sayre always told her how pretty she was, and Miss Minnie amused her with stories of "olden times," in which she passed along to Scottie the romantic traditions of her family. However, she could only visit them on the weekends, for although she still had her French governess, Scott and Zelda had placed her in the Margaret Booth School.

Scott did not go with his wife and daughter to visit the Sayres except when Zelda insisted upon his accompanying them. "Something about Montgomery makes me vaguely uncomfortable," he said to a friend. With Zelda's family he was definitely uncomfortable. Despite their courtesy to him, he felt that he was *persona non grata* with them now. He still nursed a grievance against the judge for disapproving of him and against Miss Minnie for having spoiled Zelda. The truce between Zelda and him that followed the romantic interlude at Annecy came to an abrupt end. As the skirmishes between them increased, Zelda withdrew more and more into her old life with her family and friends, leaving him to amuse himself as best he could without her. "Family quarrels," he observed in the Notebook, "are bitter things. They don't go according to any rules. They are not like aches or wounds; they're like splits in the skin that won't heal because there's not enough material."

To improve his status with Zelda's family and friends he bought, in a typical gesture, a secondhand Stutz for four hundred dollars and rented the Nick Jones house on Felder Avenue in Cloverdale. It was a large, brown, half-shingled, architecturally nondescript house, with a magnolia tree in the front yard and a garden of roses and iris enclosed by a privet hedge at the side. It appealed to him because it was not only in a fashionable residential district but it was also near the Country Club, where he spent most of his time, playing tennis or golf and drinking in the locker room.

On October 26, Scottie's birthday, her father and mother gave a party for her in their new home. Zelda floated down in a filmy pastel dress, greeted her young guests, and retired to the sidelines to act as a spectator while Scott took charge of the party. One of the games that he invented to amuse the children was a kind of mystic maze, devised from a web of cords, with a prize for the first child to find her way through it. Betty Nicrosi, the daughter of Zelda's childhood friend, Elizabeth Crommelin Nicrosi, won the prize, a book, which Betty asked Scott to autograph for her. On the flyleaf, he wrote "To Betty Nicrosi, whose cheeks are so rosy."

Scott had a way with children; he was far more successful in charming them than in charming their elders while he was living in Montgomery. The reasons for this were not wholly due to Scott's sometimes untoward conduct. Under their courteous armor, the elder generation of Southerners still bore the wounds of the Civil War and the scars of the Reconstruction. Outwardly hospitable to Yankees, they remained inwardly resentful of them, particularly of the Northerners who tried to invade the compounds of the Confederate aristocracy. Among them, "new-fangled ideas," particularly communism, immediately aroused suspicion. Intellectuals were known as "highbrows," and all artists and writers without a local pedigree were regarded as "bohemians." In polite society it was considered ill bred to talk about money or the lack of it; discussions of religion and sex were taboo.

Montgomerians had, and to a degree still have, many prejudices and conventions that seem oddly at variance with their cosmopolitan outlook and sophisticated tastes. Scott was well aware of their proscriptions and sensitive to them when he was sober; but, when he was drinking the desire to contravene them overwhelmed his better judgment and his usual good manners. He liked to talk about how much money his books had made and how much he was paid for his stories. His group therapy sessions —in the days before Parker Brothers turned such discussions into parlor games—embarrassed and annoyed his associates. He once gravely offended a friend of Zelda's who was going to have a baby by drawing her off into a corner and inquiring into the details of her pregnancy. Again, at a party he brought a dead silence over the cocktail chatter by announcing to his hostess at the top of his voice, "I often wish I were impotent so I could write more."

On the other hand, when Scott was not drinking, he could be urbane, courtly, and engaging. One evening the George Mark Woods and the Sam Cassels dropped in to call on the Fitzgeralds. Scottie's French governess answered the doorbell. "I'm sorry," she said, "but Mr. and Mrs. Fitzgerald are not in."

"We left cards and were halfway down the drive," Mrs. Wood said, "when the door of the house was flung open, and Scott called to us, 'Oh, do come in,' he said, 'we didn't know you were friends of Zelda's, and she wants to see you.' So we went back." Zelda came down, looking beautiful in an ice-blue velvet robe. She greeted George and Sam with great cordiality because they were old friends from her childhood. "Scott went out and fixed drinks for us, but none for Zelda." His attitude toward Zelda, Mrs. Wood added, "was that of an anxious parent toward a sick child. He sent her to bed at 9:30. Then he said, 'She broke down studying in the Russian Ballet.' "

Scott's work, his wife, and his daughter brought out the best in him. As a writer, a husband, and a father he commanded far more admiration than he did in his pose as a blasé, world-weary man-about-town, using sophistication as a sword and a shield in combating the disapproval of those he referred to as "Confederate feebs" and "walking neuroses."

On Saturday evenings he came to the dances at the club sometimes with Zelda, sometimes with his secretary. He was an incurable flirt; but he was now past the age for it; his style was *vieux jeu*, and his breath smelt of Sen-Sen. No matter how long he had known a girl or how many times he had danced with her earlier in the evening, when he broke on her he would tilt his head back, look down at her intently and open his gambit with that ancient chestnut, "And where have *you* been all my life?"

"Waiting for you to get a new line or stop fishing," one of Zelda's friends finally retorted.

But that did not change his standard procedure. With his usual capacity for self-deception, he attributed his waning charm not to his behavior and his threadbare clichés but to the fact that he had not published a book in six years and people were forgetting him. In writing his agent later, he remembered the months that he spent in Montgomery that year as "a horrible time," during which he was "attacked" by Zelda's family and friends.

Ignored is a more accurate word for what happened. But to Scott, filled with self-importance as he was, there was no difference between being "attacked" and ignored. Zelda tried to defend him to her family and friends. Miss Minnie, reared in the tradition in which Southern ladies accepted the wing of the chicken along with the double standard and found consolation for it in religion if they could, bore patiently with Scott and never chided or criticized him. But Judge Sayre frankly advised Zelda to divorce him. It was impossible for her to make a life with "a fella like that," he pointed out.

Divorcing Scott was easier to contemplate than to do. In the first place, Zelda and Scottie were financially dependent on Scott. Zelda's health was broken, her father dying, her family in great distress. Secondly, she had already had a taste of the kind of thing that Scott could inflict on her family in "Babylon Revisited." Again, underneath it all, in spite of their violent quarrels, their virulent charges against each other, and their momentary infatuations with others, they were still deeply in love with each other, so deeply that there was a psychic bond between them that bound them together like a pair of Siamese twins. Indeed, in their youth, they looked enough alike to be mistaken for brother and sister—and I sometimes wondered if the love between them were not essentially narcissistic.

Zelda amused herself with Scottie, with Chopin, a white Persian cat, and Trouble, a sad-faced bloodhound. After she acquired a Negro cook, who persuaded the Fitzgeralds to hire her husband, Freeman, to drive the Stutz and keep the yard, Zelda busied herself between the garden and the ballet bar. But time hung heavily on Scott's hands; the Sayres' disapproval weighed on him. Toward the end of October, a way of escape opened for him through an offer from M-G-M to come to Hollywood on a five-week contract to revise the script of Katharine Brush's *Red-*

Headed Woman. He jumped at the chance to get away. But before he left he knelt down beside Judge Sayre's bed and begged him to tell him that he believed in him. "I think you'll always pay your bills, Scott," the judge replied, politely avoiding the question at issue, which was in his mind—and had always been—whether or not Scott was capable of taking care of Zelda.

Fitzgerald left Montgomery with relief. Zelda appeared to be well, and for the moment all seemed to be serene at home. He was excited about going back to work for the movies, about returning to the glamour, the fantastic parties, and the old friends in Hollywood. But the movies and movieland had undergone cataclysmic changes since Scott was there in 1927. On August 26, 1926, the sound program presented at the Manhattan Opera House in New York had opened the possibility of talking pictures. A year later Al Jolson appeared in *The Jazz Singer*, in which not only sound effects and music were synchronized but also the dialogue. Subsequently, a technique had been developed for printing the sound track on the film itself instead of on the large wax cylinders that had hitherto been used, and a revolution broke out in Hollywood. Marlene Dietrich and Gary Cooper were on their way to stardom in *Morocco*; Greta Garbo had made her transition from the silent films to the talkies in 1930 as Anna Christie. But the advent of sound films threw out of work the scenarists who could not handle dialogue, the title writers, and the orchestras that had supplied the musical accompaniment for the films. Many of the idols of the silent screen who could not learn to speak lines or whose voices did not come through well on the sound track joined the ranks of the unemployed, John Gilbert, the Great Lover of the twenties, among them. Norma Shearer's husband, Irving Thalberg, had replaced D. W. Griffith as the wizard of Hollywood; there were new names on the studio doors, on the directors' chairs, and on the marquees of the movie theaters.

Although Zelda acquiesced in Scott's decision to leave her in Montgomery with her family, she could not conceal her anxiety over how he would behave in Hollywood, surrounded by beautiful movie stars. Even more distressing was her realization that there was no hope of her father's recovery. In *Save Me the Waltz* she remembered that:

> The doctors came and shook their heads, and so many friends came that nobody ever had more friends to bring them cakes and flowers, and the old servants came back to ask about the Judge, and the milkman left an extra pint of milk out of his own pocket to show that he was sorry, and the Judge's fellow judges came with sad and noble faces like the heads on postage stamps and cameos. The Judge lay in his bed, fretting about money.

Zelda was sobered and shaken. For all her youthful rebellion against her father's old-fashioned standards of conduct, she knew that when he was gone she would have no "last resource" except within herself, no means of support except Scott. During her illness, she had become dependent on him for more than money, for encouragement, for self-confidence, and a companionship that only someone who had shared the last ten years of her life could supply. As her resentment of her financial and psychological dependence on Scott increased, her ambivalent attitude toward him returned.

Zelda had never completely forgiven Scott for immuring her in a "nut farm." Her experience at Prangins had inflicted a psychic trauma on her from which she never wholly recovered. Had Scott called in the psychiatrists to help her or to protect himself by stigmatizing her with madness? While he was away in Hollywood, the old wounds began to fester, the old doubts to return. On the one hand, she wanted to divorce him and make an independent life for herself; on the other, she knew that holding on to him for the present was her only means of survival. She wrote to him almost every day, filling her letters with obvious flattery, praise of his writing, and protestations of her love for him, her longing for him, and her need for him. At the same time, mustering all her strength and courage, she began writing short stories again in an effort to overcome her dependence on him.

Writing with amazing speed, at the rate of "a 1000 words to a gallon of coffee," as she put it, Zelda finished half a dozen stories while Scott was in Hollywood. Without showing them to him, she sent them off to Harold Ober—an important point to remember in view of the fact that she followed a similar course in submitting the novel that she had begun to plan. Although Ober praised her stories, he could not, to Zelda's disappointment, sell but one of them, "A Couple of Nuts," which *Scribner's Magazine* bought and published in August 1932.

On November 17, 1931, while Zelda was working on her novel, her father died. As soon as she was notified, she wired Scott; but he did not come back to Montgomery for the funeral, and Zelda was left to go through another dark valley alone. When she saw her father in his casket, his face was so calm, noble, and beautiful in its immobility that she thought, "Death is the only real elegance." The flag on the Capitol flew at half mast; the entrance to the Supreme Court chambers was hung with black crepe. Miss Minnie put on mourning and pinned a widow's veil around her black hat. Zelda did not wear mourning to the funeral, but the depth of her grief showed in her face.

Long ago, when Scott was courting her, Zelda had taken him to Oakwood Cemetery to show him the Confederate graves, their iron crosses overgrown with clematis vines, the low walls around them crumbling under the ivy and roses—roses so old that the color had faded from them with the years. On a bleak November day, her father was buried there under an ancient oak, just as the sun was setting behind the dome of the Capitol.

During the judge's illness, Zelda had felt that he would leave her some final illumination before he died, some word of wisdom to guide her when he left her alone with no resource beyond herself. Perhaps, she thought, he had left some last communication to her among the papers in his bare, monastic office in the Capitol. But there was nothing there; nothing in the box with his deeds and insurance policies, except a little mildewed purse with three nickels wrapped in a piece of old newspaper—the first money he had ever earned. There was nothing hidden behind his moldy volumes of *Alabama Reports*, no notes left between the calf-bound leaves of Coke and Blackstone. "He must," she said, "have forgot to leave the message."

Her father's real life had been lived in "his cerebral laboratory," where he had toiled so long and so hard to provide for his family. He had been a noble, unworldly man, who had cared little or nothing for material things—a man of so much wisdom and so few things. At the time of his death his personal possessions had consisted of an engraving of his father, a miniature of Miss Minnie, a little bronze replica of the Lion of Lucerne, his clothes, his eyeglasses, three buckeyes from a Tennessee vacation, and a pair of gold cuff buttons among the socks and handkerchiefs in his top bureau drawer. He had left Zelda nothing but his good name, his intellectual doubts—unsolved—and his high principles. Honor, integrity, gallantry, *noblesse oblige*, personal probity—categorical imperatives of Confederate ethics—bred into the bone—or into the superego, as the psychiatrists said—it didn't matter; they were there deep inside of her, no matter how violently her ego—in competition with the other egos fighting for the assurance that fame, money, prestige, even notoriety might bring—rebelled against being hamstrung by such outworn ideals. If she never wholly yielded to the internal pressure they exerted, neither had she ever been able to throw it off. She was a carrier for them, a Typhoid Mary of Confederate tradition, she said, in the frenetic, decadent world of Scott and his friends.

That winter Zelda often drove out to Oakwood Cemetery to sit silently beside her father's grave. On the hillside above it was the "Broken Column" monument that Peyton Mathis had designed. As she passed it on her way back to the car, she thought wryly of the night that Peyton had taken her and two of her beaux out to admire it after a dance. Peyton, who was intensely proud of his sepulchral creations, thought that one of her companions failed to show the proper appreciation of the monument. "Say it's art!" Peyton ordered. When the boy laughed instead, Peyton pulled out his knife and held it against the lad's throat. "Say it's art!" The boy lunged; the knife gashed his throat. It was not a deep or serious cut but a bloody one. In their terror, they dared not take him to a doctor lest the doctor report them to the police and involve them all in a trial and a scandal. Nor could they let him bleed to death while they rode around, trying to think what to do. Finally, they decided to wake up a veterinary who had once worked for Peyton. The veterinary stopped the bleeding and sewed up the gash with catgut. It left a bad scar but no scandal.

Peyton had always had a solution for everything. He was older

and wiser than Zelda was. He had believed that the Yankee
soldiers who had invaded the town during World War I would
corrupt all that was left of the Old South after 1865. He had
warned her against Scott. So had her father. But she had convinced herself that they were merely prejudiced against him because he was not a Southerner. She was young and in love and
the only thing that mattered was to take what she wanted while
she could, to seize the promise of wealth and fame that Scott held
out to her, to marry him and escape from the restrictions of her
father's authority.

Now, as she thought of Peyton, she remembered that he had
recently persuaded the husband of a friend of hers to give her an
uncontested divorce. In hopes that he might be able to help her
or at least advise her, she went to see him. The Montgomery
Marble Works, of which Peyton was proprietor, was an imposing
building with the Egyptian wings of death sculpted in low relief
over the door. In its courtyard, among the rough headstones,
porphyry slabs, granite obelisks, and marble angels, Peyton with
his flamboyant gestures, his masterful manner, and his talent for
extravagant language and colorful invective might well have sat
for Tom Wolfe's portrait of his father in *Look Homeward, Angel*.

Generous and fearless by nature, Peyton readily agreed to help
Zelda in any way that he could. But, being also a hard-headed
business man, he pointed out that Zelda's situation and that of her
friend were very different. In the latter's case there had been no
children, no question of custody or alimony to complicate the
divorce. Peyton warned Zelda that Scott would not be publicly
humiliated by having his daughter taken from him. He was no
proper guardian for a little girl, as everyone knew, but he would
put up a fight for her custody, and a tough fight at that. On the
basis of the reports from Prangins, Scott could claim that Zelda
was mentally incompetent and financially incapable of caring for
the child. Moreover, "Babylon Revisited" was a small sample of
what he could do to Zelda and her family by means of indirection
and innuendo.

At the time neither Zelda nor her family knew that on Scott's
return from his father's funeral, after refusing to let Scottie live
with Rosalind in Brussels, he had written his Cousin Ceci from

aboard the S. S. *Olympic*, telling her that if anything happened to him while Zelda was still sick, he wanted her, Cousin Ceci, to take care of his daughter. Rosalind, who was still in Brussels at the time of her father's death, returned as soon as possible to help solve the family problems. Clotilde, Anthony, and his wife also arrived. The first question to be decided concerned Miss Minnie's future. She did not want to leave Six Pleasant Avenue, but Rosalind persuaded her that it would be more practical to give up the house and buy a small cottage that was for sale next door to Marjorie's on Sayre Street.

For the moment, apparently there seemed to be no solution to Zelda's problems. She had gone through the ordeal of her father's death with a surprising degree of fortitude and self-control. But the gloomy atmosphere that surrounded her and her family, the emotional conflict in regard to Scott, and the strain of entertaining a stream of visitors, with whom she no longer had anything in common but memories, soon began to tell on her. An attack of asthma kept her awake at night. Thinking that sunshine and salt air would cure it and against Scott's advice, she left for a stay in Florida, accompanied by a nurse.

Ever since Scott's departure, Zelda had felt an increased responsibility for Scottie; so she hurried back from Florida to spend Thanksgiving with the child and have turkey and trimmings with her at the family dinner that Miss Minnie was giving. Scottie loved holidays; Thanksgiving was scarcely over before she began elaborate preparations for Christmas that required a great deal of her mother's time and energy. When Scott returned to Montgomery just before the holidays, he found the house decorated with holly and mistletoe and the gaily wrapped presents already piled beneath the lighted Christmas tree. But neither he nor Zelda was in a holiday mood.

Since Zelda had stopped drinking completely, she found the eggnog parties intolerably dull and the tipsy chatter at the buffet suppers even more boring. Disgusted and disillusioned by his most recent failure in Hollywood, Scott had come back in a rotten humor. Although M-G-M had paid him twelve hundred dollars a week to revise the script of *Red-Headed Woman*, his version had been thrown out when he finished it. He afterward blamed his failure on the director, Marcel de Sano. "I ran afoul of a bastard named de Sano, since a suicide," he wrote Scottie, "and let myself be gypped out of control. I wrote the picture and he changed as I wrote. I tried to get at Thalberg but was erroneously warned against it as 'bad taste.' "

The trouble was that he did "get at" Irving Thalberg, the Wonder Boy of M-G-M, who became the original of Monroe Stahr in Fitzgerald's *The Last Tycoon*. At a party given by Thalberg and Norma Shearer, at which the top brass of the studio was present, Scott drank too much to allow himself to be ignored—and insisted on giving a song-and-dance exhibition. His capers embarrassed rather than amused his host, and Thalberg did not renew Fitzgerald's contract. The disastrous party furnished Scott with the material for an article, originally called "Hollywood Revisited," eventually revised into a story, "Crazy Sunday." Mencken bought the story for the *Mercury* after it had been turned down by the *Post* and *Scribner's* and thrown out by *Cosmopolitan* because the Hearst publicity men feared that it might offend the Thalbergs, Marion Davies, or John Gilbert. When Mencken finally took it, Scott said defensively that the *Mercury* bought it for the financial value of his name.

With the six thousand dollars he had netted in Hollywood, Scott planned to spend five consecutive months working on his novel. When he discovered that Zelda was writing a novel of her own, he immediately began to quarrel with her over it. He feared that she would inevitably draw upon the material of their joint experiences, which he intended to use in his own book. Zelda felt stifled by his new attempt to repress her talents. Her sense of suffocation developed into physical symptoms, and her asthma reappeared.

Whether Scott suspected that from the safety of her Montgomery citadel Zelda had been contemplating divorcing him, whether he wanted to get her away from her family and friends who were urging her to leave him, or whether he merely resorted to what he believed to be an infallible cure for their troubles, he decided to take her on a trip to the Gulf coast. Although in his Notebooks he observed that an unnamed friend was continually "running away from it all and finding that the new ménage is just the same," he

persisted in believing that by changing their geographical location he and Zelda could change the unhappy circumstances in
which they had become involved. Zelda's home town, which he
had once called "a paradise," now appeared to him as being "a
fierce little town," where he was surrounded by men wearing
panama hats, "under which burned fierce undefeated Southern
eyes." He felt that he was being attacked and threatened by a
force that he could not define. Zelda's health offered him an
excuse to get away from the psychic malaise that afflicted him
there. So he ordered Freeman to service the Stutz and drive them
south.

By their own account the Fitzgeralds' trip to the Gulf coast
proved to be a depressing one, though a few weeks later Scott
tried to convince the psychiatrists that the preceding nine months
had been the happiest of his life and, except for the grief of her
father's death, the happiest of Zelda's. From her point of view this
contention was as far from truth as hypocrisy is from holiness.
Secretly, she hoped that the publication of the novel on which she
was working might bring her the security necessary to divorce
Scott and make a new life for Scottie and herself.

The macabre second honeymoon—or was it the twenty-second?
—taken in a futile attempt to recapture the vanished magic of
youth, health, and love—did not change her mind or restore her
health. In Biloxi, "at the biggest hotel," they read *Genesis* and
"watched the sea pave the deserted shore with a mosaic of twigs."
They went on to Florida, where the wrecks of the fishing boats
disintegrating on the beaches, the scrub oaks and pine barrens of
the uplands, and wastelands of the bleak, salt marshes, "punctuated by biblical admonitions to a better life," were even more
depressing.

From the empty Don Ce-Sar Hotel on a lonely beach at St.
Petersburg, Scott wrote Max Perkins that he was replanning his
novel. It is significant that it was at this time that Scott's novel,
"The Drunkard's Holiday," became "Dr. Diver's Holiday"—eventually to emerge as *Tender Is the Night*—and Scott made a new
synopsis for it. If Zelda saw the synopsis and the character sketch
of Nicole as "Portrait of Zelda—that is part of Zelda," the knowledge of what Scott intended to do to her and her family in the

book may well have contributed to her illness. At all events, in St. Petersburg she broke out once again in the eczematous rash, her asthma grew worse, and she began to drink in order to sleep.

Scott attributed his own attacks of eczema to driving himself with black coffee. He claimed that his respiratory troubles were due to overwork, and he excused his drinking as a necessary stimulus to his writing. Yet when Zelda suffered from similar afflictions, he regarded them as symptoms of mental illness. On the way back to Montgomery, he reported that she became hysterical and began to hallucinate again. As when she first "collapsed" in Paris, her second breakdown occurred while she was alone with Scott after a violent conflict with him, away from her family, and with no other witnesses as to what she had said or done.

Early in February, Scott took her to Baltimore for treatment at Johns Hopkins. On the twelfth of the month, he entered her in its psychiatric division, Phipps Clinic, where he placed her under observation by Dr. Adolph Meyer, whom Forel had recommended to Scott. Dr. Meyer had been a student and a friend of Forel's father; and like him, the Baltimore psychiatrist had an international reputation as an authority on mental illness.

There are conflicting accounts of what took place during Zelda's observation at Phipps, some mystery as to how they were obtained, and some doubt as to their authenticity. For example, one of Zelda's biographers says that Scott gave the young resident who was later put in charge of Zelda a detailed case history. He described her youth as wild—she was "the town scandal"—and said that she had been his mistress for a year before he married her. In her youth, Zelda was the talk of the town because of her wit, her pranks, and her popularity, but she was never involved in a scandal. It is absurd to say that the daughter of a Supreme Court justice in a conservative Southern town, who was living at home, was the mistress of a shavetail lieutenant in a nearby army camp. If Scott made any such fantastic statement to the psychiatrist, he flatly contradicted his own assertion that during his courtship of Zelda, she "held him firmly at bay."

Evidently, whatever Scott may have told the psychiatrists at Phipps, neither he nor his accounts of Zelda's behavior made a favorable impression on Dr. Meyer, who antagonized Fitzgerald by diagnosing it as a dual case, *folie à deux*, a diagnosis with which Fitzgerald—but few others—disagreed. Although Scott realized that his sense of guilt in regard to Zelda's illness had driven him into despair and alcoholism, Dr. Meyer infuriated him by insisting that he was as much in need of treatment as Zelda was and should submit to psychoanalysis. After reflecting indignantly on Dr. Meyer's suggestion, Scott refused to cooperate in the treatment that the psychiatrist recommended. Obviously, by agreeing to it, he would admit that he was mentally ill himself and thus lose the upper hand he had gained over Zelda by having had her declared *non compos mentis*. The excuse that he gave was that a writer must feel, not analyze. Quite a few writers whom he knew, he said, had been psychoanalyzed and thereby ruined as writers.

Leaving Zelda at Phipps, Scott returned to Montgomery. While she was under treatment in Baltimore in the spring of 1932 she finished, in a little over six weeks, *Save Me the Waltz*, the novel she had begun in Montgomery. It was an autobiographical account of her marriage to Scott, who appeared in the original version, all too thinly disguised, as a bibulous, ineffectual painter named Amory Blaine, which was also the name of the hero of Scott's *This Side of Paradise*.

It is impossible to know whether Zelda intended to forestall the incredible implications of Scott's synopsis for "Dr. Diver's Holiday" and show him that it was a game that two can play or whether she wanted, like her heroine in "The Millionaire's Girl," to leave her husband and make a career for herself, in that "everything I do that happens to me has seemed because of him. Now I'm going to make a hit so I can choose him again." Indisputably, whether by dancing, painting, or writing, Zelda was determined to succeed on her own, to make a name for herself, and so become independent of Scott.

By the first week in March Zelda had completed the first two chapters of her novel. She showed them to Dr. Mildred Squires, one of her physicians at Phipps, to whom she dedicated the book. Dr. Squires praised it, suggested a few changes, and predicted that it would be a success. Encouraged by her approval, Zelda finished the novel at lightning speed. She afterward told Scott that, knowing he was absorbed in his own work, she had not wanted to interrupt him by asking him to read her novel any more than she had wanted to trouble him with the stories that she sent Ober while Scott was in Hollywood. While there may have been some truth in her contention, she knew that, had Scott seen the manuscript, he would not have allowed her to submit it to a publisher. Consequently, she sent it directly to Maxwell Perkins at Scribner's without showing it to Scott.

Perkins was impressed by the freshness and originality of *Save Me the Waltz*. It was one of the first, and one of the best, of the expressionistic novels. No other novel of the time so nearly achieved Hemingway's ideal of presenting "the way things were." For *Save Me the Waltz* is a remarkably accurate account of "the way things were" among the Confederates in Montgomery and the expatriates in Europe during the 1920s. It was vivid and colorful, and it had the slightly surrealistic, "real unreal" quality derived from the persistence of tradition in the South and the advent of the *avant-garde* abroad; its style was a generation ahead of its time.

Unfortunately for Zelda the novel was so patently autobiographical that Perkins felt obliged to show it to Scott at once. When Fitzgerald learned from Perkins that Zelda had subjected him to the same sort of literary dissection that he had performed on her in his first three novels, he was incoherent with rage. He regarded it as a personal attack on him, written "under a greenhouse which is my money, my name, and my love." She was, he charged, "willing to use the greenhouse to protect her in every way, to nourish every sprout of talent and to exhibit it—and at the same time she feels no responsibility about the greenhouse and feels that she can reach up and knock a piece of glass out of the roof any moment, yet she is shrewd to cringe when I open the door of the greenhouse and tell her to leave." In his anger he forgot that Zelda was under "the greenhouse" at Phipps Clinic, where she could neither leave nor take her grievances against him to the divorce court.

Further, he protested, she had portrayed him as a drunk and a nonentity in a mixture of fact and fiction that would put the most intimate facts of his private life into the hands of his enemies.

Forgetting his borrowings from her diary and letters in *This Side of Paradise*, as well as in *The Beautiful and Damned*, and her stories published under his name, he alleged that much of her material was cribbed from a novel on which he had been slaving for years. This was an absurd charge to anyone who knew Zelda's originality, which was as characteristic of her writing as of her painting. For all the help she had given Scott on his books, he maintained that she knew nothing about writing a novel and that she was merely using his name to perpetrate a personal attack on him—after his books had made her a living legend. The answer to this is that Zelda was a legend before he met her and that she furnished him with the material that gave his novels and stories much of their charm.

Scott was fond of pointing out to her, "It's a man's world; a smart woman'll always follow a man's lead." To which she once retorted, "Like I followed yours—to the gutter." Now if she was not "in the gutter," she was locked up in a psychiatric ward and helpless when Scott and Perkins decided to eviscerate her novel.

Since the original manuscript of *Save Me the Waltz* with Zelda's revisions has disappeared, there is no way of knowing exactly what they cut. At first Zelda refused to make the changes they wanted. Her manuscript, she said was "none of Scott's damn business." Scott's reaction was so violent that Dr. Squires intimated that Zelda would be better off if she left him. But how could she, particularly since Scott refused to consider the possibility of a divorce? Eventually, under pressure from Fitzgerald and Perkins, Zelda agreed to cut out the central section, which Scott termed "rather flashy and self-justifying 'true confessions,' revise the sections in which she had described him, and change the hero's—more exactly the anti-hero's—name from Amory Blaine to David Knight. The revisions on the galleys are so extensive that they indicate that Scott continued to demand many more changes.

Meantime, in April Fitzgerald had decided to move to Baltimore as soon as Scottie was out of school and the lease on 819 Felder Street expired. Early in May, after seeing the revisions that Zelda had made, he wrote Perkins from the Rennert Hotel in Baltimore, saying, "Zelda's novel is now good, improved in every way. As it is now, she has largely eliminated the speakeasy-nights-and-our-trip-to-Paris atmosphere."

Although Scott admitted that *Save Me the Waltz* might be better than even he thought, he instructed Perkins not to wire Zelda congratulations, but to keep his praise *"on the staid side."* For, he explained, "I am not certain enough of Zelda's present stability of character to expose her to any superlatives" or to encourage her "incipient egomania." Scott also requested Perkins not to discuss a contract with her until he had talked with him. Whether in social affairs or literary matters, Scott had a neurotic compulsion to take over the management; he never had been able to resist interfering in other people's activities, least of all in Zelda's.

However, once her novel had been revised to suit him and he had assumed the direction of its publication, in sending it to Perkins, he conceded, "It is a good novel now, perhaps a very good novel. It is more the expression of a powerful personality, like *Look Homeward Angel*, than the work of a finished artist like Ernest Hemingway." At that, there are those who think it quite as good a first novel as *This Side of Paradise* or *The Sun Also Rises*. And Scott probably realized it, which accounts for his first angry reaction to it, as well as for his warning to Perkins that in view of "the streaks of smallness in large personalities," he advised him not to praise it to Hemingway *"or even to talk to him about it!"* The italics and exclamation mark are Fitzgerald's and emphasize the anomaly of his strange injunction.

Scribner's published *Save Me the Waltz* in the fall of 1932, with no fanfare and a minimum of publicity. It appeared in one of the least pretentious volumes ever issued by that opulent house, printed on cheap paper and bound in green linen. It sold less than fourteen hundred copies—but today those are collectors' items. For all his apparent solicitude about Zelda's book, Scott let it go to press unpruned of the farfetched metaphors and similes that detract from it, and full of errors, typographical and other-wise—after having carefully excised the passages that did not coincide with his illusions about himself. Dorothea Brande, being a woman, must have suspected at least a little of the truth. For she pointed out in her review of it in *The Bookman*:

There is a warm, intelligent, undisciplined mind behind *Save Me the Waltz*. Mrs. Fitzgerald should have had what help she needed to save her book from the danger of becoming a laughing stock.

But as Scott had pointed out, there are "streaks of smallness even in large personalities." Both he and Hemingway were jealous of the fact that Zelda was the born "natural" and the "original" that neither of them, for all their skill in construction and craftsmanship, would ever be. Her brilliant intuitive flashes illumined a scene, a character, a situation with the same speed and clarity that lightning does a dark sky. She had the ability to soak up local color like a sponge and put it on paper in quick, bright strokes, and to delineate a character with a pungent phrase. The effects that Fitzgerald and Hemingway struggled to wring from themselves flowed from her as easily and naturally as water from an open tap. It was enough to antagonize any man, particularly "a serious writer" laboring to support a family with his pen.

It is true that Zelda had had no formal education beyond high school, no training in construction, and little knowledge of the mechanics of writing, but she had an innate artistry. She made no pretense of being the conscious craftsman that Scott was. Even so, any fair-minded critic, who can divest himself of the prejudices that accrue from Scott's reputation and compare Zelda's *Save Me the Waltz* with Fitzgerald's *Tender Is the Night*, on which he was then working, will have no doubt as to which of them had the native wit, brilliance, and originality and which one of them was the competent professional writer. All the while he was accusing Zelda of having appropriated his material, in *Tender Is the Night* he was making copious use of her letters to him from Prangins and her description of the torture she suffered from eczema there. Further, although he attributed the defects of her writings, not only to her lack of training but also to her illness, a comparison of Zelda's story, "A Couple of Nuts," which appeared in *Scribner's Magazine* shortly before Scott's "Crazy Sunday" was published in the *American Mercury*, will lead to the conclusion that her mental condition at the time the stories were written was, perhaps, better than his. Again, in contrast to Scott's criticism of her book, it is interesting to note what Zelda's family thought about it. Rosalind said:

> Joan obviously was Clotilde, more quiet and conforming than Zelda and me [*sic*] and I would say probably the most satisfactory in our parents' eyes. She had more classic beauty than Zelda's— soft-cut, lovely features, silky, creamy skin with only a trace of color, large dark eyes, and a mass of dark brown hair. Sweet and gentle, but with strong character, she walked with dignity the conventional path. Zelda's version of Tilde's lost love and her subsequent marriage is truer to life than is her story of me as Dixie, and "Randolph McIntosh." There was a boy with whom I was infatuated, and whom I helped in organizing a dancing class for grown-ups, chiefly old married couples, during the Irene-Vernon Castle era, but he was a charming young person of impeccable manners and utmost decency, and was not married, far from the undesirable character Zelda produced from her imagination to make the situation more lively.
>
> "Save Me the Waltz" is autobiography highly seasoned with fiction and some exaggeration. The descriptions of us and home stir me to tears every time I read them, so vivid they are, so full of feeling: the house that had "an affinity with light"; Papa walking to the corner to catch the tram for the Capitol every morning; Mama's sweet hands busy at one thing or another; Joan and I and Zelda; all as we were when we were there together so long ago. The keenness of her observation always astonishes me. Much of what she writes is invention but much is also true.

10. One Hundred False Starts

S COTT's decision to move to Baltimore grew out of his desire to be near Zelda while she was hospitalized there. However, after her release from Phipps Clinic, he resolved to settle down there. Baltimore appealed to him as embracing the best of both the North and the South. It was a thriving, progressive city, a flourishing port, and an industrial metropolis as well as a cultural, educational, and medical center, with world-famous institutions endowed by the immense wealth of Johns Hopkins, Enoch Pratt, and George Peabody. The city had a delightful social life, a tradition of gracious living, and a historic past. The Maryland Free State, bound neither by the rigid conservatism of the South nor the strident commercialism of the North, offered him liberty, security, and a sense of belonging. Through his father he was related by blood to the Scotts and Keys, who had lived there since colonial times, and by marriage to Roger Brooke Taney, Secretary of the Treasury and later Chief Justice of the Supreme Court, whose statue stood in Mount Vernon Place, the heart of the Monumental City.

Baltimore's verdant suburbs—Roland Park, Guilford, Towson, Rodgers Forge, and the Greenspring Valley—offered the advantages of both the city and country. After a month of house-hunting, Fitzgerald rented in May a large, decaying Victorian house, called La Paix, which stood on the Bayard Turnbull place at Rodgers Forge. In June Scott took Zelda to Virginia Beach. They stayed at the Cavalier Hotel, where the Negroes wore knee-breeches and the atmosphere was "theatrically southern," but it had the "best beach in America; at that time, before the cottages were built, there were dunes and the moon tripped, fell, in the sandy ripples along the sea-front." ("Show Mr. and Mrs. F. to Number ——") Sunshine, salt air, and sea bathing did more for Zelda than the sessions with the psychiatrists. She now improved so rapidly that she was allowed to spend half of each day at La Paix. At the end of June, she was discharged from Phipps.

When Scott had first arrived in Baltimore, he had lost no time in looking up Mencken. After Henry's marriage to Sara Haardt on August 27, 1930, H. L. had left his bachelor quarters at 1524 Hollins Street for the apartment he and Sara had taken at 704 Cathedral Street, within walking distance of the old Rennert Hotel where Scott had stayed while Zelda was in Phipps Clinic. The Menckens' apartment overlooked the velvet lawns and the fountain in Mt. Vernon Place. It was flanked on one side by the Christian Science church and the Alcazar of the Knights of Columbus on the other. But the sanctity of its location, Sara complained, did not protect them from the visits of their friends at ungodly hours. Never deterred from anything he wanted to do by consideration for other people, Scott dropped in on Henry and Sara whenever he felt lonely or in need of sympathy.

Early that spring I stopped off in Baltimore on my way to New York. Scott arrived at 704 Cathedral Street the day after I did. I had just come from Alabama after a miraculous escape from a cyclone that had taken a giant mulberry tree from the back of our house and a column from the front, but left the house itself standing. Ostensibly, Scott wanted to get details of the cyclone from me for a story he was revising, called "Family in the Wind." In reality, what he had come for was to make sure that Sara and I had the story of his most recent difficulties with Zelda from him rather than from her. Sara was less impressed by his account of the situation than I was. One of her favorite stories about the Fitzgeralds, which summed up the matter as she saw it, was of an interview that Scott and Zelda had with a psychiatrist who thought he could work out an adjustment between them. After a lengthy conference, the Fitzgeralds left, no nearer the solution of their problems than they had been in the beginning. When the door closed behind them, the psychiatrist, who was inclined to take Zelda's part in the discussion, turned to his secretary and asked, "Now, who do you think is crazy?"

"All three of you," the secretary replied.

Mencken was frequently dismayed by Scott's midnight visits, telephone calls at dawn, practical jokes, and candid questions—as well as by his capacity for self-pity and, at times, by his familiarity. Nor did Scott's references to Sara as his "favorite Venus" endear him to Henry. Scott had come to rationalize his drinking by maintaining that alcohol was to his creative talents what gasoline was to an automobile, despite the fact that, on the contrary, the doctors had warned him that it had a narcotic effect. For all his charm when he talked soberly of men and letters, two drinks turned him into a non-stop soliloquist whose failures had become obsessions. He compensated for his matrimonial disasters by endless dramatizations of them, for his undistinguished career in the army by developing a passion for military strategy, for his failure to make the football team at Princeton by a mania for gridiron tactics. No three subjects could have interested Mencken less. After an evening of listening to Scott analyze Princeton football squads, past and present, describe the coaches, lines, backfields, and the sex life of the individual players, Mencken was speechless. As the door finally closed behind Fitzgerald, Henry stubbed out the cigar he had been chewing on and turned to us. "Jesus!" was all he could say.

Scott's relations with the Menckens had been strained by his late visits and early morning calls for some time before the Hergesheimers invited them to spend a weekend at the Dower House in West Chester, where the Fitzgeralds were to be guests at the same time. Sara and Henry declined, but Scott and Zelda decided to go without them. Fitzgerald, whose talents had flowered in the fair weather of the Boom and had been nipped by the frost of the

Depression, found his host's continued success intolerable. The opulence of Hergesheimer's pre-Revolutionary Dower House, restored with impeccable taste and furnished with Sheraton, Chippendale, and Duncan Phyfe pieces worthy of the Metropolitan Museum, was in such violent contrast with Fitzgerald's homely surroundings at La Paix that it was not to be borne—or borne soberly, at any rate. Scott bolstered his ego with one glass of raw gin after another. At a party that Hergesheimer gave for them, the Fitzgeralds put on a lavish exhibition of their parlor tricks, including the rendition of a number of bawdy ballads.

There was still room behind the barn, even at cocktail parties in those days, and their uncensored versions of "Willie the Weeper," making his living as a chimney sweeper, "Colombo," who went to the Queen of Spain to ask for ships and cargo, and "The King of England," whose mind was weak and low, left sedate West Chester more aghast than amused. Before the evening was over, Scott had offended the guests, insulted Hergesheimer, and quarreled with Zelda. Between their rows, their routines, and a gastric revolt at too much of Hergesheimer's Scotch, they made a shambles of Dorothy's immaculate living room. Hergesheimer was inclined to be amused by their antics, but not so Dorothy. Next morning, despite the Fitzgeralds' elaborate apologies for their damage to her antique furniture and Sarouk rugs, Dorothy bade them a chill good-bye. It was one of those weekends of which Scott wrote in his Notebook:

> Just when somebody's taken him up and making a big fuss over him, he pours the soup down his hostess' back, kisses the serving maid and passes out in the dog kennel. But he's done it too often. He's run through about everybody, until there's no one left.

On her return to Baltimore, Zelda did not mend matters. She wrote Dorothy Hergesheimer a most courteous bread-and-butter note, sealed it in an envelope stamped "Say It with Flowers," and sent it to her hostess attached to a prickly cactus.

By the time I came back through Baltimore on my way south again, Scott and Zelda were living in the sprawling, weathered, Victorian "La Paix." Zelda described it as "a paintless playhouse abandoned when the family grew up. It's surrounded by apologetic trees and warning meadows and creaking insects and is gutted of its aura by many comfortable bedrooms."

Scott insisted on coming for Sara Haardt and me to drive us to Rodgers Forge to see Zelda, who was recuperating from another bout with asthma. Joseph Hergesheimer claimed that Mencken was the most alarming driver who ever laid hand on a steering wheel. But then he had never ridden behind Scott Fitzgerald with *Tender Is the Night* on his mind and three drinks under his belt.

When Sara cautioned Scott to drive more slowly for fear his ancient blue Stutz might suddenly suffer the fate of the one-horse shay, Scott reassured her by insisting that it was not he but Zelda who had been arrested in New York for reckless driving in their repossessed Rolls. He turned into the driveway without taking his foot off the accelerator, skidded on the gravel, and drew up in front of La Paix with a flourish. The house, whatever the color of its original paint, was a rusty gray, a veritable Hatter's Castle—and a Mad Hatter's Castle at that—with gingerbread arches, bays thrown at random, and a porch decorated with jigsaw scrollwork encircling it. Scott had a talent for picking out dreary living quarters. Even so, he had outdone himself this time. The interior of La Paix was even more depressing than its fantastic exterior. It was sparsely furnished with Victorian relics; the woodwork was dark and scarred; at rare intervals, worn carpets deadened the echoes of the bare floors; some of the windows were curtained, some were not.

The year and a half that Scott and Zelda spent there is one more example of their genius for synchronizing their lives with the times. They had been the laureates of the Jazz Age, the living images of overnight success in the Boom Era, the *jeunesse dorée* of the Gilded Twenties. The stock market crash had found them on the Riviera, deeply in debt, with Zelda on the verge of a breakdown, Scott's health ravaged by his dissipation, and their marriage cracking up under the shocking charges they hurled back and forth at each other. The Depression overtook them in that dismal Hatter's Castle at Rodgers Forge. A letter which Scott wrote to Edmund Wilson from there was headed "La Paix (My

God!)" However, Zelda said that had she named it, she would have called it "Calvin Coolidge, Jr., because it was so mute."

Scottie, who was playing tennis on the lawn, put down her racket and ran to meet her father. He obviously adored her, and his pride in her was touching. Her cheeks were still rosy, but they had lost something of the chubbiness of her childhood. Had her face been oval instead of round, she would have looked very much like Zelda at her age. "Where's your mother?" Scott asked anxiously, as if he could never be sure where or how he would find her.

Scottie shrugged. "Painting, I guess," she replied over her shoulder as she returned to her game.

Zelda had been locked in her room for two days and had only consented to emerge when Scott told her he was bringing us out to see her. He and Zelda had had a violent row over Richard Knight, whom she once described as having a head too large for his body and the most magnetic voice she had ever heard.

Knight had praised her novel extravagantly and encouraged her to go on with her ballet dancing. In a fit of alcoholic rage, Scott had quarreled with him, charged him with trying to draw her back into a world that had all but broken her, and called him a fairy. Although he had written Knight a letter of apology, admitting that his admiration of Zelda should not have irritated anyone "except the most stupid and churlish of husbands," Zelda was, understandably, indignant, not only at Scott's boorishness but also at his insistence that "she must live in a state of Teutonic morality, far from the exploits of the ego on its own." Scott's solution for the growing competition between Zelda and himself and the resultant clash of the respective egos was to cast Zelda into the role of a helpless Ophelia, whom he must protect from everything and everybody who might tend to increase her "incipient egomania"—which conflicted with his own terminal variety— a role that he was to attempt to force on her for the rest of his life.

Having warned us to be careful of what we said to her, Fitzgerald ushered us into the bare, dusty living room of La Paix and went in search of Zelda. He found her in an improvised studio adjoining his study and led us back. I had seen Scott and Zelda in Juan-les-Pins and in Paris and, more recently, in Montgomery;

but, even so, I was not prepared to find what the recent months had done to the Princeton Adonis and the most beautiful girl in Alabama. Scott's flesh had blurred the clear-cut line of his features. His muscles had gone soft; he had, in his phrase, developed "flabby arms and a fat pot." His increased girth emphasized his stocky figure and strutting walk. His hair had thinned to a kind of monk's tonsure in the back; his eyes, hard and green as chrysoprase, were bloodshot and bulging in their sockets.

Both Scott and Zelda had lost the fresh, well-scrubbed look that had marked them in their youth. Although, as ever, Zelda was immaculate, dressed in a yellow-linen dress and white espadrilles, the chic grooming of her Paris days was gone. Her once lustrous blond hair had taken on a dull red-gold tint; her skin, a grayish pallor. Illness had drained her of the vitality that lent her the splendor of a barbaric princess. The once faultless skin of her face and neck was scarred from eczema. But neither before nor since did she have "the hawk-like eyes" and "thin mouth" that Hemingway and others have ascribed to her—on what basis I do not know, for her eyes were large and luminous and her mouth the cupid's bow of a lipstick advertisement.

Beyond an exchange of Confederate amenities with Sara and me and an occasional inquiry about her family and friends in Montgomery, Zelda's conversation was confined almost wholly to her painting. A corner of her eye twitched, and her mouth twisted from the nervous strain when she spoke. From the wary glances that she cast at Scott now and then as she showed us her canvases, I gathered that Scott must be caviling that she was now becoming as obsessed by her painting as she had been by her dancing in Paris. Among the sketches of New York, of Paris, of ballet dancers, and dream gardens stacked against the wall there were two crucifixions. The face on the cross in one of them was unmistakably Zelda's. As Scott saw that Sara and I recognized the likeness, he turned abruptly and walked out of the room. If he could not face it, I could not forget it—nor the Sanhedrin of psychiatrists who had condemned her to the Calvary of a Bedlam.

To see Scott and Zelda now and to remember them in their early days together in Montgomery was like reading a palimpsest on which a stark Greek tragedy had been written over the faint traces of a romantic comedy. And it was not the way to spend a pleasant afternoon.

While Zelda was telling us about an exhibition of her work that she hoped to have in New York, Scott came to the door of his study and interrupted her to call Sara Haardt in to show her the pile of manuscript stacked up on the floor beside his writing table. It was the outline and sketches for the novel he'd been trying to write since 1926, called "Dr. Diver's Holiday" at the moment. He had high hopes for it; he had worked long and hard on it. Imprisoned there behind the bars of his leaded bow window, as he said in "One Hundred False Starts" in a vein of self-pity, "alone in the privacy of my faded blue room with my sick cat, the bare February branches waving at the window, an ironic paperweight that said Business is Good, and a New England conscience—developed in Minnesota." It had been an exhausting struggle, for it was to be a double-decker novel and one that would be both an artistic triumph and a best seller. "And it's good, good, good!" he added, pounding on the table. He spoke as if he were whistling in a cemetery to bolster his own morale. Like most egotists, Scott was basically insecure. As if to reassure himself, he said, "It *is* good, isn't it, Zelda?"

Her reply was a peal of irrelevant, mirthless laughter. For a moment I thought Scott was going to slap her. Their eyes met and locked in a conflict that had rent them both and reduced them to the tarnished specters of the golden boy and girl of the Jazz Age. Anger flashed in the dead silence between and then paled into inward desolation and despair that was no longer the mere dark night of the soul with some promised morning, however far away, but a sickness unto death.

"She's mad," Scott said huskily. Then, seeing the shock in our faces, he added hastily, as if in extenuation of his charge, "Schizophrenia, the doctors say."

Whatever Scott, the doctors, or anyone else might call Zelda's illness, the simple truth in human terms is that removed from the warmth and security of a familiar environment, plunged into a maelstrom of conflicting emotions, and faced with more professional, financial, and marital problems than she—or anyone else of her background and temperament—could cope with, she broke down. During the times when the pressures relaxed and when there was even relative harmony between her and Scott, she rebounded quickly and appeared to be her old self again.

In the beginning the split in Scott's personality had been far more apparent than that in Zelda's. In one of the shrewdest criticisms of Scott ever written, "Fitzgerald: The Double Man," Malcolm Cowley pointed out that Scott's doubleness was one of his distinctive marks as a writer. Even in his youth he had been double-minded, endowed with an uncanny ability to be both spectator and actor in an event. He once described this weird talent as being able to see himself as taking the top girl to a ball and at the same time imagining himself standing outside with his nose pressed against the window of the ballroom, wondering how much the tickets cost. Indeed, Scott once said that his idea of a first-rate man was one who could hold two diametrically opposed ideas in mind at the same time and continue to function.

Now, torn between the conviction of the futility of his efforts and the urgency of the need to struggle, the split in his consciousness had deepened until he had become, if not a Dr. Jekyll and Mr. Hyde, at least a Dr. Diver and Mr. Fitzgerald. An unhappy result of his schizoid state was his increasing tendency to project, particularly where Zelda and her family were concerned. The accusations that he hurled at them when he was drunk revealed more about Scott than about the Sayres. There is very little of Fitzgerald's experience in life that did not sift its way into his work, and a discerning eye can find more light on the origins of Zelda's illness in Scott's "One Trip Abroad," "Babylon Revisited," and *The Crack-Up* than in her family history.

On the way back to town, aware that his behavior had put him in a very bad light in Sara's eyes, Scott attempted to justify himself. He began by disparaging Zelda. Then he blamed her illness on her family, whom he taxed with bringing her up to be spoiled, selfish, and dependent—despite his continual efforts to crush her struggle to be independent of him. We tried half a dozen times to change the subject, but it was impossible to stop his scathing criticisms of Zelda and her family.

When Mencken joined Sara and me in what he called "the public rooms" at 704 Cathedral Street after our return from La

Paix, we recounted our unhappy afternoon there. H. L. summed the matter up with the wry comment: "Too bad Scott thought of having Zelda locked up first."

Nor did Scott's behavior during the ensuing year do anything to change Mencken's mind. As the political season opened, Scott's tipsy visits to Cathedral Street frequently collided with those of Governor Albert C. Ritchie, H. L.'s old friend and Maryland's favorite son. To the Sage's dismay, Fitzgerald publicly nominated him to be Governor Ritchie's Colonel House. After Edmund Wilson, who still served as Scott's "intellectual conscience," began to look favorably on communism, Mencken reported that Fitzgerald had begun to flirt with the Marxists. Like a guttering candle, Zelda's old wit flared up and she said that she had taken to horseback, but noncommittally and apologetically, because, since they had heard so much about communism at La Paix, she was not sure that it was not the horse that should be riding her.

When Scott discovered that Zelda had begun another novel, they had an epic—almost a terminal—quarrel, for she had used her psychiatric experiences as material and a clinic in Switzerland as a setting. Large sections of Scott's *Tender Is the Night* drew on the same sources. He had even used her descriptions of her sufferings from eczema and slightly paraphrased extracts from the letters she had written him from Prangins. Scott flew into a rage. He claimed that she had once more infringed upon *his* material —his because he had paid for it at the rate of a thousand dollars a month.

Meanwhile, the Fitzgeralds had been going once a week to Phipps for a conference with Dr. Meyer, who had written Dr. Forel that, while Zelda's condition continued to improve, Scott's was deteriorating rapidly. Since Dr. Meyer had failed to persuade Fitzgerald to stop drinking and to submit to psychoanalytic treatment, Dr. Thomas A. Rennie, a young psychiatrist with literary ambitions, was put in charge of the case. In her biography of Zelda, Nancy Milford says that Dr. Rennie made a one-hundred-fourteen-page transcription of his conferences with the Fitzgeralds. The transcription has now disappeared, so it is impossible to say whether Dr. Rennie dramatized the talks or reported them accurately. Scott had none of Zelda's reticence in regard to discussing their relationship. Consequently, the reports from the clinics, on which several of the Fitzgeralds' biographers have drawn heavily, reflect Scott's side of the story, which almost invariably presented a distorted—and frequently derogatory—picture of her and her family. Even so, Mrs. Milford's reports of his brutality to Zelda during their conferences with the doctors are often shocking. For example, Mrs. Milford quotes him as telling Dr. Rennie in Zelda's presence during the quarrel over her new novel that she was stealing his material, that she was "a third-rate writer and a third-rate ballet dancer." Zelda retorted that their marriage had been one long battle and that she had rather be in an institution than to try to live with him any longer.

At first Scott refused to consider the idea of a separation, for that would give Zelda free rein to say what she pleased in her novel. So he laid down the law to her: she was not to deal with any psychiatric material, nor with their joint experiences in Switzerland or on the Riviera. Further, he demanded that she stop work on her new book until he finished his novel. Chagrined at the ease and speed with which she wrote, he resorted to gin to stimulate his flagging output. As a result of his daily hangovers and nightly doses of barbiturates, he was irritable and surly. He blamed his inability to concentrate on Zelda. She needed to be disciplined, he said, even if it meant telling her to pack up and go back to Phipps. He wanted the doctors to punish her by allowing her to feel that she was utterly alone, that she had exhausted everyone's patience. When the doctors disagreed with Scott's proposed regimen for Zelda, he asked his lawyer whether he could divorce her; and if so, on what grounds. But the thought of what a court trial, a custody fight, and a broken home would do to his wife and daughter sent him back to his desk and to his battle to make yet another start on "Dr. Diver's Holiday." If Scott was tough-minded, he was also tenderhearted, particularly where his wife and child were concerned.

After a quiet Christmas at La Paix, he and Zelda went to New York for three days in January. Their room at the Algonquin was "high up amidst the gilded domes" of their lost city. They went to the theater, to an exhibition of modern paintings, to dinner with old friends in an effort to recapture the enchantment they had felt there in better years. He later explained to Max Perkins that he did not call him while in New York because he was there on a terrific binge that had put him to bed for twenty-four hours. Later in a letter to Edmund Wilson, inviting him to spend the night of Roosevelt's inauguration at La Paix, he apologized for having looked him and Ernest Hemingway up while he was in New York. He had gone there to get drunk, he said, and he assumed full responsibility for the unpleasantness of that unfortunate meeting. He and Hemingway, he added, had reached the point that when they drank together, he half-baited, half-truckled to Ernest.

Shortly before the inauguration, Dos Passos took his wife to Johns Hopkins Hospital to have her tonsils out. While he was there he saw Scott frequently. They discussed Leninism, Marxism, and the prospects of the Leftists in this country. When Dos Passos was quoted as saying, "Writers of the world unite, you have nothing to lose but your brains," he replied, "I hope I really said it. *Si non e vero e ben trovato.*" His wife had barely recovered from her operation when an attack of rheumatic fever sent Dos Passos himself to Johns Hopkins. Scott used to come around, he remembered in *The Best Times*, and sit "bleakly fidgeting" in his hospital room while he tried to talk him out of the notion that he was "high and dry on the rocks." Dos Passos added:

> Actually Scott was meeting adversity with a consistency of purpose that I found admirable. He was trying to raise Scottie, to do the best thing possible for Zelda, to handle his drinking and to keep a flow of stories into the magazines to raise the enormous sums Zelda's illness cost. At the same time he was determined to continue writing first rate novels. With age and experience his literary standards were rising. I never admired a man more. He was so much worse off than I, that I felt I ought to be sitting at his bedside instead of his sitting at mine.

When T. S. Eliot came to Baltimore to give the Turnbull lectures at Hopkins, Mrs. Turnbull asked Scott to dine with him—an invitation that pleased him greatly because he always said that he appreciated Eliot's letter to him about *The Great Gatsby* more than any other he received. After the dinner he wrote Edmund

Wilson that he had spent an afternoon and evening with Eliot and liked him very much. At Mrs. Turnbull's request, Scott had read part of *The Waste Land* aloud and pleased Eliot by his rendition of the poem's subtler nuances.

In declining a dinner invitation from Mrs. Turnbull the following September, Scott said he and Zelda had dined out exactly four times in two years. After the unhappy trip to New York, he had checked his drinking, tightened his belt, and promised himself that he would finish *Tender Is the Night* by the end of October. At that time, he promised Perkins he would "appear in person, carrying the manuscript, and wearing a spiked helmet."

11. Tender Is the Night

Ⅰ T WAS a bitter, bone-chilling winter in Baltimore. Since Sara Haardt was ill with influenza, she had asked me to take some review copies that she had sold to Siegfried Weisburger to him at the Peabody Book Shop. As I waited for the traffic light at the corner of Mt. Vernon Place, one of the green double-decker buses that plied up and down Charles Street stopped at the curb. A man, with his hat pulled down and the collar of a worn overcoat turned up against the raw wind whipping off the Chesapeake, descended from the top deck holding cautiously to the iron rail. As he stepped off, he missed the curb and landed on his knees in the slush of dirty sherbet running in the gutters from yesterday's snow. When he made no move to get up, I put down the books and went to see whether he had broken a leg. As he looked up, I saw that it was Scott.

"Oh, God," he said, with a glimmer of grim humor, "how the mighty are fallen."

"Scott? Are you hurt?" I inquired, as I helped him to his feet.

He brushed the snow off his trousers with an indignant gesture. "Did you ever fall in the gutter?" His tone implied that it was not his leg but his pride that was hurt.

"Not yet," I replied, as I picked up the books and skidded along the icy pavement. "But it could happen any moment."

"If I'd been drunk, I wouldn't care," he said ruefully. "But I'm just out of the hospital."

He fell in beside me and we walked on down Charles Street. The wind rolled the fog up off the bay and cracked the icy branches of the scraggly little trees in front of the endless rows of brick-faced, white-stooped houses that ran from the phallic column in Mt. Vernon Place to the rustica buildings of what was then Goucher College and on again to the billowing, evergreen campus of Johns Hopkins University.

The Peabody Book Shop, located in the basement of one of the brick row houses near the Peabody Conservatory, offered a cheerful haven from the dreary day and dirty slush of the streets. After Repeal, Siegfried Weisburger had paneled a room in the back of his shop, where he served beer and mulled wine to customers who wanted to browse among the books or read before the fire there. As Siegfried was out, Scott called me back to have a glass of Pilsner while I waited. He had tried to write the third section of his book on the bottle, he said, and it was no go. Hemingway had decided that Scott was an alcoholic, so Scott had made up his mind to go on the wagon until he finished his book—just to show him. Beer did not count. He could drink a dozen bottles a day and never know it. After a moment he asked whether Mencken had read Hemingway's *Death in the Afternoon.*

"He reviewed it in the December issue of the *Mercury,*" I told him.

"Did he? I didn't see it. What did he say?"

"He thought it a very fine piece of writing. But he felt that Hemingway tried to prove that he was a naughty fellow and dragged in a lot of ancient four-letter words—just for the pleasure of throwing the Oak Park W.T.C.U. into a conniption fit."

"Mencken never thought as highly of Ernest as I did. Said he was mining a thin vein. Maybe he was right." Scott stared nostalgically into the fire as if he were looking back through the flames to his early Paris days. "I used to like hell out of Ernest," he said. "Now, whenever I see him, he has to tell me what a natural he is and what a rummy I am." After he last saw Hemingway in New York, Scott had written in the Notebooks, "I talk with the authority of failure—Ernest with the authority of success. We could never sit across the same table again."

Scott drained his beer. "Ernest is so damn cocksure. Zelda could never resist baiting him," he grumbled. "There was always some kind of subtle antagonism between them."

"Subtle, did you say, Scott?"

"I guess you're right. She hated his guts."

"How is Zelda?"

"Much better lately. She gave up the novel and wrote a play—a kind of musical that the Vagabond Players are going to do."

"Good. Give her my love." As Weisburger had not come back, I left the review copies with a note for him and started out. While I was writing the note, Scott had been looking over a table of secondhand books. He turned up a copy of Mencken's *Treatise on the Gods* and said, "I'll take this along and get him to autograph it for me." Then, turning to the clerk, he added, "Never mind wrapping it. Just put it on my bill."

"To whom shall I charge it?" the clerk asked automatically.

If Scott had been suddenly slapped, he would probably have been less angry. "If you don't know who I am, you'd damned well better learn," he flung over his shoulder as he stalked out.

The clerk looked helplessly at me. "Is he somebody I'm supposed to know or just another crazy guy?"

"He's F. Scott Fitzgerald," I said, wondering as I did if Mencken had not been right in saying that it was Scott, rather than Zelda, who should have been locked up.

During the next year, 1933, every time I saw or heard of Scott he was either in or just out of the hospital. Hypochondria, apparently, is frequently one of the side effects of a writer's block. In his Notebooks under the heading of the "List of Troubles," by which he was afflicted, Scott wrote: heartburn, eczema, piles, flu, night sweats, alcoholism, infected nose, insomnia, ruined nerves, chronic cough, aching teeth, shortness of breath, falling hair, cramps in feet, tingling in feet, constipation, cirrhosis of the liver, stomach ulcers, depression, and melancholia.

Nor were things going well with Zelda. To add to her disappointment over the sales of *Save Me the Waltz*, the first night of the Vagabond Players' production of her play, *Scandalabra*, for which she had had such high hopes, went so badly that Scott called the cast together in the Green Room and attempted to revise it. His play-doctoring hurt rather than helped, and the Vagabond Players jettisoned the script.

All that came to Scott's mill was grist—ground to his own purpose—and in his Notebooks, after the failure of Zelda's play, there is a sketch for a story:

> Andrew Fulton, a facile character who can do anything, is married to a girl who can't express herself. She has a growing jealousy of his talents. The night of her show for the Junior League comes and is a great failure. He takes hold and saves the piece and can't understand why she hates him for it. She had interested a dealer secretly in her pictures (or designs or sculpture) and plans to make an independent living. But the dealer has sold only one specimen. When he sees the rest he shakes his head. Andrew in a few minutes turns out something in putty and the dealer perks up and says, "That's what we want." She is furious.

The steady progress that Scott had made on *Tender Is the Night* during the spring was interrupted in June by a fire at La Paix. In attempting to burn some old clothes in an upstairs fireplace, Zelda inadvertently set fire to the house. The blaze was readily extinguished, but not before many of their personal belongings had been lost or ruined by water from the firemen's hoses. Slight as the damage was, it momentarily staggered Scott, for he was again in financial straits. In his despair he charged that Zelda had burned her clothes and thrown away her jewelry. The only figment of truth in the allegation lay in the fact that after the success of *This Side of Paradise* Scott had given Zelda a diamond-and-platinum wrist watch, which she carelessly left on the commode in the bathroom. Somehow the watch was brushed into the toilet and flushed down the drain.

The strain of living with Scott that summer told on Zelda. Her illness and her difficulties with Scott deprived her of her spontaneity; she seemed to have lost her softness and suppleness and to have become rigid as if, like Niobe, her sorrow had turned her to stone. The penultimate blow fell in August, when her brother Anthony was the victim of a tragic accident. According to members of his family, Anthony, a civil engineer, had contracted malaria while surveying a swamp near Mobile. In his delirium he got out of bed to practice a football formation that he had thought out during his illness. He snapped the ball and in the imaginary scrimmage, plunged through an open window and was killed in the fall. In the obituaries in the Mobile and Montgomery papers, the cause of his death was not given. Nevertheless, Scott declared him a suicide. "You see," he pointed out to Sara and me, "Zelda's trouble is hereditary. It's in her family."

Obviously, Scott had forgotten that he had frequently referred to his mother as "that crazy old woman in Washington" or that he had once written Perkins asking, "Why shouldn't I go crazy? My father is a moron and my mother is a neurotic, half insane with pathological nervous worry. Between them they haven't and never have had the brains of Calvin Coolidge."

In assessing his personal relationships, given a bean, Scott could make a barrel of soup from it, particularly where his family was involved. Except as material for fiction it was impossible for him to examine his parents, his child, or his wife with any degree of objectivity. The year before, in analyzing his marriage, Scott had told Richard Knight, "our united front is less a romance than a categorical imperative." Now the united front was breaking down. Both his marriage and his career seemed to be programmed on a collision course with disaster. His royalties for the last two years had totaled fifty dollars; Zelda's royalties for 1933 amounted to only a hundred and twenty dollars. During 1933 Scott had sold only three stories, and the Depression had cut the price of those by a third.

In desperation and with or without Zelda's consent, he had sold or pawned two of her paintings to Sara Haardt and given her a receipt: "Received $100 for painting 'Morning' and one other by Zelda Fitzgerald—with stipulations in my possession—by F. Scott Fitzgerald."

As his debts piled up, he no longer pretended to confine his drinking to beer. The final revisions of *Tender Is the Night* were frequently stymied by his sprees, which always resulted in quarrels with Zelda. He had worked nine years on the novel, under various titles, and he hoped to make it his best book. Just before Christmas, worn out with the revisions and with the major portion of them behind him, he decided to take Zelda to Bermuda for the holidays. They said in "Show Mr. and Mrs. F. to Number ——":

For years we had wanted to go to Bermuda. We went. The Elbow Beach Hotel was full of honeymooners, who scintillated so persistently in each other's eyes that we cynically moved. Hòtel St. George was nice. Bougainvillea cascaded down the tree trunks and long stairs passed by deep mysteries taking place behind native windows. Cats slept along the balustrade and lovely children grew. We rode bicycles along the wind-swept causeways and stared in a dreamy haze at such phenomena as roosters scratching amid the sweet alyssum. We drank sherry on a verandah above the bony backs of horses tethered in the public square.

Memory had invested the trip with a pleasure that it had lacked for Scott. Before they sailed from New York, he had lunch with Edmund Wilson and picked another quarrel with him. Scott took a cold on the boat and developed pleurisy. As a result he spent most of his holiday in bed. It was an expensive trip and a disastrous one. On Christmas Day he wrote Perkins from Baltimore that "The month I lost in Bermuda was damn costly." *Tender Is the Night* was still unfinished, but he hoped to mail the last section to Scribner's within a week.

To have written *Tender Is the Night* under the circumstances that Scott had worked during the year and a half that he spent at La Paix was a triumph of human will over disappointment and disaster. There had been, he noted in his Ledger, "Servant trouble . . . political worries . . . almost neurosis . . . drinking increased . . . arguments with Scottie . . . quarrel with Hemingway . . . quarrel with Bunny Wilson . . . quarrel with Gerald Murphy . . . breakdown of car . . . tight at Eddie Poe's . . . sick again . . . first borrowing from mother . . . sick . . . 'The Fire' . . . Zelda weakens and goes to Hopkins . . . one servant and eating out."

Before Scott left for Bermuda, he had given up La Paix and rented more modest quarters at 1307 Park Avenue in Baltimore—in one of those depressing rows of gray houses whose white stoops always seem to be in the process of being scrubbed by shabby charwomen. In January, after the exhausting move, he had just settled down to correcting the galley proofs of his novel when Zelda broke down again.

The trip and the move had left Zelda physically worn out. Then the serialized version of *Tender Is the Night* began to appear in *Scribner's Magazine* and the galleys of the book arrived to rip open the wound inflicted on her by the synopsis she had seen in Florida two years before. Scott's merciless and distorted "portrait" of her as Nicole Diver, with its fantastic implications as to the cause of her illness, twisted the knife in the old wound. On top of it all she and Fitzgerald had an explosive quarrel over a project that was very dear to her. A friend of hers in New York named Cary Ross had offered to exhibit her paintings in his gallery on East Eighty-sixth Street. When Scott stepped in and took the arrangements for the exhibition out of her hands, Zelda was so frustrated that she went to bed and refused to get up.

Early in February Scott took her back to Phipps. As soon as she began to improve, Zelda demanded to be released from the clinic. Since she had not been legally committed, theoretically, as at Prangins, she could have left when she wanted. But she was at least rational enough to know that she could not leave without money. Scott was busy with the galleys of his novel and in no mood to have an ill wife on his hands. So he transferred her to Craig House, an expensive sanitarium in upstate New York which had been recommended. At first Zelda found it a pleasant place. It was located on the Hudson River, less than two hours from New York by train, and the doctors promised her that, if she were well enough, she could attend the opening of her show there at the end of March.

Escorted by her private nurse, Zelda went down to New York for the opening of Cary Ross's exhibition of her paintings. Scott met her there, and they stayed at the Algonquin, where a smaller showing of her work was exhibited in the lobby. Even her show at Cary Ross's gallery was not a large one—only fifteen drawings and thirteen paintings—but Zelda was elated over its success. In announcing its opening, *The New Yorker* noted the touching epigraph that she had chosen for the catalogue of her exhibit, "*Parfois la folie est la sagesse*," and described the show as one of "Paintings by the almost mythical Zelda Sayre Fitzgerald; with whatever emotional overtones or associations may remain. from the so-called Jazz Age."

As a whole, the press accounts of Zelda's exhibition were favorable, though she was chagrined to find that they featured her, rather than her paintings. Ross sold several paintings for her. The Murphys bought one, "Chinese Theater"; Dorothy Parker purchased two, "The Cornet Player," which looked like Scott, and "Arabesque," a ballet dancer that bore a striking resemblance to Zelda. Fitzgerald was particularly pleased at these sales to his friends and delighted to learn that John Biggs and Ernest Hemingway had gone to see the exhibition.

Before Zelda returned to Craig House, she went to see an exhibition of Georgia O'Keeffe's paintings and to a sumptuous luncheon given by Max Perkins to celebrate the show at Ross's gallery and the publication of *Tender Is the Night*, which was to appear the following week. While they were in New York, Zelda appeared to be cheerful and vivacious; Scott, morose and edgy. For he was nervous from anticipating the reception and the criticisms of his novel and jittery from having "finished it on the bottle," as he put it.

Scott expected that *Tender Is the Night* would have at least a *succès d'estime*. He had fought through illness, heartbreak, despair, and relative penury to finish it; he felt that he deserved a success with it. When it finally appeared on April 12, 1934, although it was in the opinion of a number of the better critics, James Branch Cabell among them, by far Fitzgerald's best novel and one of the best written by his generation, the reviews were, in general, tepid, if not hostile. Some of them even pointed to the work as evidence that Scott, like Dick Diver, had gone to pieces. Hemingway said he liked it and he did not like it. His noncommittal attitude about it cut Scott to the quick; he wrote Ernest to ask, "Did you like the book? For God's sake drop me a line and tell me one way or the other."

Hemingway replied that he found the characters in the novel to be beautifully faked case histories rather than people. When Sara and Gerald Murphy, to whom the book was dedicated, inclined to agree with him, Scott protested to Sara that it was his theory that it took half a dozen people to make a synthesis strong enough to create a fictional character. "The book," he added to Gerald, in one of the most extraordinary explanations an author ever made, "was inspired by Sara and you, and the way I feel about you both and the way you live, and the last part of it is Zelda and me

because you and Sara are the same people as Zelda and me."
Edmund Wilson's criticisms were milder than those of Hemingway and the Murphys. On the whole Scott was pleased by Wilson's comments; and he wrote him, suggesting that they have a
reunion in New York and iron out their difficulties.

Unfortunately, the publication of *Tender Is the Night* coin-
cided with Zelda's exhibition. In the April 14 issue of *The New
Yorker*, which carried another notice of her show, a hostile critic
took Scott to task for the novel. "In Mr. Fitzgerald's case," he
said, "money is the root of all novels." In the latter part of the
book, he added, "Dr. Dick Diver, having cured his schizophrenic
wife only to have her fall in love with a Gallic adventurer, goes
ingloriously to seed, and becomes merely an anatomy of moral
disintegration."

To exacerbate the bitter taste left by the unfavorable reviews of
Fitzgerald's novel, *Time* reported Zelda's exhibition in a notice
that further whetted the rivalry between her and Scott:

WORK OF A WIFE

There was a time when Mrs. Francis Scott Key Fitzgerald was a
more fabulous character than her novel-writing husband. That was
when she was Zelda Sayre, a Montgomery, Ala. girl. . . . When
she married Scott Fitzgerald in 1920, shortly after he published
This Side of Paradise she lapsed into the semiobscurity of a wife of
a famed novelist.

Zelda Fitzgerald loved motion and the dance. For a while she
studied in Paris under Maria Egorova, one time ballerina of the
Russian Imperial Ballet of St. Petersburg. But she was in her
middle 20s, too old to become a good ballet dancer. She left
school, recording her adventures in a thinly disguised autobiography, *Save Me the Waltz*. She also began to paint seriously.

Last week, in Cary Ross's Manhattan studio, Zelda showed her
pictures, made her latest bid for fame. The work of a brilliant
introvert, they were vividly painted, intensely rhythmic. A pinkish
reminiscence of her ballet days showed figures with enlarged legs
and feet—a trick which she may have learned from Picasso. An
impression of a Dartmouth football game made the stadium look
like the portals of a theatre, the players like dancers. *Chinese
Theatre* was a gnarled mass of acrobats with an indicated audi-

ence for background. There were two impressionistic portraits of her husband, a verdant *Spring in the Country* laced with telephone wires.

From a sanatorium last week which she temporarily left against the doctor's orders to see a show of Georgia O'Keeffe's art, Zelda was hoping her pictures would gratify her great ambition—to earn her own living.

Scott salved his bruised ego by leveling the same charges at Cary Ross that he had at Richard Knight and several other admirers of Zelda's.

About the same time, Fitzgerald made an entry in his Notebooks to the effect that: "The combination of a desire for glory and an inability to endure the monotony it entails puts many people in the asylum. Glory comes from the unchanging din-din-din of one supreme gift."

Glory, however, did not come to Fitzgerald during his lifetime for the nine years he had spent slaving away at *Tender Is the Night*. He was staggered and drained of self-confidence by its comparative failure; it sold only some thirteen thousand copies; and it was difficult to find a copy in the bookstores at the time of his death in 1940. Today, it is considered a classic and is required reading in most college courses in contemporary American literature. But the time was not ripe for *Tender Is the Night* in 1934, when the proletarian novel was fashionable and the social significance of a book was of prime importance. Today critics generally regard *Tender Is the Night* as a flawed masterpiece. There are too many analyses of its artistic merits and imperfections to recount them here. However, many people who know the circumstances under which Scott labored over it found that its chief flaw lay in the fact that it was written with one eye on the Book-of-the-Month Club and the other on the divorce court.

What Scott's real intention was, no one can say, but *Tender Is the Night* has as many earmarks of an attempt at self-justification as "Babylon Revisited" has. In the event that either Scott or Zelda ever made good their threats to file divorce proceedings, there was certain to be a fight over the custody of their child. It is, of course, impossible to know whether Fitzgerald deliberately wrote the offensive portions of *Tender Is the Night* to prepare a psychological defense against the threat of a divorce and a custody suit, or to retaliate for the parts of Zelda's *Save Me the Waltz*, which he and Perkins had forced her to cut, or whether he was simply slipping into the kind of projection to which he was given increasingly as he approached a crack-up.

Whatever his motive, in his sketch for Nicole in his notes for *Tender Is the Night*, he says of its heroine:

> At fifteen she was raped by her own father under peculiar circumstances—work out. She collapses, goes to the clinic and there at sixteen meets the young doctor hero who is ten years older. Only her transference to him saves her—when it is not working she reverts to homicidal mania and tries to kill men. She is an innocent, widely read but with no experience and no orientation except that he supplies her. Portrait of Zelda—that is part of Zelda.

Was it? Zelda was certainly never raped by her father nor did she ever show a homicidal mania or try to kill men.

Under the heading "Classification of the Material on Sickness," Fitzgerald lists:

A. Accounts
B. Baltimore
C. Clinics and clipping
D. Dancing and 1st diagnoses
E. Early Prangins—to February 1931
F. For Forel (include Eleuler [*sic*] Consultation)
H. Hollywood
L. Late Prangins
M. My own letters and comments

A week before *Tender Is the Night* appeared, the Menckens had returned from a Mediterranean cruise, more exhausted than when they sailed. Sara arrived in Baltimore running a fever from an infection she had picked up in Algiers and had to be hospitalized. Now that Scott had moved into town, he was once again near enough to Cathedral Street to drop in frequently on Henry. While Sara was in the Union Memorial Hospital, Mencken was left to deal with Scott and his troubles single-handedly. Although Mencken had once opined that Zelda talked too much about money, on the whole, he felt, as Sara and I did, that Scott was more responsible for their difficulties than Zelda was, and Scott's continual carping at her offended him. Nevertheless Scott looked to Mencken for consolation after the discouraging reviews of his book as he might have to Edward Fitzgerald had he been alive. He wrote Henry on April 23, 1934, complaining of the way the critics had treated it. Three days later the Sage of Baltimore replied with a courteous and encouraging letter, urging him not to be upset by "a few silly reviews" and pointing out:

> The quality of book reviewing in the American newspapers is really appalling. Reviews are printed by imbeciles that know nothing about the process of writing, and hence miss the author's intentions completely. I think your scheme is a capital one, and that you have carried it out very effectively in this book.
>
> My "Treatise on Right and Wrong" is getting the usual violent denunciations, but it seems to be selling fairly well and I am confident that it will make its way. My books always start off badly, but usually keep on selling for a long while.
>
> Please remember me to Zelda. I surely hope that she is making good progress.

For all that, William Manchester, one of the best of Mencken's biographers, reports finding in the Sage's library "an author's copy of *Tender Is the Night* with a pathetic note from Fitzgerald, begging him to read it and support him against the herding critics. At the Enoch Pratt Free Library the pages are still uncut." However, the pages of the copy in the Mencken Room had been cut when I inspected it in 1965. Whether Mencken ever actually read the book or not, no one knows. Sara, however, *did* read it while she was in the hospital. While she was impressed with Fitzgerald's admirable prose, she had grown up with Zelda in Montgomery, and she felt that the inferences to be drawn from it about Zelda and her family were as false as they were unfortunate.

After her return to Craig House, Zelda rapidly became worse. It now appeared to her as a "horrible place." Despite her efforts to cheer Scott and console him for his disappointment over the reception of *Tender Is the Night*, she herself began to despair of her ultimate recovery and urged Scott to relieve the financial burden of keeping her at Craig House by having her transferred to a state hospital. When he refused even to consider the idea, ill as she was she tried to balance the family budget by writing two articles, "Show Mr. and Mrs. F. to Number ———" and "Auction —Model 1934." Scott revised the articles and published them as the work of F. Scott and Zelda Fitzgerald. But when she wanted to begin another novel, he short-circuited her intention by proposing to have a book of her short stories and articles published. The addition of these frustrations to her worries over money, over Scott's drinking, over her separation from Scottie, and over her own illness caused Zelda to collapse. She was brought back to Baltimore from Craig House by ambulance, in what Scott described to Mencken as "a catatonic condition."

On May 19, 1934 Scott entered Zelda in The Sheppard and Enoch Pratt Hospital in Towson, Maryland. Its grounds adjoined those of La Paix, and Zelda had a horror of the place—a sinister-looking sanitarium with enclosed passageways joining its buildings, barred windows, locked doors, and dismal rooms that appeared to have been done by a decorator with a depressive psychosis. The shock of her reception there, the rough search of her person, the confiscation of her money, make-up, even her cigarettes, the callousness of the the attendants who took her clothes away and doused her in a disinfectant bath, the hopelessness of her situation there, locked in a bare ward, with no means of communicating with her family and friends—literally buried alive in a strange place—was too much for her. This time there was no doubt about it; she had broken down—or, perhaps, more accurately, after four years between the upper and the nether millstones, she had been ground down by Scott and the doctors.

At the Sheppard-Pratt, Zelda was placed under the care of Dr. William Elgin, whom she detested. Since Dr. Elgin believed Scott's side of the story and was inclined to be harsh with Zelda, her condition began to deteriorate rapidly. Dr. Elgin had forbidden Scott to visit her until she improved; she had no human being to whom she could turn; so she turned to God. To Scott and Dr. Elgin, her religious preoccupation and the experiences that accompanied it were infallible indications of a paranoid psychosis. Scott tried to resign himself to the belief that she would never be well again. "I left my capacity for hoping," he wrote in the Notebooks, "on the little roads that led to Zelda's sanitarium."

Not long after Dr. Elgin allowed Scott to see Zelda, he took her walking on the grounds of the Sheppard-Pratt. They wandered back toward the familiar lawns of La Paix where a spur track ran between the grounds of the hospital and those of the Turnbull estate. As a train approached, Scott reported that Zelda got away from him and tried to throw herself under the engine. Again, Scott was the only witness. In both of them the conflict between Eros, the life force, and Thanatos, the death urge, was strong and relentless. For every action there is an equal and opposite reaction, and the intensity of their zest for life and their love of each other provoked irresistible impulses to self-destruction in both of them. Some of their friends always thought that the suicidal impulse was stronger in Scott than in Zelda and wondered how much of his own self-destructive tendencies he projected onto her.

"Psychiatry," Zelda once said, "is worse than witchcraft." Two years before she had written John Peale Bishop *in re* the psychiatrists:

> This, they say, "is the way you really are—or no, wasn't it the other way around?"
>
> Then they present you with a piece of bric-a-brac of their own forging which falls to the pavement on your way out of the clinic and luckily smashes to bits, and the patient is glad to be rid of their award.
>
> Don't *ever* fall into the hands of brain and nerve specialists unless you are feeling very Faustian.
>
> Scott reads Marx—I read the cosmological philosophers. The brightest moments of the day are when we get them mixed up.

With Zelda behind bars again, Scott began to try to expunge her memory from his life. Between January and August he saw her only nine or ten times and then only for brief visits with her. From his Notebooks and his letters it is evident that he had begun trying to delude himself into believing that he had married Zelda reluctantly, knowing that she was spoiled and not good for him —and that he regretted it immediately. Nevertheless, finding himself in need of money and unable to drive himself to work, he rewrote her articles and sold them. In June he left her in Sheppard-Pratt and went on an extended bender in New York.

Sensing Scott's despair, Charlie MacArthur dropped everything to spend his time with him. Helen Hayes, MacArthur's wife, remembered in *On Reflection: An Autobiography*:

> Scott stayed with us at our Manhattan flat for a few nights to ease his depression. I can still see his lovely face when he told me that he had sentimentally given Zelda a bouquet which she promptly lifted to her ear.
>
> "Do you hear what they're whispering, Scotty?" she had asked.
>
> That was how he knew, once and for all, that it was hopeless. My heart went out to him, but of course I was working—I think it was in *Gilhooley*—and it was Charlie who never left his side. He drank with him and pulled him out of the black pit. It was true that when Charlie dragged him to see *Grand Hotel* their loudly voiced distaste for the production led to their being bodily removed; but at least Scott was feeling no pain and that was the whole idea.

That spree, too, ended in Johns Hopkins. On his release, he went to Virginia to visit Elizabeth Lemmon, a friend of Max Perkins, who had a lovely antebellum home, Welbourne, near Middleburg. After its spacious grace, he found returning to Baltimore by bus a humiliating experience. Scott had been drinking heavily all summer. Alone and at a loose end in Baltimore, he felt his life to be as bleak as a lunar landscape. In an effort to amuse himself, he engaged in one trivial affair and then another. After a second trip to New York to see a girl whom he had picked up there, he returned to Baltimore ill and shaken. Once more he appealed to Mencken for sympathy. H. L. called in his personal physician, Dr. Benjamin Baker. Dr. Baker tried to help Scott stop drinking; but in order to dry him out, he had to have him hospitalized again.

By the time I arrived in Baltimore late in the summer, both Sara and Henry were thoroughly outdone with Scott. In his desperation he called them at all hours of the day and night for reassurance, arrived unannounced with doubtful companions picked up in the streets, and generally made himself unpopular. Sodden with self-pity, bleary-eyed and reeling, he turned up at 704 Cathedral Street one evening while I was there. He "wasn't drunk," he explained thickly, just "staggering under the weight of a heavy heart." His hands were perspiring and trembling so that he could hardly light a cigarette. He kept wiping at the backs and palms of them with a damp handkerchief as he paced up and down. His recital of his woes sounded like a page torn from the Book of Lamentations. When at last he came to the end of it, he wanted us to go over to the Belvedere and have a drink with him. After Henry said he had some work to do, Scott insisted that Sara and I accompany him. Henry shook his head at us and told Scott that he had had enough to drink already.

"Don't try to tell me how to run my life," Fitzgerald growled, collapsing in a chair. "I can't stand any more people telling me what I should and shouldn't do."

"You're not feeling well, Scott," Henry said, as if he were talking to a fretful child. "I think you'd better get to bed."

As Scott had lost his driver's license, Mencken called a taxi and sent him home. The Sage felt very much about Scott's carousing as he did about Red Lewis's, Thomas Wolfe's, and Ernest Hemingway's; since Mencken's domestic life was well ordered, happy, and decorous, and his financial affairs were always carefully regulated, he was incapable of understanding the chronic disorder of the lives of such men. Consequently, H. L. was not as sympathetic as Scott thought he should be; so Scott's enthusiasm for Hemingway began to revive. One of the odd quirks of Fitzgerald's nature—and they were many—was that he needed an artistic or intellectual conscience, a father image, if you will, at his elbow.

Mencken found Fitzgerald's recurrent infatuation with Hemingway and the love-hate relationship between them rather odd, and Scott's long, alcoholic eulogies of the Oak Park novelist struck H. L. as tedious in the extreme. For the Sage felt that Hemingway's battle-bottle-bitch formula was destined to be short-lived. "Only too often," Mencken said, "he turns aside from his theme to prove fatuously that he is a naughty fellow, and when he does so, he almost invariably falls into banality and worse."

Unfortunately for Scott's morale, Hemingway chose to read into *Tender Is the Night* indications of Scott's disintegration and deterioration as a novelist. Six weeks after its publication he wrote Scott a sententious letter that hurt him deeply:

Forget your personal tragedy, we are all bitched from the start
. . . You see Bo, you're not a tragic character. Neither am I. All we
are is writers and what we should do is write. Of all people on
earth you need discipline in your work and instead you marry
someone who is jealous of your work, wants to compete with you
and ruin you. It's not as simple as that and I thought Zelda was
crazy the first time I met her and you complicated it even more by
being in love with her.

Later Hemingway told Arthur Mizener:

I loved Scott very much but he was extremely difficult with that
situation he got himself into and Zelda constantly making him
drink because she was jealous of his working well . . . He had a
very steep trajectory and was almost like a guided missile with no
one guiding him.

After Zelda rejected Hemingway's attentions during his visit to
the Fitzgeralds at Juan-les-Pins, there was never anything "subtle"
about the antagonism between Zelda and Hemingway. Hemingway made no bones of the fact that he thought her "several kinds
of a screwball"; and she with equal frankness described him as "a
phony he-man," a "pansy with hair on his chest" and a "bogus"
writer. Although, even after his terminal quarrel with Hemingway, Scott never came to share Mencken's or Zelda's estimate of
Ernest, he set out to do for Hemingway in a medieval romance
what he had done for Zelda in *Tender Is the Night*. In *The Count
of Darkness*, Scott attempted in Phillipe to portray Hemingway as
"the real modern man," as Stendahl had portrayed Julian Sorel as
the Byronic man in *Le rouge et le noir*. When three install-
ments of *The Count of Darkness*, which was never completed,
appeared in *Redbook*, Hemingway ignored it.

Yet, two years later, when Hemingway referred to Scott in his
short story, "The Snows of Kilimanjaro," as "poor Scott Fitzgerald" who "had once started a story that began, 'The very rich are
different from you and me,'" Fitzgerald, who could deal it out
more easily than he could take it, wrote Hemingway an angry
letter, asking him not to use his name in any future pieces of
fiction. Tongue in cheek, no doubt, Hemingway complied by having "Scott Fitzgerald" changed to "Julian" in the subsequent
printings of "The Snows of Kilimanjaro."

While Zelda was in Sheppard-Pratt, Scott spent a great deal of time at the Enoch Pratt Library, which was not far from 1307 Park Avenue. The librarians there still remember how offended he was when someone at the desk failed to recognize him. He made a practice of using the library telephone to make calls that he thought might impress the bystanders, and he never left without an armful of books and a string of important names dropped behind him. When he checked out a light novel, he was careful to explain that he was taking it to Zelda, who by her own account was reading philosophy. Fortunately, she had attracted the sympathy of Dr. Kenneth Murdock, a young psychiatrist on the staff of the hospital, who helped her to regain her self-confidence and overcome her depression. He soon began allowing her to see Scott once a week, and now and then to spend the weekend at home.

In October, with Zelda still in the hospital, Scott, in search of solace, went again to visit Elizabeth Lemmon at Welbourne. He was in a "mood of terrible depression and despair," which all her graciousness failed to allay. "The trouble about women," he reflected wryly after he returned to Baltimore, "is that when a man needs them most they are never in a receptive mood" . . . "it's just the old story that when he feels like weeping on their shoulder, he is usually in such a state of mind and body that nobody wants him to weep on their shoulder."

Next month, on learning that Gertrude Stein was returning to America on one of her rare visits, Fitzgerald sought consolation in another quarter. He not only put himself at Miss Stein's disposal while she was to be in Baltimore but he also begged for as many hours and occasions as she would be willing to give him. Eventually, he arranged to have her come to tea at 1307 Park Avenue on Christmas Eve. Zelda, who had recovered sufficiently to be home for the holidays, did not look forward to the party with the same enthusiasm that Scott did. Although she was accustomed to being the center of attention in any gathering of men at which she was present, Zelda in Paris had been among the wives who were left to talk to Alice B. Toklas while Miss Stein held forth to their husbands on art and letters. Consequently, she had never regarded Miss Stein as one of the major prophets of contemporary literature. To Zelda Miss Stein did not appear to be an oracle but a stout, dumpy old woman with her hair cut short and brushed

forward like a French barber's. Her remarks struck Zelda not as
literary conversation but as sententious gibberish.

As part of her Southern heritage, Zelda was endowed with a
pride that would not let her truckle to the great and near great as
Scott did—a trait that sometimes offended those who felt entitled
to obeisances. It was the kind of *hubris* that invites *nemesis*, and
it was probably the tragic flaw in Zelda's character. Certainly, it
was the one that did much to alienate Scott. Whenever he hurt
her pride, which he did all too often, she lashed back at him with
a cold fury that could, if he was drinking, drive him to violence.
It was pride rather than jealousy which sometimes made her
appear aloof and indifferent with certain of Scott's literary friends
to whom she felt that he was being too deferential.

After an exchange of fulsome compliments between Scott and
Miss Stein, Zelda served tea and sat back to listen silently while
they discussed literary theories.

"Sentences," Miss Stein averred, "must never leak."

"Explain just what you mean by that," Scott countered.

"They must not have bad plumbing."

At that, Zelda laughed, as well she might. But scenting a danger signal, Scott said hastily, "Give us an example, Gertrude."

"Well," Miss Stein hesitated, aware of the tension. "Your dedi-
cation to *The Great Gatsby*—'Once again to Zelda,'" she said
tactfully. "It's complete, it holds together, it doesn't leak."

Scott thanked her and did a double shuffle, an American version of the Irish jig, that he did when he was pleased or flattered.
But how a sentence, minus such an integral part of its plumbing
as a verb, could be complete or fail to "leak" baffled Zelda. "But, I
don't see . . ." she began.

To head off what he feared might be a sharp retort from Zelda,
Scott turned to her hastily and said, "Why don't you show Gertrude your paintings?"

Zelda brought in some of her canvases, which Miss Stein politely admired. "You can have a couple of them, if you'd like,"
Scott volunteered without consulting Zelda. "Take whichever
ones you please."

Miss Stein studied the canvases and picked out the two that she liked best. "I'm sorry those are the two you like," Zelda apologized, "because they're the ones I promised to give my doctor."

"Don't be silly," Scott interjected. "Don't you understand that Gertrude will take the pictures back to Paris? She'll hang them in her salon and make you famous. Besides, she's been kinder to me than almost anyone else, and I want to give her something."

"Give her anything you please," Zelda riposted. "If she's been as good to you as my doctor has been to me, you ought to give her everything you own. But she can't have those two paintings that I've promised him."

In the end, for all Scott's protests, Miss Stein was forced to choose two other paintings. Despite repeated invitations from Scott, she did not pay another visit to 1307 Park Avenue. In an effort to smooth matters over, he wrote her a flattering letter, apologizing for his having been "stupid-got" with Christmas spirit and telling her, "It meant so much to Zelda, giving her a tangible sense of her own existence, for you to have liked two of her pictures enough to want to own them." The sentence leaked—in an unctuous way.

The Fitzgeralds celebrated Christmas with a small tree for Scottie, but with little holiday spirit to enliven it. Then, despite her protests, Scott tore Zelda away and took her back to the Sheppard-Pratt.

"If I get a pimple on my face, Scott puts me in the hospital," Zelda complained to her family. "He's nothing but a big Irish policeman."

"You can't go on being tied to a dead hand forever," he said in extenuation of his action. He needed "the custody of his leisure hours," which he had to sacrifice to Zelda when she was with him.

12. Taps at Reveille

WHILE Scott was in the midst of correcting the proofs for *Taps at Reveille*, a book of his short stories that Scribner's was to bring out in the spring, he wrote Max Perkins that his doctors had given him "what amounted to a sentence of death" by telling him that he was threatened with cirrhosis of the liver. He was so frightened about himself that he actually stopped drinking. By driving himself with Coca-Cola and black coffee he managed to correct the proofs. After he mailed them to Max Perkins, one night in February he threw some clothes into a battered briefcase and fled first to Tryon and then to Hendersonville, North Carolina, to escape from the raw, wintry weather in Baltimore.

"The history of my life," he once said, "is the history of the struggle between an overwhelming urge to write and a combination of circumstances bent on keeping me from it." There was nothing in Hendersonville to prevent his buckling down to work; but his good resolutions weakened under the strain of his financial worries and loneliness, and he soon began to drink again. Forced to live cheaply, he took a single room in the Skylands—a drab hostelry that overlooked the marquee of a movie house, on which a glaring electric sign, studded with burned-out bulbs, advertised, *The Crusades: The Flaming Passion of a Woman Torn*

Between Two Camps. In his Notebooks, he recorded that his food totaled eighteen cents a day. He lived off potted meat, oranges, and dry soda crackers, known as Uneeda Biscuits, washed down with beer, and thought wryly of the thousands of appetizing meals that he had sent back untasted in better years. Every night he washed his two handkerchiefs and his shirt, but he could not part with the pajama pants he wore for underwear or the socks he used for slippers at night long enough to launder them. Before his visit was over they had become so "notorious" that he considered presenting them to the Hendersonville Museum. But he professed not to mind the interlude of poverty there; the air was fine and bracing, and it was not so bad to be poor when he didn't have enough liver power for an appetite, anyhow. He was amused by the deference of the hotel clerks and shopkeepers, who imagined that he was a rich city dude from the East, when at the time he was thousands of dollars in debt and overdrawn in his bank account, with only forty cents in his pocket, saved to pay postage on a story to be sent to *McCall's*. It was a "bankrupt's comedy," he told himself, "and one that had probably been enacted many times in the U.S. during the last four years of the Depression."

When Nora and Lefty Flynn came to call on him, they were as startled by his pallor and listlessness as by his living quarters in the Skylands. Empty cigarette packages, potted-meat tins, and half-eaten crackers littered the top of the dresser; books and papers were piled up on the chairs and on the floor; his clothes hung from the bedposts. Nora Flynn, whom Scott described as "one of the world's most delightful women," was a member of the distinguished Langhorne family and a relative of Lady Astor. Chic, handsome, and well bred, she knew all the people that Scott considered worth knowing in England and America. Tactful as well as charming, she concealed her dismay at the "bankrupt's comedy" and tried to cheer him in "her brave, gay, stimulating way." Maurice, or Lefty, as Scott called him, had lived a life almost as adventurous and exciting as Ernest Hemingway's. He had been an outstanding athlete at Yale, a star in the silent films, and a naval aviator in World War I. Both he and Nora knew how to charm and how to entertain. They had a fund of stories about the celebrities they had known, from the Queen of England to

Bertrand Russell, and they could mimic them in such a hilarious way that they made Scott double up with laughter and forget his troubles when he was with them. Nora issued him a standing invitation to dinner with them in Tryon, but, alas, a taxi to their house there cost four dollars.

By the first of March he had finished a story about them, called "The Intimate Strangers," and had accumulated enough money to check out of the Skylands Hotel and to get back to Baltimore. He returned feeling worse than when he left. In his absence his troubles had multiplied: *Taps at Reveille* was not selling; Zelda was worse; Scottie was failing in two of her subjects at school. At the end of his tether, he turned again to the Menckens for help. Sara Haardt had been hospitalized with pleurisy. The emotional turmoil occasioned by Sara's long illness had given Mencken a deeper insight into the effects of Zelda's breakdown upon Scott and created a new sympathy for him.

Despite Mencken's aid and encouragement, Scott sank into despair and fell ill again. He was so pale and lifeless that Mencken insisted on his seeing Dr. Baker, who ordered him to have X-rays of his chest made at once. The X-rays revealed not only that Scott had suffered from mild tubercular lesions in 1919 and 1929, but also that he now had a serious cavity in one lung. In May Dr. Baker quietly packed him off and put him under the care of Dr. Paul Ringer, a lung specialist in Asheville, North Carolina. Scott did not care to have his publishers know that he was tubercular, so he told Perkins only that he was closing up the house at 1307 Park Avenue and going away somewhere for awhile. He did not want to see anyone he knew, not even Hemingway, for he realized that he was not very pleasant company of late. He explained, "Zelda is in very bad condition and my own mood somehow reflects it."

Zelda's anxiety at being left alone in Baltimore in the hospital, where no one but Scott was allowed to visit her, precipitated another acute phase in her illness, which had in turn reacted on Scott. The recurrence of tuberculosis in Fitzgerald alarmed both Sara and Henry. On May 23, 1935, Mencken wrote to Scott, who had installed himself in an expensive suite in Asheville at Grove Park Inn, telling him that Sara had contracted what appeared to be a mild case of flu. Henry planned to take her to the Adirondacks, but Sara was stricken with a splitting headache and the trip to the mountains had to be postponed. H. L. rushed her to the Union Memorial Hospital, where a spinal tap revealed that she had been stricken with tubercular meningitis. She died a week later, on Friday, May 31, 1935.

After her death Henry wrote me to come to Baltimore to go through her things and choose whatever I wanted from them. I was then on a motor trip through the West, and it was not until the middle of September that I returned to Baltimore. Since the Stafford Hotel was nearer to 704 Cathedral Street than the Belvedere, I stopped there. Henry had asked two of our mutual friends, Anne and Edmund Duffy, to have lunch with us at his apartment. Since our hearts were still too full to talk about Sara, I asked about Scott and Zelda. Henry and Edmund Duffy shook their heads over Zelda and gave me a somber account of Scott's latest escapades.

That evening, I had just come in when the telephone in my room at the Stafford rang. It was Scott; he was also staying there and had seen my name on the register. "I've been calling you all afternoon," he announced. "Where the hell have you been?"

"Henry and I went to the cemetery to take some flowers to Sara's grave."

"Then I know you need a drink. Come on up to my room and I'll fix you a highball."

"Sorry but that's out of bounds for me, Scott."

"Oh, don't be that way. Listen, baby, I'm low as the devil and I need somebody to talk to."

"I'm afraid I'd be a Job's comforter; I'm in no happy mood myself this evening."

"You know what I've always said about you, don't you?"

"No, and I tremble to think."

"You needn't." Scott turned on his charm and gave me the benefit of his talent for blarney. "I've always said that you had the most beautiful voice I ever heard—not exactly Southern, not exactly English, but something wonderful in between."

"Thanks, but I'd rather have your gift for words, Scott."

"It doesn't do me much good with you; you'd never even flirt with me. But, at least, do this much for me, come down and have a drink with me in the bar."

"All right, but I can only stay for a minute. I'm going to dinner with Henry at seven, and I have to dress."

Scott was waiting for me in the lobby, looking haggard and hung over. "How's Zelda?" I asked, as he steered me into the bar.

He shook his head. "I don't think she'll ever be any better. She's been going downhill ever since April."

"Can I see her?"

"She's not well enough to have visitors—and hasn't been in months." He ordered a beer for me and another for himself. Then he said rather pettishly, "You always liked Zelda better than me. Why?"

"I've known her so much longer," I countered.

"You think I'm a son of a bitch, don't you?"

"Why, Scott! What makes you say that?"

"Because most of Zelda's friends think so. Sometimes I think so myself. I had a talent, baby, a beautiful talent, and I bitched it." He lighted one cigarette from another. The first two fingers of his left hand were stained dark brown down to the palms. He blew the smoke out between his teeth and pushed away the glass of beer. "And the hell of it is, I don't give a damn any more. Not about anybody or anything. Not even beer. But I keep on drinking it. Sometimes three dozen bottles a day."

"Do you row out of it, swim out of it, or sail out of it?"

"I wish I'd bailed out of it before I did. God, what a summer!" After Scott had concluded a bowdlerized account of his latest romance, he ordered a straight whiskey, gulped it down, and chased it with the remains of the beer. "I didn't think I could face Zelda. How I got through with it, I don't know. She was very sweet, but I think she suspected something." He put his head down in his hands. "What shall I do about her? What *can* I do about her?"

"Why don't you get her out of the hospital and let her go back to Montgomery, Scott?" I suggested. The longer I listened to him the more certain I was that Dr. Meyer had been correct in diagnosing the trouble as a dual case—*folie à deux*, the mental disorder in which two intimately associated people develop the same obsessions, as the weaker and more submissive yields to the stronger; usually the "infected" person relinquishes his or her delusions when separated from the other. But since that was not a thing one could tell Scott without infuriating him, I said instead, "I've heard that there are some gypsies who can't live outside the tribe; and, I suspect, the same thing is true of a great many Confederates. They don't transplant well as a rule."

"Maybe you're right. Sometimes I think if I'd left Zelda down South, let her marry one of her rich Babbitts, some kind, simple fool who'd always give her her own way, she might have been happier. We came out of different worlds, you know that, and she never could adjust to mine—nor I to hers."

"She's never had a breakdown when she was at home with her family, has she?"

"No, but I couldn't take it there—with her family looking down their aristocratic noses at me—I tried it. But Sara Haardt adjusted to it here in Baltimore, so I don't see why Zelda can't."

"Sara Haardt was half Confederate, half German; so is Henry, and so is Baltimore. That makes a difference."

Scott leaned across the table and took my hand. "Tell me something?"

"If I can."

"Are you going to marry Mencken?"

"Don't be absurd. Henry's old enough to be my father—and almost like my father as my father was."

"I didn't know a little thing like blood relation was a barrier to you Confederates."

"Not according to the Yankee novelists, at any rate," I retorted.

He cut a bloodshot eye at me. "I really didn't think so," he said blandly. "You know what a man said to me once while I was at Camp Sheridan?"

"No telling."

"He said the only virgins in that part of the world were those that could outrun their brothers."

"And where was he from, may I ask?"

"Pennsylvania."

"I should have guessed Minnesota."

Scott flushed to the roots of his hair. "Well, I suppose I asked for that one. But I didn't say it, he did. Honestly. Drink up and let's have another beer."

"Sorry, but I have to go. Give Zelda my love and tell her that I'd like to see her as soon as she's well enough to have visitors."

Scott felt at home in Baltimore. "I belong here," he said, "where everything is civilized, gay, rotted, and polite. In a few years Zelda and I will snuggle up together under a stone in some old graveyard here." The idea, however, did not appeal to Zelda at all. Although she began to improve rapidly after Scott's return from Asheville, she wanted to go back to Montgomery. Scott refused to go or let her go. Indian summer in Baltimore was warm and pleasant. Scottie was in the Bryn Mawr School there. So toward the latter part of September, he took "an attic," as he called it, on the seventh floor of the Cambridge Arms Apartments, overlooking the campus of Johns Hopkins University.

Zelda balked at the idea of Scottie being left alone at the Cambridge Arms with Scott. The dissension between Zelda and Scott aggravated the nervous troubles of both of them. Zelda went through what Scott described as a terrible crisis; she was very, very depressed, he told Perkins. On May 14, 1935, he wrote Verner Haldene, "Zelda has been sick and unproductive since her art exhibit last fall [sic]. In fact the Fitzgeralds are slowly rotting like the other survivors of our period. [We] had a hell of a good time when [sic] it lasted though which is more than can be said for your generation."

On learning that he had recovered from tuberculosis, Scott "cracked like an old plate" as he later wrote in "The Crack-Up." He could neither sleep nor work. In his nervous condition, he became increasingly sensitive to noise. The crackle of static on the radio, the screech of car brakes from the streets, and Scottie's loud dance records drove him wild. Perhaps the noblest facet of Scott's character was his solicitude of his daughter and his struggle to rear and to educate her in the face of overwhelming odds. However, he resented having to be both father and mother to her. He loved her deeply, but he was overanxious about her, especially after she began having dates. Fearing that she might go the way he and Zelda had gone and wear out young, he lectured her constantly on the dangers of drinking, petting, and joyriding. He wanted her to be among the best of her race and not waste herself on trivial aims. To be useful and proud—was that asking too much? Between his anxiety for her and his irritation at having his work interrupted by the noise that she and her friends made in the apartment, he was often stern and sometimes irritable.

Many years later, after reading over her father's letters to her, Scottie said:

> In my next incarnation, I may not choose again to be the daughter of a Famous Author. The pay is good and there are fringe benefits, but the working conditions are too hazardous. People who live entirely by the fertility of their imaginations are fascinating, brilliant, and often charming, but they should be sat next to at dinner parties, not lived with. Imagine depending for your happiness upon a Bernard Shaw or a Somerset Maugham, not to mention such contemporary stars as Norman Mailer. I have the impression that the only people quite as insufferable as writers are painters.

In reflecting on her problems with her talented parents, Scottie tried to analyze the traits which make writers difficult:

> I have puzzled much over the why of this, and have compiled a few tentative answers. First, I suppose it is impossible to form the habit of inventing people, building them up, tearing them down, and moving them around like paper dolls, without doing somewhat the same thing with live ones. Good writers are essentially muckrakers, exposing the scandalous condition of the human soul. It is their job to strip veneers from situations and personalities. The rest of us accept our fellow beings at face value, and swallow what we can't accept. Writers can't: they have to prod, poke, question, test, doubt, and challenge, which requires a constant flow of fresh victims and fresh experience.

The two other reasons that Scottie gave in explaining the vagaries of writers were that there is nothing that anyone else can do to help a writer and that "successful writers, like all successful people, are spoiled and indulged by everybody with whom they come in contact. They are, at the same time, spared the rod of discipline imposed by other occupations. . . . Between the writer himself and doom stands no one but his creditor."

In the winter of 1935 Scott's creditors were once more at his heels. His stories were being steadily rejected. His agent, Harold Ober, complained that several of them, written while Scott was drinking, were illegible as well as incoherent. Once again he had overextended his flank, overdrawn on his resources, physical and financial, intellectual and spiritual. In assessing his tragic situation, he found material for the three articles, "The Crack-Up," "Handle with Care," and "Pasting It Together," which appeared in *Esquire* in the spring of 1936. He was living, he felt, "in a world of inscrutable hostilities and inalienable friends and supporters." But among them there was no one who could help him.

In his despair a glimmer of the truth began to haunt him. His success as a writer dated from the time that Zelda had shown him the diary and letters that he had used to rewrite "The Romantic Egotist" into *This Side of Paradise.* In some strange way his talent for fiction was bound up with his love for her. By his treatment of her and his merciless psychological dissections of her, on which his novels and many of his stories were based, he had not only killed the thing he loved but he had also dried up the wellsprings of his literary success.

Zelda now lived much of the time in a realm he did not understand and with which he had no patience. One by one she had pricked the iridescent bubbles of this world's illusions: fame, money, and a big time. Left to face the blank wall of another life beyond the purgatory of a psychiatric hospital, Zelda, in Scott's phrase, had "gone religious" on him, which, as a lapsed Catholic and a vaunted agnostic, he regarded as a kind of *lèse majesté* and a sign of mental deterioration. Her return to the faith of her fathers widened the breach between them and increased his sense of isolation. He had a feeling, he said, "that someone, I'm not sure who, is sound asleep—someone who could have helped me to keep my shop open. It wasn't Lenin and it wasn't God."

One night late in the fall, harassed and despairing, driven by a need to escape from people, to be absolutely alone, and insulated from his ordinary cares, Scott suddenly shut up shop and took sanctuary again in the Skylands Hotel at Hendersonville, as far as possible from the troubles that pursued him as relentlessly as the Furies did Orestes. Every day there was as dull as Sunday in a blue-law state. He hated the nights when he could not sleep and hated the days that ended in wakeful nights. Sunrise or sunset made no difference; "In a real dark night of the soul," he said, "it is always three o'clock in the morning, day after day."

Despite his gloom, his dismal surroundings, and his illness, he returned to Baltimore at Christmas for a celebration of sorts with Zelda and a tree for Scottie and her friends. Scottie's faith in him was all that kept him going through those dark holidays.

The year 1935, which marked the nadir of Fitzgerald's fortunes, went badly from the beginning. He was in such dire straits for money that, despite his vow that he would never return to Hollywood, he began negotiating with Samuel Goldwyn about doing a ballet picture. Because of Zelda's experience, he considered himself an expert in ballet and uniquely fitted for the job. He evidently intended to draw heavily on *Save Me the Waltz*, for on February 8 he wrote Harold Ober, "Please don't have anybody read Zelda's book because it is a bad book. But by glancing over it yourself you will see that it contains all the material that a tragedy should have, though she was as incapable of realizing where tragedy lay as she was incapable of facing it as a person." The self-revelatory portions of the three "Crack-Up" articles, "the trilogy of depression," as he called it, which began to appear in February, made the movie moguls back off and impeded his getting a Hollywood contract to bolster his shattered finances. Then his old standby, the *Post*, began to turn down his stories. The editors were not impressed by the serious, pessimistic tone of them. But under the circumstances, even the thought of writing about young love paralyzed him. Further, in the thirties, the focus of public attention had shifted from social and intellectual rebellion to political and economic revolt. Now both Mencken and Fitzgerald, the idols of the twenties, found themselves relegated from the spotlight to the penumbra and forced to turn to potboilers.

When Rosalind came to Baltimore that spring, she was shocked to find that Zelda had fallen off until she weighed only eighty-nine pounds. The doctors at Sheppard and Enoch Pratt Hospital told Rosalind that Scott interfered with their care of Zelda so persistently that it was impossible to do anything for her. However that may have been, it was obvious to Rosalind that Zelda was going rapidly downhill there; and at her sister's instance, Scott had Zelda removed to the Highland Hospital in Asheville.

At Scott's request, Rosalind went through Zelda's trunk to see whether there was anything that she might want to take with her to the Highland. It was one of the saddest experiences of Rosalind's life. "What I found," she said, "was a bit of old clothing, a brass candlestick, and a musical powderbox with a Pierrot on top that turned with the tune."

Highland proved to be not only a less expensive but also better hospital than Sheppard-Pratt. Pleasant quarters provided the patients with homelike surroundings that did away with the institutional atmosphere. The staff demanded and received the cooperation of those under their care. Zelda's charm and intelligence enlisted the sympathy of Dr. and Mrs. Robert Carroll, who ran the sanitarium. Under their care and affection, she began rapidly to improve. To while away the time, she painted, modeled, and wrote. "Zelda bloomed again," Rosalind said, "and on several visits to me in New York during that period [she] was almost like her old self, beautiful once more, still interested in music, the theater, and art, but toned down to an almost normal rhythm. Any thought of gay life was now far behind her, but she still retained a zest for living that was characteristic of her."

13. The Crack-Up

THE BEST portrait that we have of Fitzgerald, according to Henry Dan Piper, is to be found in his autobiographical essays and sketches. Certainly, the three "Crack-Up" articles provide a very fine subjective delineation of his state of mind in 1935. But the man whom they depict is a very different one from that revealed by the earlier ones—"Outside the Cabinet Maker's," "My Lost City," "Show Mr. and Mrs. F. to Number————," "Sleeping and Waking"—and the later ones—"Author's House," "Afternoon of an Author," "An Author's Mother," "Early Success," "Financing Finnegan," and "The Lost Decade." Further, Fitzgerald's picture of himself in the "Crack-Up" essays differs greatly from a more honest appraisal of his own character made in a letter to John O'Hara:

> I suppose this is just a confession of being a Gael though I have known many Irish who have not been afflicted by this intense social consciousness. If you are interested in colleges, a typical gesture on my part would have been, for being at Princeton and belonging to one of its snootiest clubs, I would be capable of going to Podunk on a visit and being absolutely bowed and overawed by its social system, not from timidity but simply because of an inner necessity of starting my life and my self-justification over again in whatever new environment I may be thrown.

Matthew Bruccoli, one of the best and most knowledgeable of Fitzgerald's critics, says that the "Crack-Up" essays "are frightening exercises in self-dissection and come as close as a man can to exposing the painful truths about himself." But they are, after all, his own views of himself prepared for publication, and the sheer brilliance of writing often distracts the reader from the terror of these essays. Bruccoli believes that a more realistic account of Fitzgerald's breakdown is to be found in the "independent daily log" of a woman whom Scott met at Grove Park Inn in Asheville in the summer of 1935, Laura Guthrie Hearne. Shortly before he was introduced to Mrs. Hearne, who was then telling fortunes at the Inn, Scott had become entangled with a married woman from Memphis. At a party given by a school of hairdressers, he asked Mrs. Hearne to read his inamorata's palm, but she declined. Later, however, after Scott had made Mrs. Hearne his secretary, nurse, and confidante, she aided and abetted him in his courtship of the lady from Memphis.

It was a tragicomic affair, complicated by the presence of his inamorata's sister, with the Demon Lover running true to form. Since Mrs. Hearne has recorded the affair in all of its sensational details in excerpts from her diary that were published in *Esquire*, it is unnecessary to go into it here except to point out those phases of it that throw an important light on the origins of Zelda's illness and Scott's crack-up.

When Fitzgerald began to tire of his new inamorata, he made advances to her sister, who was outraged and reported them to the lady. Infuriated by what he regarded as treachery, Scott declared that the sister was out of her mind. He then tried to persuade his former ladylove to send her sister to a psychiatrist in New York. To his way of thinking, Zelda or any other woman who questioned the right of the Demon Lover to do as he pleased, was crazy. Threatened with the arrival of her suspicious husband, his ladylove begged him to run away with her. Thoroughly alarmed by the advent of her husband, Scott armed himself with a number of sharp beer openers and tried to close out the affair by telling the lady that he could never desert Zelda. The love between him and Zelda was "the love of the century." He had given Zelda all the youth and freshness that was in him. And it was a sort of investment, he added, that was as tangible as his talent, his child, his money. The fact that his present companion had a visceral appeal for him, he said, did not change his love for Zelda.

The affair ended abruptly when the lady had a nervous break-down. Her husband flew to her bedside, bringing her personal physician with him. They took her away to White Sulphur Springs to recuperate and eventually had to put her in Dix Hospital. Scott, with his unlimited capacity for self-deception and projection, blamed her collapse on her self-indulgence. Women, he maintained, were by nature weak and unstable. A man could stand the stress and strain of a great passion, but women break down under it. Then, typically, he added that it was a hell of a thing for him, but he would get over it, and someday, he would make something out of it—a story or maybe a chapter in a book.

Scott, for all his nonchalance, had not escaped totally un-scathed from the affair. He reproached himself for having forgot-ten Zelda even for a few weeks. In a recurrent dream, he was brought before the bar to answer for his love life to a stern, white-haired judge. Thirty-six bottles of beer a day failed to allay the suppuration of an ulcerated conscience. He suffered from insomnia and had to take chloral hydrate or amytal to sleep. A rash broke out on his chest and, convinced that he had syphilis, he suffered torments from the thought of the effect his infection might have on the lives of other people. In order to keep his fears from his doctors in Asheville, he went to Spartanburg, South Carolina, to have a Wasserman test taken. Apparently, syphili-phobia was part of Scott's guilt reaction to his extracurricular affairs, for he told Laura Guthrie Hearne that this was the fourth time he had had a Wasserman made. The Spartanburg test, like the others, proved to be negative. Ironically enough, the rash on his chest was diagnosed as eczema. Although Zelda's affliction with eczema had always appeared to him as being a visible proof of a psychosis, he did not relate his own attack of eczema to his own mental condition.

In his Notebooks, Scott observed, "There never was a good biography of a good novelist. There couldn't be. He is too many people, if he's any good." Mrs. Hearne's account of him, as well as others' accounts of him at this time, bear him out. His "Crack-Up" articles suggest that it is also impossible for a good novelist to write a good autobiography. All a conscientious biographer can do is to cite his views, compare them with the views of others and point out the inconsistencies between them.

The reaction to the "Crack-Up" articles gave Scott a bad jolt. Not only had it stymied his Hollywood contract but also some people, he complained, saw the articles as evidence that he was "a complete moral and artistic bankrupt." To Hemingway they were proof that Fitzgerald had turned out to be "the rummy" he suspected him of being. Further, Ernest criticized Scott for whining in public and "shamelessly" exposing his private life. Then in an effort to cheer him up, Hemingway invited Scott down to Key West to go fishing with him. If Scott were really as depressed as he sounded, he could get himself heavily insured, Hemingway said, and they could take in the next revolution in Cuba, where he promised to get Scott killed and to write a fine obituary. Malcolm Cowley would seize upon the best parts of the notice for the *New Republic*; Hemingway himself would take Scott's liver out and give it to the Princeton Museum, send his heart to the Plaza Hotel, and take one of his lungs to Max Perkins and the other to George Horace Lorimer, editor of the *Saturday Evening Post*. Scott was in no mood for such macabre jesting. Then "The Snows of Kilimanjaro," with Hemingway's unfortunate reference to "poor Scott Fitzgerald," appeared. Coming at the time it did, it was a stunning blow to Scott—and one without the mercy of a *coup de grâce*.

In retaliating, Scott ran true to form. He wrote Perkins that in reply to his request, "in the most measured terms," that Hemingway refrain from using his name in fiction, Hemingway had written him "a crazy letter," telling him about what a great writer he was and how much he loved his children. Hemingway, he said, had completely lost his head. About the same time, he wrote another friend, Beatrice Dance, that Hemingway was quite as nervously broken down as he was but that it manifested itself in different ways. Ernest's neurosis inclined him toward megalomania and Scott's toward melancholy. Hemingway's diagnosis of Zelda's mental state had boomeranged—but too late.

Fortunately for Scott's sagging morale, not all his friends agreed with Hemingway's criticisms of the "Crack-Up" articles. Alec Woollcott, Julian Street, G. B. Stern, Nancy Hoyt, and James Boyd wrote him letters of praise. John Dos Passos, who had tried to persuade Scott not to publish the three articles, later declared that *The Crack-Up* turned out to be one of his best books. Certainly, they were among the best things he ever wrote alone and unaided. They are not, however, the honest confessions, the candid examinations of conscience that they are sometimes held to be; rather they are an *apologia pro vita sua*. For in them he attributed his emotional bankruptcy to a reckless giving of himself, drawing on resources that he did not possess, mortgaging himself physically and spiritually up to the hilt; but he evaded the fact that his crack-up was the direct result of extravagance, dissipation, and drinking.

Not long after the articles appeared in *Esquire*, Lane Carter, a staff writer on *The Birmingham News*, who interviewed Fitzgerald in his apartment at the Cambridge Arms, gave a revealing account of him. The receptionist had been told to say that Fitzgerald was ill and not seeing visitors; so Carter took the freight elevator to the floor on which Scott lived and rang his bell. Scott answered the door in his pajamas and invited the newsman in. Fitzgerald appeared to be "slightly dumbstruck," Carter said. "He was not as handsome as I had believed. His face seemed smaller. The features were not as chiseled as I had seen in photographs and his hair was not the bright auburn that I had expected. He was pale and thin."

Carter found Scott's conversation disappointing, too. "The sentences came out laboriously, connected with long, drawn-out 'an . . . ds.'" After hearing Fitzgerald talking so affectionately of Zelda and Scottie, Carter could not reconcile the conversation with Scott's attitude toward his daughter when Scottie came in, looking very pretty and very chic:

> She was wearing dark blue crepe de Chine and looked as if she had dressed for church.
>
> Her father gave her a long, critical, stern, disgusted look and demanded, "Where did you get that snootful?"

Scottie stood with chin proudly raised, looking straight before her, and didn't answer.

I detected no evidence of any "snootful."

Fitzgerald directed her to "go clean up your room."

"They go out and dance all morning," he explained to me in disgust after she departed. This judgment of the younger generation from the historian of the Jazz Age and exponent of the flapper I found amusing.

The incident also revealed Scott's increasing tendency to project his own failings on others, particularly on those who were nearest and dearest to him. He was a very sick man, Carter said. Scott stood up suddenly and staggered toward his bedroom, his face strained with pain and despair. Carter hastened to support him and tried to assure him that a bright future still lay ahead of him. "That's in the lap of the gods," Scott replied despondently.

While Fitzgerald stayed in Asheville during the summer of 1935, his attitude toward Zelda showed the same tendency to project and the same ambivalence that he had displayed in dealing with Scottie. According to Laura Guthrie Hearne, he spoke of his wife frequently and lovingly. "Life," she quoted him as saying, "ended for me when Zelda and I crashed." He swore that he would never desert her, but he seldom went to see her. On her birthday he sent Mrs. Hearne out to buy three birthday presents and take them to her, but he did not go himself. In analyzing their relationship, he tended to blame her for his misfortunes.

In the end it was, I think, Scott's admitted passion for self-justification that hurt Zelda more than his self-indulgence. He convinced his friends that she was "helpless and pitiful," that she was so inclined to do away with herself that she could not be trusted out of the hospital without a nurse, and that her tragedy weighed so heavily upon him that he had to resort to liquor to put it out of his mind. During the summer he saw little of her. He excused himself for not taking her out more often by saying that in his own nervous condition he could not endure the strain of adjusting himself to the limited world in which she now lived. Consequently, he had to resort to his old friend John Barleycorn to sustain him whenever he saw her.

After one of his visits with her, she wrote him a beautiful letter, which Scott forwarded to Harold Ober so that he might "gauge the awful strangling, heart-rending quality of this tragedy that has gone on now more than six years, with two brief intervals of hope":

Dearest and always Dearest Scott:

I am sorry too that there should be nothing to greet you but an empty shell. The thought of the effort you have made over me, the suffering that this *nothing* has cost would be unendurable to any save to a completely vacuous mechanism. Had I any feelings they would be bent in gratitude to you and in sorrow that of all my life there should not even be the smallest relic of the love and beauty that we started with to offer you at the end.

You have always been so good to me—and all I can say is that there was always that deeper current running through my heart; my life, you.

You remember the roses in Kenney's yard—you were so gracious and I thought—he is the sweetest person in the world—and you said "darling." You still are. The wall was damp and mossy when we crossed the street and we said we loved the South. I thought of the South and a happy past I'd never had and I thought I was part of the South. You said you loved this lovely land. The wisteria along the fence was green and the shade was cool and life was old.

I wish I had thought something else—but it was a Confederate, a romantic and nostalgic thought. My hair was damp when I took off my hat and I was safe and home and you were glad that I felt that way and you were reverent. We were glad and happy all the way home.

Now that there isn't any more happiness and home is gone and there isn't even any past and no emotions but those that were yours where there could be my comfort—it is a shame that we should have met in such harshness and coldness where there was once so much tenderness and so many dreams. Your song.

I wish you had a little house with hollyhocks and a sycamore tree and the afternoon sun imbedding itself in a silver tea-pot. Scottie would be running somewhere in white, in Renoir, and you will be writing books in dozens of volumes. And there will be honey still for tea, though the house should not be in Granchester.

I want you to be happy—if there were justice you would be happy—maybe you will be anyway.

Oh Do-Do, Do-Do.

I love you anyway—even if there isn't any me or any love or even any life—

I love you.

After Fitzgerald moved back to Grove Park Inn in the summer of 1936, he told Scottie that her mother looked five years younger and much prettier than when he last saw her. He began to hope that she might still come all the way back. And had Scott held to his good resolutions, the chances are that she might have done so. He had gone to Asheville with the avowed intention of devoting the summer to Zelda, but he saw her only five times, and each visit turned out to be more disastrous than the last.

On one unfortunate occasion, he took Zelda to Baltimore to see Scottie, who was to be graduated from the Bryn Mawr School there in June. Before Zelda could unpack, Scott began drinking and trying to pick a quarrel with her. Leaving him in a stupor, she walked out on him. When he came to and found that she had left him, he dumped the contents of her suitcase into the middle of the hotel room and systematically tore up one piece of her clothing after another. Zelda was eventually found, sitting calmly in the station, reading her Bible, and waiting for the train to take her back to the Highland. And it was Scott who had had Zelda hospitalized.

He must, however, have had some insight into his own condition that summer, for he employed a registered nurse to look after him and help him control his drinking while he was at Grove Park Inn. In July, in an attempt to show off in the pool there, he tried a swan dive off a fifteen-foot diving board and dislocated his shoulder—or, according to his story, "broke" it. While his shoulder was still in a plaster cast, he slipped on the bathroom floor, where he lay on the tiles until he could get help. As a result, he caught a cold, developed a form of arthritis, and kept to his bed for ten weeks, during which he drank steadily.

In September, when his mother died in Washington, he gave his illness as an excuse for not going to her funeral. Instead he bought a secondhand Packard roadster on the strength of his inheritance. His share of his mother's estate was seventeen thousand dollars, but the legal formalities of the settlement delayed payment of it for six months. In order to pay his medical bills,

Zelda's fees at the hospital, and Scottie's tuition at the Ethel Walker School in Simsbury, Connecticut, which she was to enter in September, he had to borrow money from Oscar Kalman. He said it was the only time in his life that he had ever asked a friend for a loan—a statement which is open to question.

He had, he told Kalman later, "completely ceased to give a good Goddamn." Perkins, who had refused to advance him more money on novels that were unlikely to be written, suggested expanding the "Crack-Up" articles into an autobiographical book, but Scott objected that a number of people thought that the articles had already damaged him. Indeed, indirectly they almost put a period to his career.

Impressed by the self-revelatory, confessional tone of the articles, the editors of the *New York Post* decided to send a reporter, Michael Mok, to get an interview from Fitzgerald on his fortieth birthday, on September 24, 1936. Mok tracked Fitzgerald to Baltimore and eventually ran him down in Asheville at Grove Park Inn. Scott's shoulder was still in a cast. As a result of his accident and of the alcohol and sedatives he had taken to relieve the pain, he was in no state to be interviewed. But pleased at the idea of talking to reporters again and won over by Mok's flattering overtures, Scott invited Mok up to his room. During the interview, despite the warnings of his nurse, Fitzgerald made frequent trips to the bottle cached in the highboy and allowed Mok to draw him into confessions even more damaging than those in the "Crack-Up" articles.

On September 25 Mok's interview with Fitzgerald, entitled "The Other Side of Paradise," appeared on the front page of the *New York Post*. "The poet-prophet of the post-war neurotics," according to Mok, spent his birthday as he spent all other days, "trying to come back from the other side of Paradise, the hell of despondency in which he has writhed for the last couple of years." Then, almost as if he were deliberately trying to pay Scott off in his own coin for the things he had said about Zelda, Mok continued, "But whatever pain the fracture might still cause him, it did not account for his jittery jumping off and onto his bed, his restless pacing, his trembling hands, his twitching face with its pitiful expressions of a cruelly beaten child." The article went on to say that Fitzgerald admitted having lost confidence in himself and faith in his star. In conclusion, Mok quoted Scott on the nightmarish, apocalyptic fate of his generation, " 'Some became brokers and threw themselves out of windows. Others became bankers and shot themselves. Still others became newspaper reporters. And a few became successful authors.' His face twitched. 'Successful authors!' he cried. 'Oh, my God, successful authors.' "

Scott had once said that there are no second acts in American life; but he was mistaken, at least in regard to his own. The first act had been ironic comedy; the second, a stark tragedy. And the curtain rang down on it in Asheville that summer. When Scott read Mok's article, he threatened to kill him. He protested that he had not made any of the remarks that Mok attributed to him. They were, he said, taken word by word from the first "Crack-Up" article; and the photograph of him, supposedly taken on his fortieth birthday, was faked. Shortly afterwards *Time* appeared with an equally devastating piece based on the interview in the *New York Post*. Scott wired Miss Walker to keep it from Scottie. Then his rage gave way to shame and despair. His nurse had left morphine, intended to be given hypodermically to relieve the pain in his shoulder, on the table beside his bed. In a black moment, he swallowed the entire contents of the vial. But the lethal dose nauseated him and frustrated his attempt at suicide.

"Show me a hero," he once said, "and I'll write you a tragedy." By this time, however, Scott's losing battle against his weaknesses and the misfortunes they engendered had drained him of the heroic qualities to which he had aspired in his youth. "This general eclipse of ambition and determination and fortitude, all of the very qualities on which I have prided myself, is ridiculous," he wrote Perkins in October, "and, I must admit, somewhat obscene."

In his own eyes Scott had become an anti-hero. And the third act in the saga of an anti-hero is not tragic but tragicomic. The last four years of Scott's life were anticlimactic; "once you get to the point where you don't care whether you live or die—as I did —" he explained, "it's hard to come back to life," and despite his dogged fight to come back, his efforts were doomed to end in one bizarre contretemps after another.

As a votary of the Bitch Goddess, he confessed, once success turned her back on him, he tried to regain her favor by pouring down a libation of two quarts a day. He lay in bed in a darkened room at Grove Park Inn, brooding over his troubles of the previous year. When Perkins sent Marjorie Kinnan Rawlings, the novelist, to see him, she found him "nervous as a cat." But, for the time being, he had had his nurse hide his liquor, and at lunch he confined himself to sherry and table wine. He was, Mrs. Rawlings said, still hurt by Mok's story and Hemingway's crack about "poor Scott Fitzgerald," which they agreed was part of Hemingway's sadistic desire to knock people down. Despite Hemingway's postmortems on Scott's career, Fitzgerald, she noted, did not consider himself ruined by a long chalk; nor did she think that "his masochisms" would interfere with his work. "He has thrown himself on the floor and shrieked himself back in the face and pounded his heels—as most of us do in one way or another—" she concluded, "but when it's over he'll go back to his building blocks again."

The visit cheered him. He began to drive out now and then to see Lefty and Nora Flynn, who still lived in Tryon, some twenty miles from Asheville. Although Zelda was well enough to go to a football game with Scott and the Flynns and to appear in a fashion show at Grove Park Inn, Fitzgerald insisted on keeping her at Highland Hospital. Her mother evidently began to suspect that Zelda's condition was better than Scott's, and she insisted that Scott let Zelda come home for Christmas. Scott had promised to let her go to Montgomery with Scottie and a nurse to spend the holidays with Miss Minnie. On his return to Baltimore, however, he decided that before they went south, it was up to "old dowager Fitzgerald" to give a tea dance for Scottie at the Belvedere. As usual, Scott drank too much, staggered about the floor trying to dance with Scottie's teen-age friends, and generally made a laughingstock of himself.

After that "ghastly tea-dance," as she called it, Scottie and her friend Peaches Finney went home on the verge of hysteria. Mr. and Mrs. Finney fed and consoled them, and Scottie said:

> Within two hours we were dressed, curled, and deposited by them at the door of the next Christmas party. Meredith Boyce, then the best sixteen-year-old dancer in Baltimore, actually stopped dancing long enough to ask me to sit down.

"How can you seem so *cheerful?*" he asked. He was a very good friend; in fact I flattered myself that we had a case of puppy love. "After what happened this afternoon."

"Nothing happened this afternoon," I said.

"Are you being brave? Smiling through the tears?"

"Not at all. It just never happened, that's all."

He told me much later that he had been shocked by my detachment that evening. I asked him why.

"Because kids should care more about their parents," he said. "He was so drunk, and so pitiful, and you acted as if he wasn't there."

"Meredith, I *had* to," I said. "Don't you see that if I had allowed myself to care, I couldn't have stood it?"

Realizing how much he must have embarrassed Scottie, Fitzgerald went on a tear and landed in the hospital again. This time the doctors kept him there until he was completely dried out. Sobered and humbled, he faced his situation squarely for once. The past year had been his most unproductive since 1926. He was forty thousand dollars in debt. Even if he cut his expenses and Zelda's to the bone, the novel he had been planning would have to wait until he could clear up his debts. He still had too much pride to heed the friends who advised him to put Scottie in a public school and Zelda in a state hospital. His only possible way out of his troubles, he again decided, was through Hollywood.

14. West of Paradise

IN AUGUST Fitzgerald had had an offer of fifteen hundred dollars a week to go to Hollywood to work on a young love script, but he had been forced to decline it because of the injury to his shoulder, which he later described as a broken back. However, when Zelda and her mother arrived at Grove Park Inn to visit him during the first week of the month, they found him walking around and writing upon a specially contrived board that the manager of the hotel had rigged up for him. Nevertheless, he continued to complain of his injuries and to use them as an excuse for his dwindling output. During 1936 he had devoted most of his time to writing articles for *Esquire*, which did not bring in as much as his stories. As a result his income for the year fell to ten thousand, one hundred eighty dollars. His inheritance from his mother had helped to amortize part of his debt, but plainly something had to be done. Here he was, he wrote Ober, worrying about his weekly hotel bill, though even the dullest hacks were making a thousand dollars a week in Hollywood.

While he was waiting for Ober to get a movie contract for him, Scott went back to North Carolina. Instead of taking another suite at Grove Park Inn, he lived in a thirty-five-dollar-a-week room in Tryon at Oak Hall, a rambling, gray hotel with spacious porches

and rooms like monks' cells. He ate at Misseldine's Drug Store,
which he celebrated in a rhyme, written there on a paper napkin:

> Oh Misseldines, dear Misseldines,
> A dive we'll ne'er forget.
> The taste of its banana splits
> Is on our tonsils yet.

His appetite was fitful and capricious; he lived on banana splits,
malted milks, and chocolate fudge sundaes, but he stopped drinking entirely. By substituting Coca Colas for beer and gin, he
remained completely sober for six months, put on weight, and
regained something of his good looks, gaiety, and charm. After
having been creatively dead for three years, he said, he was
beginning to come alive again.

In June Harold Ober succeeded in getting him a contract from
M-G-M as a screenwriter at a thousand dollars a week. Before he
left for the West Coast, he saw Hemingway briefly in New York.
They patched up their difficulties over a few drinks, which halted
Scott's ride on the water wagon. From the train enroute to Montgomery, where Scott was taking Zelda and Scottie for a visit with
Miss Minnie, he wrote Hemingway on June 5, 1937, that he
wished that they might meet more often; he felt as if he did not
know him at all any more. Going south, he added presciently,
always seemed to him rather desolate, fatal, and uneasy, while
going north was a safe, dull feeling.

Late one night, shortly after his arrival in Montgomery, Scott
called Pitt Tyson Maner, a mutual friend of ours who was president of the Young Democrats and asked him to endorse a check
for him. He was angry and distressed because the clerk at the
Jefferson Davis Hotel had refused to cash it for him. "But I'm
Scott Fitzgerald," he had protested.

"I don't care who you are," the clerk had replied. "We don't
cash checks for strangers."

How was it that he could be called a stranger in a town in
which he had lived a few years before and in which he had been
greeted and fêted as a celebrity? Fame was a fickle wench, as he
well knew; yet to come back to Montgomery and find himself
treated as a stranger made him feel like an exile from his former
"paradise."

Nor did his reception by the Sayres alleviate his vexation. They were courteous, but cool. Miss Minnie, who had hitherto been pleasant, even cordial, to him, had now definitely aligned herself on Zelda's side. Nor did Zelda find as warm a welcome as she had before *Save Me the Waltz* appeared. Tom Wolfe was not the first nor the last writer to find that you cannot go home again and be received with open arms after putting your family and friends into a book. In the final pages of her novel, Zelda had satirized the gossips holding forth at a party in Montgomery. One of them was the social editor of a local journal, an old lady with young ideas, fond of remarking, "Free love is coming and coming fast. But I'm afraid I'll be too old to enjoy it when it gets here." Zelda had described her, with a very slight variation in the spelling of her name, as having "short white hair and the face of a satyr." Zelda's friends were more shocked than amused. They laughed at her quips, but they were wary of her for fear they might also find themselves ridiculed in print.

The tension in Montgomery was too much for Scott. He fled precipitately. Aboard the train to Hollywood, he wrote Scottie, "What an exit! Horrors of life in the sticks—nothing could have turned around there except a model T. Ford. Sorry to leave you and Grandma in such a mess." His Alabama visit had evidently reminded him of his riotous days there during the war, because he continued sententiously, "For premature adventure one pays an atrocious price. As I told you once, every boy I know who drank at eighteen or nineteen is now safe in his grave. The girls who were what we called "speeds" (in our stone-age slang) at sixteen were reduced to anything they could get at marrying time. It's in the logic of life that no young person ever 'gets away with anything.' They fool their parents but not their contemporaries." His projection of his fear of emotional bankruptcy into anxiety over Scottie and the *non-sequitur* that followed it are an indication of his state of mind at the time. "It was in the cards that Ginevra King," he said, speaking of the girl he had been in love with while he was in Princeton, "should get fired from Westover—also that your mother should wear out young."

When I saw Zelda briefly in Montgomery early that summer, I must say she looked far from "worn out," nor was she fantastically dressed "in the outworn robes of the twenties." If Zelda had ever owned "a hat like a child's bonnet with the strings carefully tied under the chin," she had discarded it for a tennis visor. She wore a sleeveless white sharkskin dress and spectator pumps, and she had a racket and tennis shoes with her as she waited beside the pool at the Country Club for the friends with whom she was to play. Her meridional tan was becoming to her, and she looked far healthier and happier than she had in Baltimore. Her manner was easy and gracious. There was nothing even slightly offbeat in what she said and did. After she told me that Scott wanted her to go back and stay at Highland Hospital while he was in California, I wondered why he had not taken her with him. Six months later, when I saw Scott in Hollywood, I no longer wondered.

Far too much has been made of Scott's difficulties in Hollywood. In 1937 the thousand dollars a week that M-G-M paid him was worth twice that amount today. His troubles with the movie moguls were no greater than those of most screenwriters. Zelda and Scottie were both in the East; he no longer had them to interrupt his work. He was certainly not lonely. Many of his old friends turned up in Hollywood—Robert Benchley, Charlie MacArthur, John O'Hara, Donald Ogden Stewart, Dorothy Parker, and Ernest Hemingway.

When Hemingway blew into town, Scott was back on the wagon again. Dorothy Parker invited them both to have a nightcap at her house after a dinner party at the Fredric Marches'. At first Scott declined, because, he said, "I'm afraid of Ernest, I guess, scared of being sober when . . ." Lillian Hellman, who finally persuaded him to go, described their meeting:

> We went into the hall and turned left to the living room. Nobody saw us come in because the four or five people in the room were all turned toward Ernest, who stood with his back to the door, facing the fireplace. I don't know why he did it, or what had gone on before, but as we started into the room, Hemingway threw his highball glass against the stone fireplace. Fitzgerald and I stopped dead at the sound of the smashing glass: he stepped back into the hall and turned to leave, but I held his arm and he followed me through a swinging door as if he didn't know or care where he was going. Dottie and [Dashiell] Hammett were in the kitchen talking about Errol Flynn as they watched Alan Campbell, Dottie's husband, grow irritable about ice trays.

I said, "Ernest just threw a glass."

Dottie said, "Certainly," as she kissed Fitzgerald.

I moved toward Dash and said in a whisper, "Please help Mr. Fitzgerald. He's frightened of Ernest and the glass throwing didn't help."

Hemingway's visit left Scott unhappy. However, he stuck to soft drinks while he played and partied with Hollywood's great and near great that summer. On July 26 he reported to Mrs. Harold Ober that he had met Miriam Hopkins, Greta Garbo, Marlene Dietrich, and Shirley Temple, talked with Robert Taylor, and danced with Ginger Rogers. He added that he had also visited in Rosalind Russell's dressing room, wisecracked with Robert Montgomery, drunk ginger ale with Zukor and Lasky, lunched alone with Maureen O'Sullivan, watched Crawford act, and lost his heart to a beautiful half-caste Chinese girl whose name he had forgotten. "So far," he said, "I've bought my own breakfasts."

In August he arranged with Helen Hayes to bring Scottie out to spend a month with him. Everything went beautifully, he wrote Max Perkins. Scottie had the time of her life, dining with Joan Crawford and Norma Shearer and talking to Fred Astaire, her favorite star. After she returned to the East, Scott went to Alabama and took Zelda on a four-day trip to Charleston, South Carolina. At Christmas he went east again to spend the holidays with her in Miami.

Scott had just come back from Florida when I ran into him at a party in Hollywood, given by Pitt Tyson Maner, who had come to the West Coast to see the University of Alabama football team play in the Rose Bowl. As we came into the Trocadero, where the party was held, the first person we saw was Scott. He had a beautiful blonde with him, who looked enough like Zelda to be mistaken for her at a distance. Disengaging himself from her, he hastened over to speak to us and assure us that he was now "sitting on top of the world."

A few days later Margaret Sullavan, who had once acted in a summer theater of which I was a director, took me to the M-G-M commissary for lunch. While we lingered there over our coffee, Clark Gable came over to our table to discuss the casting of *Gone With the Wind*. Peg introduced him to me and I said, "How do you do, Mr. Gable," and not wanting to interrupt their shop talk, let it go at that. After he left us, Scott, who had been sitting at another table with the beautiful blonde, left her and rushed over in Gable's wake. Wheeling me around by the shoulder, he said, "Do you know who that was? That was the King! That was Clark Gable!"

"I know, Scott, but what do you want me to do, salaam, curtsey, or fall in a faint?"

"At least, turn on your charm." Scott pulled up his chair and sat down. By contrast with the exotic clothes, the loud sport coats, Hawaiian shirts, and plaid trousers then in vogue in filmland, he was dressed like a college boy in a pale-green shirt, dark-green tie, tan pullover, brown trousers, and saddle shoes. Although he was in good spirits, he was evidently not well. He had lost weight, and his face was pale and lined. In fact, he looked like a specter of the Jazz Age laureate reincarnated in the image of Pat Hobby, the protagonist of his later-day stories.

"How do you like Hollywood?" he asked.

"It's not like home," I laughed.

From its acres and acres of studio lots with their false-front buildings, papier-mâché castles, and cloak-and-suit geniuses to the stucco palaces of the stars in Beverly Hills, the concrete chuck wagons, brown derbies, windmills, and bulldogs from which food and drink were dispensed, the glaring streets studded with palms that looked like up-ended feather dusters, the endless rows of bastard-Spanish bungalows, the garish temples of myriad offbeat religious sects, the swarm of seers, fortunetellers, swamis, the hordes of flesh peddlers, and the throng of starlets on Vine Street with silver-fox capes over their shoulders and run-down heels on their shoes—Hollywood appealed to me as one great sideshow. In no other gold-plated clip joint in the world does the surface glitter so reveal the cheapness and sordidness at the core. But to have said so would have started an argument with Scott. Instead, I asked, "Have you ever noticed how much Clark Gable looks like Hemingway in his early days?"

"Yes," he agreed, "but Gable's better looking; Ernest's getting fat and losing his hair. He came out here last summer with a documentary he'd helped make on the Spanish Civil War. He was taking up a collection for the Loyalists—when he wasn't trying to pick a fight. He's always trying to knock somebody down these days. Had a fight with Max Eastman in Scribner's office. Success has gone to his head. He's living in a world of his own these days."

"And how's Zelda?" I asked, with an irony he could not miss.

For a moment, he was flustered. Then he said shortly, "She's better," as if in "the voices fainter and fainter—how is Zelda, how is Zelda—tell us—how is Zelda," he had begun to hear a deliberate reproach. He hastily changed the subject by asking Peg whether she had ever thought what a perfect Nicole she would make if *Tender Is the Night* were filmed. When she thanked him so coolly that it was evident that his suggestion had not flattered her, he looked hurt for a moment. Then, since Peg's husband, Leland Hayward, was Scott's agent, he launched into an uncalled-for explanation of his life and works. He had, he said, just returned from taking Zelda from the Highland to Montgomery for Christmas—a quiet, sober Christmas—before they went on to Miami and Palm Beach. He was on the wagon now for good, writing like mad to finish the script he was working on—which, by the way, was the best he had done. M-G-M had renewed his contract. It was amusing to remember that Hollywood had assumed that he was through after "The Crack-Up" appeared. Hemingway, too, had thought that he was washed up. Well, he would show him. Hemingway had cracked up himself, but did not have the insight to realize it—a complete megalomaniac now, if there ever was one—one of those people who are always right. According to Scott, he was the only sound nut in a bowl of cracked ones.

After he took his departure, leaving behind him a trail of carefully dropped names—Helen Hayes, Norma Shearer, Joan Crawford—Peg told me that Scott was "shacked up," as she put it, with the beautiful blonde at the Garden of Allah Apartments.

"I thought it was strange he didn't introduce her to us either here or at Pitt's party. Who is she?" I asked.

"Sheilah Graham, the glamour girl of the Fourth Estate," Peg told me. "Scott met her a week after he arrived here at a party Bob Benchley gave to celebrate her engagement to the Marquess of Donegall."

Sheilah was as radiant and lovely as Zelda had been in the first days of her marriage to Scott. The beauty and the glittering history of the young columnist had completely enthralled Fitzgerald. She had been reared in London, she told him, by an aunt, who lived in an elegant Georgian house in Chelsea, overlooking the Thames Embankment. Her aunt had sent her to an exclusive finishing school in Paris. After making her debut in London, she had been presented at court and married to a retired major of the British army who was twice her age. Now she had divorced him and become engaged to the Marquess of Donegall, a wealthy playboy, who amused himself by writing a gossip column for a London paper. Notwithstanding, she had plunged into a headlong love affair with Scott. And in October he told Scottie triumphantly that Sheilah had broken her engagement to Donegall.

With Zelda safely locked away in Highland Hospital and Scottie at the Ethel Walker School, where she was preparing to take her entrance examinations for Vassar, he was free to do as he pleased in Hollywood. There were no questions asked at the Garden of Allah, a rambling aggregation of pink-stucco buildings, once the home of the Russian movie actress, Alla Nazimova, who had designed the swimming pool there in the shape of the Black Sea to remind her of her birthplace on its shores. Many of Scott's famous friends had stayed at the Garden of Allah while they were in Hollywood. Therefore, although ostensibly he was in Hollywood to recoup his finances, he felt that he must put up there, too, even if the rent for the top floor of a bungalow there was one-fourth of the total amount that he had put aside for Scottie, Zelda, and himself to live on while he applied the rest of his salary to his debts. Not only did it give him a certain prestige to stay at the Garden of Allah, where so many noted writers and artists lived, but also in its bohemian atmosphere there would be no objection to his open liaison with Sheilah Graham.

Until Scott ran into trouble while he was working on the script for Erich Maria Remarque's *Three Comrades*, Sheilah was able to exert a stabilizing influence on him. She was attractive, industrious, sober, and kind. Edmund Wilson, who met her when she and Scott visited him and his wife on a trip to the east, said of her:

So not only did she rouse in him the sense of romance without which he could not flourish; she was able, with her affection and common sense, to do everything a woman could to console him, to keep up his morale and to provide him with the necessary conditions for work—all of which meant making it possible for Fitzgerald to insulate himself from the distracting, and, for him, humiliating life of the motion-picture world. And she was admirable in her relations with Fitzgerald's daughter. . . ."

While Scott worked at studying the technique of writing for the talking pictures and revising the script for *A Yank at Oxford*, Sheilah prevailed on him to confine his drinking to holidays and weekends. But then came his disappointment over Joseph Mankiewicz's revisions of *Three Comrades*, Fitzgerald's first important assignment, for which he hoped to get a film credit and possibly even an Academy Award. He had given Mankiewicz, the producer, a drawing, he complained, and Mankiewicz had touched it up with chalk. When he finished reading Mankiewicz's revisions, he added, there were tears in his eyes, not for the heroine but for Margaret Sullavan, who was to star in it and who would have to speak those *"re-fined,"* sentimental lines. When the hope of a possible Academy Award was snatched from him, he began to console himself with bathroom potations, ill concealed by Sen-Sen and cloves.

Sheilah kept him away from parties and tried to help him regain his self-control. But while he was working on *Infidelity*, a picture for Joan Crawford, his actions became so erratic that his friends were alarmed. For example, in reply to a student who wanted to do a study of his life and asked for information, he sent a list of fictitious reference books:

> *F. Scott Fitzgerald: His Youth and Parentage*—C. B. Ansbrucher, Berlin, Privately Printed.
> *F. Scott Fitzgerald: The Image and the Man*—Irene Kammer Thurston, Brentano's, 1937.
> *Fitzgerald As I Knew Him*—J. B. Carstairs, Scribner's, 1928.
> *F. Scott Fitzgerald and the Rise of Islam.* Harcourt, Brace and Howe.
> *The Women Who Knew F. Scott Fitzgerald*—Marie, Comtesse de Segours, Editions Galantière, Paris.

At the end of February he went on a three-day binge in New York. He was still drinking heavily when he met Scottie and Zelda for a holiday at Virginia Beach. He promptly broke up their tennis and golf lessons and quarreled with both of them. His violent behavior so frightened Zelda that she reported to the hotel that he was a dangerous maniac and tried to have him certified. But she had the disadvantages of being without funds, a woman, and a patient in a mental hospital; no matter what she had to endure, there was no redress for her. Scott returned her to Highlands and told Dr. Carroll that the outworn pretense that they could ever come together again was better forgotten. The mainsprings of the love that had once been between them were gone. He had, he added, "no desire ever again to personally undertake her supervision. That period has gone, and each time I see her something happens to me that makes me the worst person for her rather than the best, but a part of me will always pity her with a deep sort of ache that is never absent from my mind for more than a few hours; an ache for the beautiful child that I loved and with whom I was happy as I never shall be again."

The pattern of Scott's relationship to Zelda and to his inamorata in Asheville repeated itself in his love affair with Sheilah Graham. Once the first glow of passion faded, his attitude became ambivalent, polarized between love and hate, compassion and cruelty. The object of his love became a specimen to be dissected, analyzed, observed, and used for another chapter in another book.

In the course of the quarrels with Sheilah that followed his sprees, Fitzgerald discovered the cracks in her glamorous façade. He subjected her to a ruthless inquisition, broke down her story, and wormed the truth out of her. She *had* been born in London, but not as Sheilah Graham. Her real name, Lily Sheil, was as hateful to her as the memory of a basement in a London slum that smelled of laundry soap and boiled potatoes—a basement, which she and her mother shared with a washerwoman. Her mother had put Sheilah in an orphan asylum and kept her there until she needed someone to nurse her after she had undergone an operation for cancer. After her mother's death Sheilah worked as a parlor maid, a demonstrator, a clerk, and a showgirl in one of Charles Cochrane's reviews. At seventeen, she married the major. During her marriage to him she began to write occasional pieces for the papers, which eventually led to a job writing a Hollywood column for the North American Newspaper Alliance.

The pathos of her story appealed to a latent tenderness in Scott. The revelation of her humble origins gave him a sense of superiority, which he badly needed at the time. She catered to him and looked after him as though he were a sick child. As he became more and more dependent upon her, his resentment at being tied to Zelda increased. Yet he protested that he would never divorce "his invalid" or allow her to feel deserted as long as she was ill. But, after an argument with Dr. and Mrs. Carroll as to how much time Zelda was to spend in and out of the Highland Hospital, Fitzgerald wrote Scottie that "they threaten to release her altogether to me which would be a catastrophe—I can't work and look after her. And she wouldn't obey any companion unless the hospital has authority back of the companion. Mrs. Sayre wants her to come and sit beside what will soon be a deathbed and I can't see that as any promising future (I don't mean Mrs. Sayre is sick but she is almost so)." Under these transparent evasions, it is clear that Scott wanted Zelda kept in the East at all costs. He dared not tell her that he was sending Scottie to Europe and renting a cottage at Malibu Beach for Sheilah and himself that summer, and he warned Scottie not to do so because Zelda would feel as if they were happy and she was in prison.

At the beach Scott lived openly with Sheilah Graham. In his Notebooks there is a telling comment on the summer, *"Honi soit qui Malibu."* As Ernest Boyd shrewdly pointed out, Scott was a character out of his own fiction. His confessions, if he ever wrote any, Boyd added, would be permeated by the conviction of sin, which Boyd believed to be happier than the conviction that the way to Utopia was paved with adultery.

As his guilty mood deepened, Scott took it out in baiting Sheilah, moralizing to Scottie, and disparaging Zelda. Scottie's reasoning, he wrote her, had lately become more like her mother's than his: "Never in her whole life did she have a sense of guilt, even when she put other lives in danger—it was always people and circumstances that oppressed her." He was outraged because, after Scottie was graduated from Ethel Walker's, she and a friend, who was also staying on at school to study for college entrance exams, thumbed a ride to Yale to have dinner with the latter's fiancé. They were seen and reported by their Latin teacher. Although Scottie had already received her diploma, as a result of that ridiculously innocent escapade she was asked to leave the school. Her father wrote her a bitter letter, in which he blamed Zelda for his own shortcomings as well as Scottie's:

> When I was your age I lived with a great dream. The dream grew and I learned how to speak of it and make people listen. Then the dream divided one day when I decided to marry your mother after all, even though I knew she was spoiled and meant no good to me. I was sorry immediately that I had married her but, being patient in those days, made the best of it and got to love her in another way. You came along and for a long time we made quite a lot of happiness out of our lives. But I was a man divided—she wanted me to work too much for *her* and not enough for my dream. She realized too late that work was dignity, and the only dignity, and tried to atone for it by working herself, but it was too late and she broke and is broken forever.
>
> It was too late also for me to recoup the damage—I had spent most of my resources, spiritual and material, on her, but I struggled on for five years till my health collapsed, and all I cared about was drink and forgetting.
>
> The mistake I made was in marrying her. We belonged to different worlds—she might have been happy with a kind simple man in a southern garden. She didn't have the strength for the big stage —sometimes she pretended and pretended beautifully, but she didn't have it. She was soft when she should have been hard and hard when she should have been yielding. She never knew how to use her energy—she's passed that failing on to you.
>
> For a long time I hated *her* mother for giving her nothing in the line of good habit—nothing but "getting by" and conceit. I never wanted to see again in this world women who were brought up as idlers. And one of my chief desires in life was to keep you from being that kind of person, one who brings ruin to themselves and others.

Sheilah Graham was made of tougher stuff than Zelda. Even so, as she admitted in *Beloved Infidel*—her account of her liaison with Fitzgerald, published after his death—Scott sometimes drove her to the verge of despair. He quarreled with her at home and with his colleagues at M-G-M. "Writing for Joan Crawford is difficult," he complained to Gerald Murphy. "She can't change her emotions in the middle of a scene without going through a sort of Jekyll and Hyde contortion of the face, so that when one wants to indicate that she is going from joy to sorrow, one must cut away and then back. Also, you can never give her such a stage direction as 'telling a lie,' because if you did, she would practically give a representation of Benedict Arnold selling West Point to the British."

When *Infidelity* was stymied by the censors, Scott was put to work turning Clare Boothe Luce's play *The Women* into a scenario for Norma Shearer. This was a more pleasant job for him, not only because the lines of Mrs. Luce's witty comedy amused him but also because he had Donald Ogden Stewart as a collaborator, and Stewart could always make Scott laugh—even when he parodied him as he had done in "The Courtship of Miles Standish In the Manner of F. Scott Fitzgerald."

After his divorce from the former Beatrice Ames, Stewart married the widow of Lincoln Steffens and espoused her devotion to the Marxist cause. Both he and she took part in the activities of the Popular Front in Hollywood and tried to interest Scott in them. But while he liked to hear Stewart's humorous accounts of the fellow travelers' antics, Scott said that after his experiences with the Communists in Baltimore, he declined to be involved with them again. Yet after he finished polishing Stewart's script for *The Women*, he wrote Scottie, who was going on a visit to Baltimore, that there was a strong left-wing movement there and that he did not want her to set herself against it. He added that he was known as a left-wing sympathizer, and he would be proud if she were, too.

As Scott verged on another crack-up that summer, his mind and his moods changed more and more often. In one letter to Scottie he would be tender, gay, and cheerful; in another, hypercritical and severe, even contumacious. One evening he would go to a party for Thomas Mann, whose works he greatly admired, and charm the author with his scintillating appraisal of them; the next morning he would appear at the studio as silent and morose as he had been effervescent and genial the night before.

James M. Cain, the noted novelist and a former editor of *The New Yorker*, once told me about meeting Scott while they were both working at M-G-M. Cain went to his office early to put in a quiet hour on his assignment. He had not been in Hollywood very long. However, he said:

> My name was already on the door, but I had it [the office] all to myself as not even the secretary had reported yet. Then there came a knock at the door, and when I called "Come," it opened, and this collegiate-looking character, in Hollywood slacks and lounge coat came in, and said: "Mr. Cain?" "Yes," I said. He held out his hand, and said: "I'm Scott Fitzgerald—just dropped in to say hello and welcome you to the lot." "Oh!" I said. "Well! Well say—thanks." "Well," he said, and backed out the door. Then I thought to myself: "Well & well & well—that was a hell of a way to greet Scott Fitzgerald." So I thought: "What can you do to retrieve it?" So around 12, I went down the hall, found his name on the door, and knocked. He said "Come in," and I went. He wasn't doing anything, just walking around. No secretary was there, that I saw. I suggested lunch, and without saying anything he nodded, came out, and fell into step beside me. We went to the commissary, I chatting amiably along, but in a minute or two I realized that he hadn't said anything. He hasn't said anything yet. He just sat there staring at me. Later someone who knew him told me: "He probably thought you were pitying him for being a has-been, and inviting him to lunch for that reason." Whatever it was, it was perhaps the most uncomfortable hour I ever spent in my life. . . .

Scott was often equally morose with his colleagues at the studio. Sometimes he was truculent, even hostile to them. Consequently, the studio replaced him before he finished doing the script for *Madame Curie* and refused to renew his contract at the end of the year. He loafed for a few weeks and began making notes for another novel. But he was in need of money; so he took the job of polishing the script of *Gone With the Wind* for Selznick-International. Although he thought the novel interesting, if not particularly original, he disliked the idea of rewriting a script that had already been worked over by a dozen other writers. Moreover, he told Max Perkins, it annoyed him to have to thumb through Margaret Mitchell's novel as if it were scripture and to copy out her words that applied to scenes covered in the script because he had been strictly forbidden to use any words but those of the novel's author. By the time he had finished his work on *Gone With the Wind,* he was ill in mind and body. He was disgusted with the motion-picture industry and disappointed over his failures in Hollywood. As usual he had a physical reaction to a psychological crisis. He began having night sweats and running a slight temperature, which he feared indicated that his old tubercular lesion had become active again.

In February 1939, when Walter Wanger offered to send him to Dartmouth to collaborate with Budd Schulberg, the son of a Hollywood producer, on a scenario based upon the Winter Carnival, he made what he afterward called the most stupid mistake of his career. Ill as he was, he agreed to go. Schulberg's father saw them off at the airport and wished them bon voyage with a magnum of champagne. The champagne sent Scott off on a bender. He switched to gin and began drinking in earnest. Sheilah Graham, who had accompanied him and Schulberg on the plane as far as New York, tried to curb him, but he was completely out of hand. The trip to Dartmouth turned out to be an alcoholic fiasco that landed Scott in Bellevue Hospital, but not before he had disgraced himself at Dartmouth, been fired by Wanger, and furnished Budd Schulberg with the material for *The Disenchanted,* a satirical novel based on the trip to Dartmouth.

Fortunately, Sheilah Graham was still in New York, and as soon as Scott was well enough to travel, she took him back to Hollywood. There he faced new troubles; he was worried about Scottie, who had been put on probation at the end of her first semester at Vassar, depressed by Scribner's rejection of his proposal to put out three of his novels in an omnibus volume, and despondent over having to borrow on his life insurance again. He drove himself, he wrote Mrs. Frank Case, through March and April on a quart of gin a day, three teaspoons of chloral, two Nembutals, and forty-five drops of digitalis at night. Edgy and irascible as a result of the alcohol and drugs, exhausted from the work that he and Don Stewart had done on the scenario for *Air Raid,* he quarreled with Stewart and broke off his affair with Sheilah.

After Sheilah left him, Scott was so lonely that he decided to take Zelda on a trip to Cuba. Knowing that he was in no state of mind or body to look after Zelda, her family wrote Dr. Carroll, expressing their doubts as to the advisability of letting her make the trip with him. But, as her husband, Fitzgerald had the legal right to take her out of the hospital whenever he chose, so Dr. Carroll had to let her go.

Scott was tired, ill, and drinking heavily before he and Zelda left for Havana. There, as the result of an attempt to stop a cock fight, he was worsted in a free-for-all with some Cubans who resented his interference. Zelda managed to get him back to New York and nursed him in the Algonquin Hotel until he drank himself into a manic state and began to break up the furniture. Since Zelda had Scottie and a school friend with her, she called her sister, Clotilde Sayre Palmer, who was then living nearby in Larchmont, and asked if she might bring the two girls out there. The three of them spent the night with the Palmers. Next morning Zelda, who had overstayed her leave from Highland, took the train back to Asheville alone.

Alarmed at Scott's condition, Mrs. Frank Case, wife of the Algonquin's host, sent for a physician, who took Scott to Doctors Hospital, sobered him up, and told him that he would be dead in a year if he did not stop drinking. As soon as he began to improve, Mrs. Case called Sheilah Graham, and between them they arranged for his transportation back to Hollywood, where Sheilah generously forgave him, took him back, and resumed nursing him.

15. The Effulgent Legend

AFTER Scott's return from Cuba, he wrote Zelda, who had loyally defended him to Scottie and to the doctors at Highlands, saying: "You are the finest, loveliest, tenderest, most beautiful person I have ever known, but even that is an understatement because the length that you went to there [in New York] at the end would have tried anybody beyond endurance."

As his attitude toward Zelda softened, Fitzgerald became more difficult with Sheilah. Convinced that Scott would be better off and less inclined to drink if they did not move back to Hollywood, she had rented a place for him in the San Fernando Valley. "I'll be damned if I'll believe anyone lived in a place called 'The Garden of Allah,'" Thomas Wolfe had once said to Fitzgerald, who was then living there. But, after giving up the cottage at Malibu, Scott moved to the Edward Everett Horton place at 5521 Amestoy Avenue in Encino, which was even more incredibly named "Belly Acres." As Sheilah's job required her to spend much of her time in Hollywood, Scott was bored, lonely, and jealous. He and she carried on a running battle with each other at "Belly Acres," where, to use her own euphemism, she was matriculating in the "F. Scott Fitzgerald College of One."

According to Sheilah's account of her liaison with Scott in *Be-*

loved Infidel, knowing how she hated to see him drink, he would frequently pay her off for her absences by going on a binge. On one notable occasion, she returned from Hollywood to find that he had a pistol. Realizing that he was too depressed to allow him to keep it, she tried to take it from him. A scuffle over the gun ensued, during which Scott struck her.

Not long afterward she came in one afternoon to find him drinking with two stumblebums whom he had picked up on Ventura Boulevard. He had fitted them out in some of his clothes and had laid places for them at the table. When Sheilah ordered them to leave, Scott lost his temper. In his rage, he threw a bowl of soup on the floor, kicked the nurse, and slapped Sheilah. She kept her head until he began to taunt her by dancing around the table, chanting the name that she had tried to forget, "Lily Sheil! Lily Sheil! Lily Sheil!" Then she flew at him. In the imbroglio that followed, Scott threatened to kill her. He dived into his room, looking for his pistol. When he found that she had hidden it, he became so violent that she was forced to call the police to subdue him.

That night Sheilah left him and refused to see him or to speak to him on the phone. When Scott's entreaties failed to move her, he sent her threatening notes, warning her, "Get out of town, Lily Sheil, or you'll be dead in 24 hours" and again, "Leave town or your body will be found in Coldwater Canyon." That was the last straw to Sheilah. She made up her mind to have no more to do with him and kept her resolution until Scott bombarded her with letters, promising her that whether she went back to him or not, he would stop drinking.

Scott believed that he had been successful in keeping the knowledge of his liaison from Zelda; and in his letters to Scottie, he was constantly warning her not to tell her mother anything that might arouse her suspicion. For instance, when Sheilah gave Scottie a fur coat of hers, which Scott had had his secretary's father, who was a furrier, make over, Scott told Scottie to invent some story about the coat to tell her mother and not to let her know where it came from. But to judge from the leading questions that Zelda asked me when I came back from Hollywood, she was not fooled. Naturally, I told her nothing except that I had seen Scott and that he had seemed to be working hard and in good spirits. I feel sure that Scottie, who had made two trips to the coast to visit her father, was equally discreet. However, in a letter to Mrs. Bayard Turnbull, the owner of La Paix, written after the publication of the fragment of Scott's *The Last Tycoon*, whose heroine was drawn from Sheilah Graham, Zelda said that she did not like the heroine, who seemed to be the kind of person who knew very well how to capitalize on the unwelcome advances of the iceman and who smelled a little of the rubber shields in her dress. Possibly the "rubber shields" was a pun on "Lily Sheil."

To add to the chagrin that it must have caused Zelda for Scott to be living openly with his mistress in Hollywood, Sheilah made a bid for Scottie's affection by entertaining her in Hollywood and sending her presents while she was in school. Zelda sensed that the three of them were allied against her. She also realized that Scott wanted her kept at Highland at any cost, and she taxed him with thinking of her as an enemy and with having paranoid and self-defensive motives in continuing her hospitalization.

As a conciliatory measure, Scott proposed to send Zelda to attend Scottie's graduation from the Ethel Walker School. Zelda was pleased with the idea, and Scott was relieved because she would take his place at the exercises and he would not have to make a trip to the East; but Scottie objected to the arrangement. It was not that she did not want to see her mother, she explained, but it seemed pointless for Zelda to make the long trip merely to see her daughter walk up the aisle and get her diploma. Further, her mother probably did not have the proper clothes for the occasion, nor did she have a car. And she would have to stay at some farmhouse miles away from the school and without any conveniences such as running water. Ignoring Scottie's protests, Fitzgerald replied firmly that her mother and her Aunt Rosalind would appear at her commencement, chicly dressed and in a chic limousine.

Since Scottie had been elected to several positions in her class and had passed her college board examinations, Scott soon forgave her for her New Haven escapade and continued with his plan to take her abroad that summer. However, he found that his

work on the scenario of *The Women* would keep him in Hollywood; so he arranged to send Scottie to Europe with a party. He
promised to meet the boat when she returned and to take her and
Peaches Finney to Hollywood for a visit before Vassar opened.
Evidently, Scottie knew of her father's affair with Sheilah, for he
instructed her that Sheilah was to be referred to only as a "great
friend" because his personal affairs were none of Peaches' business. In the same letter he announced that Zelda would be in
New York about September 20 and would ride up to Vassar. It
gave her so much pleasure to think that she was contributing to
her daughter's education that it would be a kindness to carry on
the illusion. He promised that Rosalind would come with Zelda
and that they would no more interfere with Scottie's activities
than they had last June at commencement.

Although Scottie says that she "was not a perspicacious teen-
ager, and in fact was probably more self-preoccupied than most,"
in many ways she was wise and compassionate beyond her years.
The vagaries of her parents were a heavy cross for her to bear, yet
she made few complaints or criticisms of them. Scott, she said,
was "a born manager," and she was understandably often exas-
perated at being managed. "My mother and I," she added "were
dolls who frustrated him by not behaving according to the script
he had written for us." Her father, Scottie realized, "was not only
a genius but a great man in his way, despite his partly self-in-
flicted torments and his gigantic sins." Likewise, she appreciated
the fact that her mother had been a brilliant and beautiful woman
who had broken down under intolerable stress and strain. The
only way for Scottie to preserve her own equilibrium was to
ignore their tragedies when she could. Remiss as her father sometimes was in doing his duty toward Zelda while she was so ill, he
insisted upon Scottie's meticulously fulfilling hers to her mother
by shopping for her, writing her once a week, and sacrificing the
time to visit her in Asheville or Montgomery during the vacations.
Naturally, Scottie sometimes chafed under the obligations that
her father imposed upon her. Once, after a visit with her mother,
she did criticize her. But afterward, seized by regret, she wrote
her father that she realized that her mother was very charming
and twice as intelligent and well informed as she was; consequently, she was sorry that she had tried to judge her.

In his Gwen stories, "Too Cute for Words" and "Inside the House," Scott had attempted to write about his daughter, but found that he could not do it. In explaining to Kenneth Littauer of *Collier's* why it was impossible to go on turning out stories about young girls, Fitzgerald told him that he had a daughter who was very smart, very pretty, and very popular but that her problems and her point of view seemed dull and uninteresting to him. After Scottie entered Vassar, however, his attitude began to change. He literally relived his own youth in hers; and his letters to her are full of advice about her problems—her studies, her dates, her reading, her conduct, her clothes, and her trips to proms. "Old Dowager Fitzgerald" was almost as involved as Scottie when she made her debut at the Bachelors' Cotillion in Baltimore, escorted by Eben Finney, Peaches' father. But Scott warned Scottie that she should not boast about it at Vassar because the Bachelors' Cotillion did not mean as much as it did ten or twenty years ago.

With any woman he cared for, whether it was his sister, his wife, his daughter, or his ladylove, Scott liked to play Professor Higgins to Eliza Doolittle. Between the studies that he outlined for Scottie at Vassar and those that he had Sheilah Graham poring over in his "College for One," Scott virtually put himself through another undergraduate course.

In the notes that Scott made for *The Last Tycoon* during 1938, there is one in which he said that the novel was to be for two people, Scottie and Edmund Wilson. Both of them were very much on Fitzgerald's mind that fall. After a visit to New York, he and Sheilah Graham went on to Stamford, Connecticut, to spend the night with Wilson and Mary McCarthy, whom Wilson had recently married. Scott found Wilson relatively unchanged. With his clear features, domed forehead, auburn hair, and wide eyes, he was still handsome. His mischief—he had a taste for sleight-of-hand tricks—his elfish humor, his immense erudition, his shrewd insights, and his judicial criticisms made him Scott's favorite companion as well as his "intellectual conscience." After dinner they renewed old times and talked of Princeton, of mutual friends in New York, of recent poetry, of Kafka, and of Scott's new novel. After he returned to California, Scott wrote Wilson that the evening had been a delight and had meant more to him than anyone could imagine.

Back in Encino and encouraged by Wilson's kindness and by *Collier's* interest in serializing the novel, Scott set to work on it in earnest. After his reconciliation with Sheilah, he controlled his drinking, a thing that was much easier for him to do when he was working. A writer who was not writing, he once observed, was a maniac within himself. Unfortunately for his work, in December he had a flare-up of the old tubercular lesion, and in the spring he had to be hospitalized after his disastrous trip to Dartmouth and again after his return from Cuba. By May he had sufficiently recovered to work two hours a day. He had blocked out several outlines for the novel, which he discussed with Perkins on a flying visit to New York, but it was not until early in the fall that he finally settled on one and began to write the first chapter. His final outline for *The Last Tycoon* called for nine chapters, composed of short scenes of some twenty-five hundred words each. The total length of the book was to be about fifty-one thousand words.

Due to a number of complications, Fitzgerald's progress on the novel faltered. He and Sheilah were still at odds. The Sayres began to press more and more urgently for Zelda's release. After Scottie had a slight attack of appendicitis, he insisted on her going to Asheville to have an appendectomy there where Zelda could be with her during her convalescence. Although Scottie considered the operation to be totally unnecessary, she later remembered it as a rather pleasant experience. While she was in the hospital she read *Anna Karenina* and *The Forsyte Saga*, discovered Somerset Maugham, and drew closer to her mother. Scott's reason for sending her to Asheville was that he wanted her to be near her mother. But to his dismay, the result of Scottie's talks with her mother there was to have her adopt what her father derided as "the Montgomery point of view" and join the Sayres in urging him to allow Zelda to go home and live with Miss Minnie. He asked the doctors at Highland to talk to Scottie because his relationship to her would be adversely affected if she continued to side with the Sayres. Moreover, he urged them to point out to her that her mother would probably not be able to maintain her equilibrium when she went through the menopause.

Scott could be extremely arbitrary and capricious with his daughter at times. For example, while she was recuperating in Asheville, the July 1939 issue of *Mademoiselle* appeared, in which Scottie made her debut as a writer with an article entitled "A Short Retort." Despite the numerous times that Scott had drawn his material from life and despite his having encouraged Scottie in her writing, the publication of her article threw him into a temper tantrum. "All this talk about modern youth being streamlined and hardboiled is nonsense," she contended and proceeded to compare her generation with that of her parents. Her father wrote Harold Ober that he did not care for the article or for the idea of having her sit on his shoulder and beat him over the head with a wooden spoon. Further, he would like to see anything that she wanted to publish in the future. Henceforth, he asked Scottie to please sign her articles with some name other than his.

The next thing that happened to impede Scott's work was a break with Harold Ober, who had been his friend, agent, and loan officer since 1920. Ober and his wife had been like another set of parents to Scottie, and when she was to be operated on, Fitzgerald asked Ober for a five hundred dollar advance. Ober sent it to him, but told him that he thought it would be a bad idea to continue to borrow money from him now that Scott had paid up the debt that he owed him before he went to Hollywood. In July, after sending Ober two more stories that he could not sell, Scott asked for another advance. This time Ober declined to give it to him. On August 2, 1939, Scott wrote him that he was stunned by his refusal and his sudden change in policy. He was, he added, living off the money obtained from pawning his second-hand Ford, and he would have to send his stories and articles directly to the magazines in order to eat. From now on he would act as his own literary agent.

A few weeks later *The Hollywood Reporter* carried a vicious attack on Sheilah Graham. Scott took up the cudgel in her defense, drank too much, and tried to call out the editor of the *Reporter*, who merely laughed at the idea of fighting a duel with him. Scott could never resist the temptation to live dangerously and extravagantly for very long. With his bank balances down to five, ten, and fifteen dollars, in desperation he left off work on his novel, turned back to the movies, and worked for a short while on the script of *Raffles*.

Descartes' great discovery was not *"Je pense, donc je suis"* but the fact that writers can work better in bed than anywhere else. By propping himself up with pillows and reclining in bed, Scott found that he could stretch his working time from two hours to five. Balancing a lapboard on his knees, he wrote in longhand on a legal cap pad. He had no definite time for working but wrote only when he felt like it, boiling the pot by grinding out Pat Hobby stories for *Esquire*. And while they are far from being his best stories, they are valuable as evidence that Fitzgerald was a master of black humor thirty years before it became a literary fashion.

In September Kenneth Littauer wired Scott that if *Collier's* liked the first fifteen thousand words of *The Last Tycoon*, it would pay him thirty thousand dollars for the serial rights to the novel. Overjoyed by the prospect of being released from hackwork and having the time and money to devote to his novel, Scott's health improved. He hired Frances Kroll as his secretary and began dictating to her. During October and November he completed the first chapter of his novel. On October 31 he told Scottie that he had begun to write something which might be great. He was not drinking; and he believed if he stayed on the wagon, he could finish the book in three or four months. But, by November 20, he was in such desperate financial straits that he sent Littauer the first installment, hoping that he might get an advance on it. Since it ran only six thousand words instead of the fifteen thousand that Littauer had wanted to see, he wired Fitzgerald that the verdict would have to be deferred until the story was further developed.

Scott received his telegram on November 28 and immediately wired Max Perkins, asking him to send a copy of the manuscript to the *Post* by air mail. When the *Post* also declined to give him an advance on it, Scott went "berserk," as he later apologetically admitted to Sheilah, and set out to drown his sorrow. He took his frustration out on Sheilah, picked a quarrel with her, and said incredible things to her. After she left him he sent an abusive telegram about her to her employer, John N. Wheeler of the

North American Newspaper Alliance. When Sheilah refused to return a silver-fox jacket that Scott had given her, he broke into her closet and took it away. In an undated letter he told her that when he finally came to himself he found something of hers, presumably the fur jacket. Then he had gone into her room, trying to find whether she had not left something more of herself there. He had not meant the cruel things that he had said to her; they came from the fever, the liquor, and the sedatives. In another note, written after he had had a slight heart attack, he told her that he wanted to die and that the end was very close. On December 10 he wired John Wheeler, apologizing for the telegram about Sheilah that he had sent him and asking him to consider it as coming from a man who was far from himself. At the time, he said, he had had a temperature of a hundred two degrees, a good deal of liquor in him, and some personal difficulties with Sheilah; as a result, he had behaved very badly.

On the same day Scott had Frances Kroll write Sheilah that he was himself again after six days in bed. Everything that he had done in the walking nightmare in which he had lived after his quarrel with her now seemed abominable to him. He wanted to know whether there was any material way in which he could repair the damage that he had done and whether it would help her for him to leave Hollywood. He did not know where she was, and he had no intention of trying to see her; he merely wanted to compensate as far as possible for the unhappiness that he had caused her.

If things had gone badly for Scott during 1939, Zelda's lot had definitely improved. Since she had shown that she was capable of taking care of herself on the trip to Cuba, she was now allowed to leave the hospital with Scottie or Rosalind. Her relations with Scott were so much better that he even thought of bringing her out to the West Coast to make him a visit. Instead, however, he sent her on a trip to Florida and to Virginia Beach. That summer during the Rhododendron Festival her paintings were exhibited by the Asheville Artists' Guild. In an editorial the *Asheville Citizen* praised her abstractions:

There is an arresting and imaginative quality about this painter's use of vivid color and abstract circular design to portray pure emotion that sticks in the observer's mind long after he has left the gallery. And there is a velvety effect about her handling of oil paint which suggests the visions one conjures up by pressing the palms of the hands over the eyeballs in a dark room.

One of Scott's biographers to the contrary, Highland was not to be Zelda's permanent home for the rest of her life. In 1939 she returned to Montgomery to live with her mother at 322 Sayre Street. At Dr. Carroll's behest, she was finally released from the hospital in April 1940 on condition that she promise to live quietly in Montgomery and make no attempt to rejoin Scott in California.

Grover Hall, Jr., one of Zelda's Montgomery friends, once extended the limits of Paradise to include his home town in the springtime: when he called a friend who was then in New Orleans, she asked, "Where are you?"

"I'm in heaven," he replied; "I'm in Montgomery."

Free, safe, and recuperating in her mother's garden that spring, Zelda must have felt that she was once more just this side of Paradise. April in Paris or Cherry Blossom time in Washington are considered by many people to be perfection in time and place —but not by anyone who ever spent an April in Montgomery. The oak-vaulted streets are then garlanded with purple and white wisteria; the Paul Scarlet roses bloom against the columns of its antebellum homes, the redbuds, dogwoods, and Japanese magnolias burgeon around the most beautiful state house in America; the gardens are ablaze with azaleas, hydrangeas, and flowering quinces; the artesian water bubbling from the fountains foams over the pansy beds around them like champagne from a magnum; the fields are blanketed with pink primroses; and the air is heady with kiss-me-at-the-gate, tea olive, and honeysuckle.

During Scottie's first year at Vassar, her father advised her to take a course in botany, urging her to "Think of the enormous pleasure amounting, almost, to the consolation for the tragedy of life that flowers have been to your mother and your grandmother."

Miss Minnie, who was now well, robust, and overflowing with

energy, encouraged Zelda to work in the garden with her and to build a little patio there, where she could paint the flowers and listen to the white doves to which she was so attached. It was probably better therapy than any prescribed by the psychiatrists. However, Zelda conscientiously followed Dr. Carroll's suggestions for continuing her improvement. One thing that he thought would be helpful was bicycle riding. So she bought a wheel; and her friends were fascinated to see her riding all over town, dressed in bright, exotic clothes, and attracting attention wherever she went. For a while she resumed her dancing lessons, but she preferred dancing alone so that she could invent her steps. Besides, the regular ballet exercises knotted the muscles of her legs, so she abandoned the lessons and began instead to take a long walk every day. Livye Hart frequently joined her in her walks, for she and Zelda liked to reminisce about the carefree, light-hearted days of their youth.

When Livye and other old friends came to see Zelda, Miss Minnie would make them stay for a meal. Her Negro cook took pains to prepare the kind of food they liked, and Zelda often went into the kitchen to fix some special dish for them. In the evenings she and her mother read, took in a movie, or simply sat and talked. Miss Minnie had a fine mind; she kept well posted on new books and current events as long as she lived, and Zelda enjoyed discussing them with her.

Pleasant as it was to be at home again, it must have been difficult for Zelda to reconcile herself to leading such a quiet life, particularly after Scott abandoned the idea of bringing her to Hollywood. One reason that Scott decided against that idea was that he and Sheilah had had a reconciliation; another was that, at the time, he could not have afforded the expense. During the last six months he had turned out seventeen Pat Hobby stories for Arnold Gingrich of *Esquire*, but they only brought between two and three hundred dollars apiece. And when Scott sent him a story called "Three Hours Betweeen Planes," Gingrich said he could not publish it until he had run the rest of the Pat Hobby stories that he had on hand. Only Max Perkins's generous offer to lend Fitzgerald $1,000 staved off disaster. As it was, before Perkins could mail him the check, Scott had to draw a draft for $205 on him to pay his rent for January and to borrow money from Gerald Murphy to keep Scottie in Vassar.

In his anxiety over how to pay his next month's bills, Scott sent another story to Gingrich with a covering letter, asking:

> Why don't you publish it under a pseudonym—say John Darcy. I'm awfully tired of being Scott Fitzgerald, as there doesn't seem to be so much money in it, and I'd like to find out if people read me just because I am Scott Fitzgerald or, what is more likely, don't read me for the same reason. . . . My ambition would be to get a fan letter from my daughter.

Toward the end of the month, however, things began to look up for Fitzgerald. Lester Cowan, a free-lance producer, paid him eight hundred dollars for the film rights to "Babylon Revisited." When Columbia Pictures became interested in backing Cowan in filming it, they offered Scott twenty-five hundred dollars to do a film script from the story, with a bonus of an equal sum if the script were accepted. He wrote Scottie "You have earned some money for me this week because I sold "Babylon Revisited," in which you are a character, to the pictures (the sum received wasn't worthy of the magnificent story—neither of you nor of me—however, I am accepting it)." He said that working on it was more fun than anything else he had ever done in pictures; he sobered up and labored over it all spring. To his chagrin Columbia eventually shelved his script. In 1947, when Cowan asked a scenarist to revise it, the writer told him that it was the most perfect script that he had ever read. Cowan replied that the scenarist was absolutely right and that he would pay him two thousand dollars a week to stay there and keep him from changing a word of it.

By April Scott was so ill and exhausted from working six hours a day on "Babylon Revisited" that he spent most of the time in bed. Although he kept his promise to Sheilah never to take a drink again as long as he lived, he was so sick that she was afraid to leave him at Encino, particularly during the fierce summer heat there, because he was once more running a temperature and having night sweats. Therefore she moved him to 1403 Laurel Avenue in Hollywood, where he and she both rented apartments, one above the other. With a compassion and patience that few women could have mustered under the circumstances, she nursed him through the next seven months, during which he was bedridden most of the time.

Despite the fact that he had taken the smallest apartment that would not permit him to look poor, which he felt he could not afford to do in Hollywood, he was soon forced to take a job at Twentieth Century-Fox working on the scenario for "Brooklyn Bridge" and then on one for a screen adaptation for *The Light of Heart*, a play by Emlyn Williams. Although both screenplays were scrapped, Scott had made enough money from his work on them to go back to his novel.

Before Fitzgerald sent Scottie to Montgomery to visit her mother and her grandmother in June 1940, he warned her that she would be interviewed on her arrival there, for she was on the way to becoming a celebrity herself. She had sold another story, which *The New Yorker* published, founded the OMGIM—an acronym for Oh-My-God-It's-Monday—a Vassar club, done the book for the club's musical comedy, *Guess Who's Here*, and projected a biography of her parents. Scott promptly vetoed the biography and asked her to please not discuss her mother or himself with the press. So when a reporter from the *Advertiser* duly arrived to interview her, Scottie obeyed his wishes and confined herself to saying that her father did not wish her to talk about her parents. She wanted to be a writer, she explained, but in case it did not pay, she was preparing herself to teach school. She discussed education in the machine age, life in Paris, and the flapper. The chief difference between the flappers of her mother's youth and the young girls of today, she observed, is that the flappers were no longer unique. "Way back there when a girl bobbed her hair or smoked she was put in a class by herself. Today," she added, "nobody notices, that's all."

Scottie had learned early how to handle the press. She loved Montgomery and the South, she said. She went on to point out that the people there took so much more trouble to be friendly and kind than they did in the East. Another thing that she liked was the way that people seemed so much happier here. In the East everybody was talking and worrying about the war, and some of her more cynical beaux were beginning to take the attitude that nothing mattered very much since they were probably going to get killed very soon anyway. The interviewer returned the bouquets by describing Scottie as a glamour girl, with honey-colored curls, round blue eyes, a lovely complexion, and sense of purpose that was in startling contrast to her beauty. In addition, her quick wit and charming manners, the reporter concluded, had made her "about as popular a girl as has ever visited here."

Just before Scottie arrived in Montgomery, Zelda had had a "toxic attack" that had depressed her and given Miss Minnie a sense of defeatism that was unusual with her. But Scottie's visit cheered them both, and she reported to her father that they were happier now. With her mother she had been an angel, complete with a halo, she said, even going so far as to discuss marriage with her in order to make her feel that she had some ideas to contribute. Between Zelda's studies of the cosmological philosophers and the existentialist theologians, her ideas were so complex and elaborate that Scottie did not think that they were even remotely comprehensible to most people; and yet they were too far out to be of interest to really knowledgeable men and women. Consequently, her mother sometimes felt like a fish out of water, she added.

The generation gap was not peculiar to the Fitzgeralds or to the 1960s and 1970s. But all things considered, Scottie felt that she and her mother had gotten along very well that summer; and indeed they must have, for her mother asked particularly to see her again before college opened. In August Scott decided that it would be better for Scottie to go back to Montgomery because to send Zelda north to see her would mean sending two people. He said he knew that it would be dull "going into that hot little town in September," but Scottie would be helping him if she went. "Even invalids like your mother have to have mileposts—" he continued, "things to look forward to and back upon. It gives her more pride there in Montgomery if you come to see her, something to talk about. Only think how empty her life is and you will see the importance of your going there."

Apparently it did not occur to him to go himself instead of sending Scottie, who had gotten a job for the summer with *Har-*

per's Bazaar. He was pleased to see a picture of her in the *Bazaar,* but he objected to her calling herself Frances Scott Fitzgerald because it "does push me into the background. It calls attention to my being of my generation, which is not too good since I hope to have a big book out in a year." He was also glad that Scottie had the job, but that did not prevent him from sending her to see Cousin Ceci in Norfolk and Zelda in Montgomery.

When I saw Zelda in Montgomery late that summer, she was subdued and a little sad. After all, it was a devastating experience to have to come back to her home town, where she had been a belle in her youth, as a semi-invalid, many of whose friends had been alienated by her book and alarmed by the stories Scott had spread to justify himself. He sent her thirty dollars a week to pay her board to Miss Minnie, dress herself, and cover all her other expenses. Needless to say, there was little, if any, money left over for entertainment. When I met her, she was coming out of St. John's Episcopal Church, where she told me she frequently went on weekdays and sat "in peace and serenity" for hours "because there's no place else to go and think unless I take a streetcar and ride to the end of the line and back." She had a Bible in her hand and her forefinger between the pages as if she had been reading it in the church.

"Do you have any convictions anymore?" she asked, hesitantly, almost apologetically.

"Too many, I'm afraid. But convictions about what, particularly?"

"About religion, I mean. So few people do these days. And it's my only strength—my only strength."

"If you find peace and serenity in your faith, why care whether other people share your convictions or not?"

"Scott doesn't. He doesn't believe in anything—even prayer, anymore. And it irritates him when I pray. And I have to pray to —to live."

"Then pray for him, too, Zelda."

She told me that she had begun to write another novel, based on a religious theme, which she hoped would explain her *Weltanschauung* to Scott. The novel, which was to be called *Caesar's Things*, was never finished, and it is highly improbable that Scott ever saw it or even parts of it. But had he done so, it is even more improbable that she would have succeeded in convincing him that her conversion and her mystical experiences were not symptoms of her illness.

On Sundays she went to the Church of the Holy Comfortor, which she usually attended and for which she was painting a picture. One morning she met some friends outside the church and asked them to sit in the pew with her. They noted that she had brought some paper with her and wrote steadily all during the sermon. But whether she was working on the novel or writing religious letters to her friends, they did not know. In one such letter, written to Judge William Wallace Hill, there is a poignant expression of her religious feeling at the time:

> Though the late sun bled with tragedy and roads were drenched with heartbreak and worlds were lost in the dust of history, God sent the Spirit of Truth.
> One is grateful for the magnamity [*sic*] of His love. Christ said "Love God" and "Love one another". . . . There are many ways of loving one another: There is the way of reverencing the soul as a symbol of efforts made and of traditions served; there is the way of impersonal gratitude for poetic harmonies and there is the way of sympathy.

For a time Zelda studied Catholicism and probably would have become, according to Livye Hart, a devout Catholic if Scott had shown any interest in proselytizing her. But he wrote to Scottie that he had as little patience with Zelda's taking instruction as with what he called her "early Chaldean-rune worship," and he spoke of people like her as "mere guests on earth, eternal strangers carrying around broken decalogues they cannot read."

In the last months of his life, Scott was so immersed in his novel that he found no time to spend with Zelda, but he tried to send her a weekly letter. At the end of September he wrote her that he was going out in society the next day for the first time in several months—to a tea given by Dorothy Parker for the Countess Tolstoy, Don Stewart's ex-wife. Inwardly, he had not only drawn away from Zelda but also from Harold Ober, Max Perkins, and even Hemingway. When Hemingway sent him a copy of *For Whom the Bell Tolls*, however, Scott thanked him with a brief note signed, "With old affection." But was it? If so, after *For Whom the Bell Tolls* was chosen by the Book-of-the-Month Club, "old affection" was replaced by old rivalry, for Scott intimated to Zelda that he did not think much of it and that Hemingway's present eminence was a far cry from his old days over the sawmill in rue Notre Dame-des-Champs. From Scott's wry comments, it is not difficult to imagine what his reaction would have been had he lived to see Hemingway awarded the Nobel Prize. On the other hand, Hemingway's reaction in *A Moveable Feast* to Fitzgerald's posthumous fame was a distinct surprise—and an unpleasant one —to their mutual friends.

At a time when Scott's novels were part of the required reading in almost every college course in freshman English in the United States, Hemingway's post-Nobel fame had begun to fade. Possibly it was the fabulous posthumous popularity of Scott's novels and the adulation of his biographers that revived Hemingway's early jealousy of Fitzgerald to such a point that he forgot the jovial image of "Papa," which he had so carefully fostered in his later years, and launched a virulent attack on both Scott and Zelda in *A Moveable Feast*.

After Scott's letter to Hemingway, thanking him for sending him a copy of *For Whom the Bell Tolls*, there are no more letters from him to Scott in the Princeton collection; and, apparently, their correspondence ended some months before Scott's death. Hemingway had long since decided that "Poor Scott Fitzgerald" was a rummy, and the "Crack-Up" and the Pat Hobby stories had done nothing to change his mind.

In November 1940 Scott had an attack of avitaminosis, which gave him the feeling that a heavy weight was pressing on his shoulders and upper arms. He doubtless also had a cardiac spasm at that time. One evening when he had walked over to Schwab's drug store to get some cigarettes, as he was standing at the counter, everything suddenly went black. He was so frightened by the way he had felt that he subsequently stayed in bed, stopped drinking Coca-Colas, and tried to take better care of himself. Since the doctor advised him not to climb steps, Sheilah moved him downstairs to her apartment.

There, writing in bed on a lapboard, he continued his heroic attempt to finish *The Last Tycoon*. Although he was weaving the story of his romance with Sheilah Graham into the novel, Scott, like its protagonist Monroe Starr, was in love only with the memory of his wife and with death. Yet he worked on, bravely and persistently, driven by a desperate need for money and the encouragement of another successful novel. On December 13 he told Perkins that the novel was progressing and progressing fast; he had resolved not to stop until he completed the first draft of it, which he hoped to send him about the middle of January.

By Friday evening, December 20, Scott had finished the first part of chapter six. By way of a celebration, he and Sheilah went to see *This Thing Called Love* at the Pantages Theater. On their way out of the theater, Scott suddenly said, "I feel awful." The crowd seemed to fade out before his eyes. He stumbled against his seat and caught the back of it to support himself. Sheilah helped him home and put him to bed. He had a good night's sleep and felt better the next morning. That afternoon, while he was waiting for the doctor, he sat by the fireplace, eating a chocolate bar and making notes on the football team on a copy of the *Princeton Alumni Weekly*. Without a word, he rose abruptly, swayed against the mantelpiece, gasped, and fell.

Scott's final heart attack lasted only a few minutes. When his Cousin Ceci asked if he had received supreme unction, Sheilah told her that his death had been so sudden that there was no time to send for a priest. She did not want to say that Scott had abandoned Catholicism years before and that she did not think that he would have wanted to have the last rites of the church administered to him. Yet, curiously enough, he had expressed a desire to be buried beside his father and mother in the cemetery of St. Mary's Catholic Church in Rockville, Maryland.

In his will, written in June 1937, Scott had said "Part of my estate is first to provide for a funeral and burial in keeping with my station in life." Later, he wrote over "for a funeral" and so forth in pencil "the cheapest funeral," adding, "the same to be without undue ostentation on unnecessary expense." His body was taken to a mortuary chapel in downtown Los Angeles and laid out, not in the chapel but in the William Wordsworth room, which as Frank Scully—one of the few friends who came to pay his last respects—remarked, "must have seemed to the morticians to be the most suitable place for the last rites of a literary man." There Scully found him "laid out to look like a cross between a floorwalker and a wax dummy in the window of a two-pants tailor. His hair was neatly parted on one side. None of it was gray and no lines showed in his face, but his hands were wrinkled and thin —the hands of an old man."

Scott's remains were shipped from Los Angeles to Baltimore. The local papers reported that he was to be buried there. When Mencken could not learn from them when or where the funeral was to be, he called Dr. Baker, but he could not give Mencken any information. Actually, since there was no mortuary chapel in Rockville, Scott's body was taken to Tichnor's Funeral Home in nearby Bethesda. Because he had renounced Catholicism, died without supreme unction, and his books had been proscribed, the bishop refused to allow him to be interred in hallowed ground. Therefore, his family decided that he should be buried in the Rockville Union Cemetery, a small Protestant cemetery nearby.

After a simple service at the funeral home in Bethesda, the cortege wound through the rain to Rockville. The shock of Scott's death had been too great for Zelda to undergo the ordeal of his funeral. Sheilah and Scottie agreed that it was best for Miss Graham not to come to Rockville. There were twenty or thirty people at the service: Scottie; her cousins, the Hume Taylors and the Charles Abeles from Norfolk, Virginia; Newman Smith, Rosalind's husband; the Murphys; the Obers; Max Perkins; John Biggs; Ludlow Fowler; the Turnbulls; and a few more of Scottie's friends from Baltimore. The Turnbulls lingered at the cemetery until the casket was covered. Then Mrs. Turnbull laid some pine branches from La Paix over the grave.

At the time of Scott's death, Zelda was in Montgomery, where Harold Ober called her and tried to break the news to her as gently as possible. Her replies to the telegrams and letters of condolence she received indicate that she remained remarkably controlled in the face of shock, grief, and the uncertainty of her health—and of her livelihood until Scott's estate could be settled. Immediately after his funeral, Scottie left for Montgomery to be with her mother and help her make plans for the future.

Scott's will remained in probate for almost four years. According to the laws of California, half of his estate went to his widow. Ultimately, Zelda received some fifteen thousand dollars. At the instance of Judge John Biggs, whom Scott had named as his literary executor, after depositing a small sum in the bank to provide for unforeseen contingencies, she invested her money in an annuity, which would yield her fifty dollars a month as long as she lived. Judge Biggs had assured her that she and Scottie would not be allowed to suffer for lack of money while the estate was being settled. Even so, they were pinched for ready cash. Oddly enough, Zelda did not pin her hopes for easing their straitened circumstances on her own unfinished novel but on the publication of Scott's *The Last Tycoon*, which was also unfinished. As much as she disliked its heroine, she urged Edmund Wilson to edit it and Maxwell Perkins to publish it.

In retrospect, her admiration for Scott's work increased and she predicted that his books would win him an enviable place in American literature. Her attitude toward him personally softened, until looking over their years together she said that it seemed to her that he had always been planning happiness for her and her daughter—books to read and places to go. Although she and Scott had not been close for some time before his death, she now felt that he was the best friend a person could have. He was, she added, as "spiritually generous" a soul as ever lived.

From her reply to a note of condolence from Mr. and Mrs. John Peale Bishop it is evident that Zelda was as spiritually generous as Scott. Further, it also shows that she was aware of the circumstances under which he died in Sheilah Graham's apartment, and the dignity and restraint of the letter are indicative of her character and her relationship to Scott:

> Scottie and I are grateful for your sympathy and remembrance. There are few consolations as deep as old friends' tributes.
>
> Life makes its exigence, and death descends like the closing of a porte-cullis where had been a gate-way to fair possibilities. Nobody had higher hopes or a heart more full of promises than Scott. He loved his friends and loved his work and I grieve that he should have died in rooms full of suit-cases and unintentional accumulations who had so faithfully provided [for Scottie and me?].

Maybe he wanted his rest: come unto me all ye that labour and are heavy laden and I will give ye rest.

The poignancy of human aspirations and the significance of purposes long pursued were Scott's deepest inspiration and I am glad that he is so kindly remembered.

With equal restraint, on the same day, she wrote a note of thanks to the Class of 'Seventeen, Scott's class at Princeton:

Dear Sirs—

In times of grief and duress there are few consolations as deep as the warmth of one's fellow-men's good will.

Scott Fitzgerald and Zelda Fitzgerald are grateful to you for your flowers and appreciate the tribute and remembrance.

Few women have ever been placed in such a painful position as that in which Scott placed Zelda. She bore it so loyally, with such proud dignity and Spartan fortitude that it should have won her more respect and admiration than she has received from the critics. Almost without exception they represent Zelda in her last years as an eccentric recluse, leading an aimless, vegetative life. But their reports do not tally with those of her family and friends.

It is true that she lived quietly, but her years from 1941 to 1948 were neither as tormented nor as rash and improper as one would infer from the biographical and fictional accounts of her. Admittedly, she was not as happy as she had been at times while she was living with Scott, but neither was she as desperately wretched as she had been upon numerous occasions when she was with him.

"Down here," she said, "the little garden blows remotely poetic under the *voluptés* of the late spring skies. I have a cage of doves who sing & woo the elements and die." But the tenor of her later life was not always scored in such plaintive tones. She took pleasure in reunions with her family, in gardening, in making her own clothes, in painting, and taking part in various civic and religious activities. Scottie's visits were a great joy. Before she arrived, Zelda went to the beauty parlor "to be made presentable for her daughter." Although she avoided cocktail parties now, she liked to go out and have tea with Mrs. Nash Read at Hazel Hedge or to stop in for coffee at the George Mark Woods' on her way home from her dancing lessons. At Mrs. Wood's request

Zelda gave a program at a meeting of the Bluestockings, the top-flight study club. "She delivered an inspired discussion of religion," Mrs. Wood said. "Her choice of words and her wonderful vocabulary made it delightful, and her voice was beautiful, too."

During World War II, when Virginia Cody, the sister of one of Zelda's old beaux, was asked to organize an elite Red Cross unit, she invited Zelda to attend the first-aid classes. Zelda came regularly and took a lively interest in the proceedings. Sometimes, according to her instructor, she showed flashes of her old brilliance; but at other times she seemed preoccupied in a way that made her friends wish they could find some magic word—some open sesame—that would admit them into the remote realms into which she often retired—or that they could bring her back to their everyday world. It was difficult for them to realize that time and tragedy had tempered the light-hearted, outgoing Zelda of the Jazz Age into a serious contemplative, who was pioneering in mysticism, abstraction, and surrealism twenty years before they became popular. But, at least, they realized that Zelda possessed unique gifts.

Her paintings became prized possessions of her friends. On the wall of Lawton Campbell's house in Bronxville there is Zelda's watercolor of a rhododendron in bloom. "Several people have wanted to buy it," he said, "but I won't sell it. I think it is lovely and also it was something she gave me. The frame, the cord and everything are just as she gave them to me." Elizabeth Crommelin Gunster felt the same way about a beautiful Mediterranean scene of Zelda's that graced her drawing room. And among my souvenirs, there is a small painting of the Capitol in Montgomery, which Zelda did on a compact and which I have been advised to keep in the bank vault.

Nor was the appreciation of Zelda's painting confined to her friends. In November 1942 the Montgomery Museum of Fine Arts exhibited twenty-six of her pictures and held a reception in her honor. To the reporters who covered it, she explained that while she was in Paris she had studied the paintings of Picasso, Matisse, Cézanne, and Gauguin. Stimulated but not unduly influenced by their work, she had developed a style of her own. Her pictures were not intended to represent an actual likeness of their subject; they were psychological impressions of things as she saw them. In the circus pictures, she had deliberately elongated and neutralized the figures so that they would not dominate the scene. The legs of her ballet dancers appeared swollen and distorted on the canvases because that is the way a dancer's legs felt after hours of practice at the ballet bar. A dreamy study in which the cotton bolls resembled soft, blue bubbles she entitled "Hope" to suggest a planter's vision of the harvest.

Recently, in reproducing six of Zelda's pictures in his magazine, Arnold Gingrich of *Esquire* said of her, "There will never be an end to the incense." And it is still burning steadily. In the spring of 1969 the Montgomery Museum of Fine Arts set up a memorial to her—a glass case, standing near her painting of the cotton bolls, and filled with reminders of her—a soft scarf, a copy of *Save Me the Waltz*, a gold-beaded bag, a perfume atomizer, an overturned wine glass, and a pair of white doves.

Shortly after the exhibition of her paintings in Montgomery, Zelda found additional happiness in Scottie's announcement of her engagement to Ensign Samuel J. Lanahan, USN, whom she had been dating ever since she was in Vassar and he in Princeton. Although Scott did not live to meet his future son-in-law, on the basis of Scottie's accounts of him and his background, her father had approved of her attachment to the young Princetonian. Scottie's marriage to him took place in the church of St. Ignatius Loyola in New York on February 13, 1943. It was a wartime wedding, with the groom and his groomsmen in their dress uniforms and Scottie in a white bridal dress. The wedding announcements, embossed with the Fitzgerald coat-of-arms, read, "Mrs. Francis Scott Fitzgerald has the honor of announcing the marriage of her daughter. . . ," but Zelda was not well enough to be present.

Late in the summer, Zelda felt herself slipping and returned to Highland for a six months' stay. She was forced to go back there again in the spring of 1946. While she was still at Highlands, Scottie's first child, Thomas Lanahan, was born on April 26, 1946. Zelda had set her heart on having Scottie present her with a grandson, and she "positively beamed" over his birth. By summer she was well enough to make a trip to New York to see the baby. Afterward she observed:

> It is completely incredible to me that one of my generation should be a grandmother: time is no respecter of persons and goes on as if behaving in a rational manner. I do not know of anything . . . which is as gratifying as the purpose and direction which a child brings into life and am rejoiced, and immeasurably pleased about my grandson.

Had she lived to see her first granddaughter, Eleanor Lanahan, who was born in January 1948—just a few weeks before her grandmother's death—Zelda would doubtless have been equally pleased with her.

Early in the summer of 1947, Scottie brought her husband and her little son to Montgomery for a visit with her mother and grandmother. Zelda gave a luncheon for them at the Blue Moon, an inn on the outskirts of town, which had been noted for its cuisine ever since she was a girl. Mrs. George Mark Wood, who was one of the guests, remembers that it was quite a large party, over which Zelda presided with dignity and grace.

Between June 1940 and the time of her death, I saw Zelda only once. After I came back from covering the formation of United Nations in 1945, I went home through Montgomery and stopped by to see her. She was just coming out of the house as I drove up. Although it was Indian summer and very hot, she was wearing black, possibly because she was still in mourning for Scott. With her was the spastic child of a neighbor. Every morning Zelda took the afflicted girl to walk with her. She told her stories, painted her pictures, and treated her with a tenderness and compassion that reminded me of Zelda's care for me some thirty-odd years before on that same Sayre Street hill. A few years ago, when I saw the girl again, she still could not talk of Zelda without crying—nor could I listen to her account of Zelda's kindness to her without tears burning at the back of my own eyes. If Zelda was sometimes "The Beautiful Lady Without Mercy" to the strangers who tried to hunt her down, to her own people she was gracious and loving —and was deeply loved by them.

In the fall of 1947, realizing that she needed treatment, Zelda returned to Asheville and put herself under Dr. Carroll's care. She stayed only a few weeks before going back to Montgomery; but after an attack of asthma and aware that her condition was deteriorating again, she arranged to return to Highland once more. Her mother, her sister Marjorie, and Livye Hart had gathered on the porch of the Rabbit Run, as Miss Minnie called her little cottage. After they had said goodbye to Zelda, she started toward the car. Livye thinks that Zelda must have had a premonition of the tragic fate that awaited her, for she ran back to the porch, threw her arms around her mother and said, "Mama, I'm not afraid to die."

While Zelda was at Highland during the winter of 1948, she wrote her family cheerful letters, repeatedly telling them how eagerly she was looking forward to being at home in the springtime. Even in her last days, she appealed to an old friend from Selma as "a very real and vibrant person." He continued:

> I was with Zelda in Asheville, N.C., about an hour before her death. We had been to a hospital dance and, really, all of us had a wonderful time.
>
> I have no idea what Zelda's clinical diagnosis was, nor do I particularly care. At the time of her death her mind, to me, was as clear as a bell. She was attractive, gracious, and charming. I considered her my friend instead of just an acquaintance.
>
> When I first arrived, she came up and introduced herself and the other patients who were present. When she found out that I was from Selma and that we had mutual friends and acquaintances, she was overjoyed. . . .
>
> Whatever problems she had were either well concealed or licked. Of course, she wanted to leave the hospital, but since she couldn't, she certainly made the best of it and helped the morale of the other patients. She did not talk too much about Scott, but when she did, there did not appear to be any bitterness. I believe she was at peace with herself.

On the night of March 10, fire broke out in the diet kitchen of the hospital. The flames rapidly enveloped the building. Since it was almost midnight before the first alarm sounded, most of the patients were asleep. The locked doors and barred windows hampered the rescue efforts. Before the firemen could bring the flames under control, the hospital was a shell of blackened stone and twisted metal. Most of the patients on the lower floors were rescued, but the ruins were too hot for the firemen to reach those on the third story. Of the ten women trapped there, one managed to break open a window and jump from it. The nine others perished in the fire. Among them was Zelda Sayre Fitzgerald.

Over forty firemen continued to pour water on the hospital all night. By the time the ruins had cooled sufficiently to allow the rescue squad to remove the charred bodies of the patients, there was nothing left that could be positively identified as Zelda's remains. One would like to think that when the flames freed her spirit, they transmuted all that was mortal of her into her natural elements of fire and air.

The ashes that the doctors believed to be hers were sent to the same mortuary chapel in Bethesda in which the funeral services for Scott had been held. On a chill March day, Scottie and her husband, Jack Lanahan, Rosalind and Newman Smith, Clotilde and John Palmer, John Biggs, Mrs. Turnbull, Peaches Finney, the Harold Obers, the Stanley Woodwards, and a number of friends from Baltimore and Washington gathered in the chapel. An Episcopal minister read the Order for the Burial of the Dead from the Book of Common Prayer. As its beautiful, sonorous cadences reverberated through the chapel, they seemed particularly apposite for Zelda's funeral services. "I am the resurrection and the life, saith the Lord: he that believeth in me, though he were dead yet shall he live. . . . and though this body be destroyed, yet I shall see God; whom I shall see for myself, and mine eyes shall behold and not as a stranger." At the graveside in the Rockville Union Cemetery in Rockville the service continued with another especially fitting passage: "Man, that is born of woman, hath but a short time to live, and is full of misery. He cometh up, and is cut-down, like a flower; he fleeth as it were a shadow, and never continueth in one stay. . . . Of whom shall we seek succor, but of thee, O Lord, who for our sins are justly displeased? . . . Thou knowest, Lord the secrets of our hearts . . . suffer us not, at our last hour, for any pains of death, to fall from Thee."

Zelda's grave and Scott's are now marked by one simple headstone, inscribed "Francis Scott Key Fitzgerald and His Wife Zelda."

Time, in a terse notice of her death, described her as "the brilliant counterpart of the heroines" of Scott's novels. In her obituary in *The Montgomery Advertiser*, Grover Hall, Sr., the Pulitzer prize-winning editor of the paper, came forth with a fact that Scott's biographers have omitted to mention, but Zelda's friends have long known: "Mrs. Fitzgerald had collaborated with her husband on some of his books . . ."; in fact, on all of them except the unfinished fragment of *The Last Tycoon*. Among those who knew both Scott and Zelda well, very few will disagree as to which of the Fitzgeralds had genius and which of them talent and a knowledge of the writer's craft.

So great has been the resurgence of the Fitzgeralds' popularity that Scottie gets over a thousand letters and queries a year about them. At the time of Scott's death, his works were hard to find on the booksellers' shelves; but now, they have not only been reissued many times in English, but they have also been translated into ninety-seven languages. Even more amazing than the present-day sales of Fitzgerald's books are the number of courses in both American and European universities that are now devoted to the study of them and the number of scholarly monographs on them that appear each year.

One explanation of the Fitzgerald revival is that Scott and Zelda anticipated many of the current literary trends; another is that their liberal convictions and their rebellion in the Jazz Age foreshadowed the leftist sympathies and the revolt of youth in the sixties. Perhaps a third explanation is that, taken together, their self-revelatory writings constitute one of the most significant contributions to the understanding of the first half of the twentieth century.

Indeed, Cyril Connolly observed some years ago that "apart from his increasing stature as a writer, Fitzgerald is now firmly established as a myth, an American version of the Dying God, an Adonis of letters . . . flowering in the twenties, the Jazz Age, which he prefectly expressed and almost created, and then quietly wilting through the thirties—to expire as a deity of spring and summer should—on December 21, 1940, at the winter solstice and the end of an epoch."

Edmund Wilson says that after he edited *The Crack-Up* and *The Last Tycoon*, he received a steady flow of letters about Scott, which indicated that Fitzgerald had become "the object of a cult that had gone beyond mere admiration for literature. He had taken on the aspect of a martyr, a sacrificial victim, a semi-divine personage. . . . I realized that it would be quite impossible for such worshipers to form any realistic idea of what Fitzgerald had been like, and that they had better have been left with their myth."

However that may be, Scott was more than candid about his human frailties. The Catholic rite of confession was so deeply ingrained in him that as long as he lived he felt the need to shrive himself by talking and writing about them. Yet, on the other hand, he wanted so deeply to leave them shrouded in the effulgent legend that he had created for himself that one wishes that he had lived to see the revival of the Fitzgerald cult and hear the critics discuss his deification. Scott would have laughed, but he would have loved it.

Bibliography

MANUSCRIPT MATERIAL

Baltimore. Enoch Pratt Free Library. Mencken collection.
Cambridge, Mass. Houghton Library, Harvard University. Fitzgerald
  papers.
New Haven. Beinecke Library, Yale University. Van Vechten papers.
Montgomery, Ala. State of Alabama Department of Archives and
  History. Sayre and Fitzgerald papers.
Princeton, N.J. Firestone Library, Princeton University. F. Scott Fitz-
  gerald's Ledger.
Princeton, N.J. Firestone Library, Princeton University. F. Scott Fitz-
  gerald's Notebooks.
Princeton, N.J. Firestone Library, Princeton University. Fitzgerald
  papers.
Princeton, N.J. Firestone Library, Princeton University. F. Scott Fitz-
  gerald. "The Romantic Egotist."
University, Ala. Amelia Gayle Gorgas Library. University of Alabama.
  Mayfield collection.

WORKS OF F. SCOTT FITZGERALD

Fitzgerald, F. Scott. "Afternoon of an Author." *Esquire*, August 1936.
————. *Afternoon of an Author, A Selection of Uncollected Stories and*

Essays. With an Introduction and Notes by Arthur Mizener. New York: Charles Scribner's Sons, 1957.

―――. *All the Sad Young Men.* New York: Charles Scribner's Sons, 1926.

―――. "A Short Autobiography." *The New Yorker*, May 25, 1929.

―――. "Author's House." *Esquire*, July 1936.

―――. "Babes in the Woods." *Nassau Literary Magazine*, May 1917, and *The Smart Set*, September 1919.

―――. "Babylon Revisited." *The Saturday Evening Post*, February 21, 1931.

―――. *Babylon Revisited and Other Stories.* New York: Charles Scribner's Sons, 1960.

―――. "Benediction." *The Smart Set*, February 1920.

―――. "Family in the Wind." *The Saturday Evening Post*, June 4, 1932.

―――. "Financing Finnegan." *Esquire*, January 1938.

―――. *Flappers and Philosophers.* New York: Charles Scribner's Sons, 1921.

―――. "How to Live on $36,000 a Year." *The Saturday Evening Post*, April 1924.

―――. "May Day." *The Smart Set*, July 1920.

―――. "My Generation." *Esquire*, October 1968.

―――. "Our Own Movie Queen." *Chicago Tribune*, June 7, 1925. [Written by Zelda, but revised and signed by Scott.]

―――. *Tales of the Jazz Age.* New York: Charles Scribner's Sons, 1922.

―――. *Taps at Reveille.* New York: Charles Scribner's Sons, 1935.

―――. *Tender Is the Night.* New York: Charles Scribner's Sons, 1934.

―――. *The Apprentice Fiction of F. Scott Fitzgerald.* Edited with an Introduction by John Kuehl. New Brunswick, N.J: Rutgers University Press, 1965.

―――. *The Beautiful and Damned.* New York: Charles Scribner's Sons, 1922.

―――. *The Crack-Up.* Edited by Edmund Wilson. New York: New Directions, 1945.

―――. "The Cruise of the Rolling Junk." *Motor*, February, March, and April 1924.

―――. "The Debutante." *Nassau Literary Magazine*, January 1917, and *The Smart Set*, November 1919.

―――. "The Diamond as Big as the Ritz." *The Smart Set*, June 1922.

―――. "The End of Hate." *Collier's*, June 22, 1940.

————. *The Great Gatsby*. New York: Charles Scribner's Sons, 1925.

————. *The Last Tycoon*. Edited by Edmund Wilson. New York: Charles Scribner's Sons, 1941.

————. *The Letters of F. Scott Fitzgerald*. Edited by Andrew Turnbull. New York: Charles Scribner's Sons, 1963.

————. "The Millionaire's Girl." *The Saturday Evening Post*, May 17, 1930. [Written by Zelda, but signed with Scott's name.]

————. *The Pat Hobby Stories*. With an introduction by Arnold Gingrich. New York: Charles Scribner's Sons, 1962.

————. "The Rich Boy." *Redbook*, January and February 1926.

————. *The Vegetable or from President to Postman*. New York: Charles Scribner's Sons, 1923.

————. *This Side of Paradise*. New York: Charles Scribner's Sons, 1920.

Scott Fitzgerald. *Letters to His Daughter*. Edited by Andrew Turnbull, with an introduction by Frances Fitzgerald Lanahan. New York: Charles Scribner's Sons, 1965.

WORKS BY F. SCOTT AND ZELDA FITZGERALD

Fitzgerald, F. Scott and Zelda. "Auction—Model 1934." *Esquire*, July 1934.

————. "Looking Back Eight Years." *College Humor*, June 1928.

————. "The Changing Beauty of Park Avenue." *Harper's Bazaar*, January 1928.

————. "The Girl the Prince Liked." *College Humor*, February 1930.

————. "The Girl with Talent." *College Humor*, April 1930.

————. "The Original Follies Girl." *College Humor*, July 1929.

————. "The Poor Working Girl." *College Humor*, January 1931.

————. "Southern Girl." *College Humor*, October 1929.

————. "Show Mr. and Mrs. F. to Number————." *Esquire*, May and June 1934.

————. "What Became of Our Flappers and Sheiks." *McCall's*, October 1925.

————. "Who Can Fall in Love after Thirty?" *College Humor*, October 1928. [Although these works were signed by both Fitzgeralds, Scott credited them chiefly to Zelda.]

WORKS OF ZELDA FITZGERALD

Fitzgerald, Zelda. "A Couple of Nuts." *Scribner's Magazine*, August 1932.

————. "Eulogy of the Flapper." *Metropolitan Magazine*, April 1922.

————. "Miss Ella." *Scribner's Magazine*, December 1931.

————. "Review." *New York Tribune*, April 2, 1922.

————. *Save Me the Waltz*. New York: Charles Scribner's Sons, 1932. Reprinted Carbondale, Ill.: Southern Illinois University Press, 1967.

SPECIAL WORKS

Baker, Carlos. *Ernest Hemingway: A Life Story*. New York: Charles Scribner's Sons, 1969.

Bruccoli, Matthew Joseph. *The Composition of "Tender Is the Night": A Study of the Manuscripts*. Pittsburgh: University of Pittsburgh Press, 1963.

Cowley, Malcolm. "Fitzgerald: The Double Man." *The Saturday Review of Literature*, January 15, 1951.

Cowley, Malcolm, and Cowley, Robert. *Fitzgerald and the Jazz Age*. Scribner's Research Anthologies. New York: Charles Scribner's Sons, 1966.

Fabre, Geneviève et Fabre, Michel. "Tender Is the Night." In *Francis Scott Fitzgerald*. Présentation par Bernard Poli. Collection U2. Paris: Librairie Armand Colin, 1969.

Fadiman, Clifton. "F. Scott Fitzgerald." In *The New Yorker*, April 14, 1934.

Fitzgerald/Hemingway Annual, 1969. Edited by Matthew J. Bruccoli. Washington, D.C.: Microcard Editions, 1969.

Graham, Sheilah and Frank, Gerold. *Beloved Infidel*. New York: Henry Holt and Co., Inc., 1958.

Graham, Sheilah. *College of One*. New York: Viking Press, 1967.

————. *The Rest of the Story*. New York: Coward-McCann, 1964.

Goldhurst, William. *F. Scott Fitzgerald and His Contemporaries*. Cleveland and New York: World Publishing Co., 1963.

Hearne, Laura Guthrie. "A Summer with F. Scott Fitzgerald." *Esquire*, December 1964.

Hoffman, Frederick J., ed. *The Great Gatsby: A Study*. New York: Charles Scribner's Sons, 1962.

Kazin, Alfred, ed. *F. Scott Fitzgerald: The Man and His Work*. Cleveland and New York: World Publishing Co., 1951.

Kiley, Jed (John Gerald). *Hemingway: An Old Friend Remembers*. New York: Hawthorne Books, Inc., 1965.

Le Vot, André. "The Great Gatsby." In *Francis Scott Fitzgerald. Présentation par Bernard Poli. Collection U2.* Paris: Librairie Armand Colin, 1969.

Milford, Nancy. *Zelda.* New York: Harper & Row, 1970.

Mizener, Arthur, ed. *F. Scott Fitzgerald: A Collection of Critical Essays.* Twentieth Century Views. Englewood Cliffs, N.J.: Prentice-Hall, Inc., 1963.

―――. *The Far Side of Paradise.* Boston: Houghton Mifflin, 1951. Revised edition, New York, 1965.

Piper, Henry Dan. "F. Scott Fitzgerald: A Check-List." *The Princeton University Library Chronicle,* Summer 1951.

―――. *F. Scott Fitzgerald: A Critical Portrait.* New York: Holt, Rinehart and Winston, 1965.

―――. "Zelda Sayre Fitzgerald: A Check-List." *The Princeton University Library Chronicle,* Summer 1951.

Shain, Charles E. *F. Scott Fitzgerald.* University of Minnesota Pamphlets on American Writers, n. 15. Minneapolis: University of Minnesota Press, 1961.

Trilling, Lionel. "F. Scott Fitzgerald." *The Liberal Imagination.* New York: The Viking Press, 1951.

Tomkins, Calvin. "Living Well Is the Best Revenge." *The New Yorker,* July 28, 1962.

Turnbull, Andrew. *Scott Fitzgerald.* New York: Charles Scribner's Sons, 1962.

―――. *Thomas Wolfe.* New York: Charles Scribner's Sons, 1967.

Warren, Dale. "(Signed) F. S. F." *The Princeton University Library Chronicle,* Winter 1964.

Wilson, Edmund. "Literary Spotlight." *The Bookman,* March 1922.

Wilson, Edmund. *The Shores of Light.* New York: Vintage Press, 1961.

Wilson, Edmund, *Bit Between My Teeth.* New York: Farrar, Straus and Giroux, 1965.

GENERAL WORKS

A Guide to the City of Montgomery. Montgomery, Ala.: Walker Printing Co., Inc., 1969.

Birmingham, Stephen. *The Right People: A Portrait of the American Social Establishment.* Boston and Toronto: Little, Brown and Company, 1968.

Callaghan, Morley. *That Summer in Paris: Memories of Tangled Friendships with Hemingway, and Some Others.* New York: Coward-McCann, 1963.

Chanler, Mrs. Winthrop. *Autumn in the Valley.* Boston: Little, Brown and Company, 1936.

Cooper, Wyatt. "Whatever You Think Dorothy Parker Was Like, She Wasn't." *Esquire,* July 1968.

Dos Passos, John. *The Best Times: An Informal Memoir.* New York: New American Library, 1966.

Ford, Hugh, ed. *Nancy Cunard; Brave Poet, Indomitable Rebel, 1896–1965.* Philadelphia: Chilton Book Company, 1968.

Forgue, Guy Jean. *H. L. Mencken: L'Homme, L'Oeuvre, L'Influence.* Paris: Minard Lettres Modernes, 1967.

Gish, Lillian, with Pinchot, Ann. *The Movies, Mr. Griffith, and Me.* Englewood Cliffs, N.J.: Prentice-Hall, 1969.

Hayes, Helen, with Sanford, Dody. *On Reflection: An Autobiography.* New York: M. Evans and Company, Inc., 1968.

Hellman, Lillian. *An Unfinished Woman: A Memoir.* Boston: Little, Brown and Company, 1969.

Hemingway, Ernest. *A Moveable Feast.* New York: Charles Scribner's Sons, 1964.

Koeper, H. F. *Historic St. Paul Buildings.* St. Paul, Minn.: St. Paul City Planning Board, 1964.

Kohn, Peter [John]. *The Cradle: Anatomy of A Town—Fact and Fiction.* New York, Washington, and Hollywood: Vantage Press, 1969.

Loos, Anita. *A Girl Like I.* New York: The Viking Press, 1966.

Mencken, H. L. *Letters of H. L. Mencken.* Selected and annotated by Guy J. Forgue, with a personal note by Hamilton Owens. New York: Alfred A. Knopf, 1961.

Moore, Grace. *You're Only Human Once.* Garden City, N.Y.: Doubleday Doran & Co., Inc., 1944.

Phelps, Robert and Deane, Peter. *The Literary Life: A Scrapbook Almanac of the Anglo-American Literary Scene from 1900 to 1950.* New York: Farrar, Straus and Giroux, 1968.

Robertson, W. G. *Recollections of the Early Settlers of Montgomery County and Their Families.* Montgomery, Ala.: Excelsior Printing Company, 1892.

Wood, Mattie Pegues. *The Life of St. John's Parish.* Montgomery, Ala.: The Paragon Press, 1955.

PERIODICAL FILES

Alabama Journal.
Fitzgerald Newsletter.
Life.
Princeton Alumni Weekly.
Redbook.
Scribner's Magazine.
The Baltimore Sun.
The Birmingham News.
The Bookman.
The Montgomery Advertiser.
The New Yorker.
The New York Times.
The Mobile Register.
The Princeton University Library Chronicle.
The Saturday Evening Post.
The Saturday Review of Literature.
The Smart Set.
Time.

Acknowledgments

Exiles from Paradise is based in part upon unpublished letters, diaries, notes and clippings, as well as upon available published sources for which permission has been obtained. A heavily documented and bibliographed manuscript of the book has been deposited in the Mayfield Collection in the University of Alabama Library for the use of scholars.

For permission to use the unpublished letters, diaries, notes, and clippings in the Mayfield collection in the Amelia Gayle Gorgas Library of the University of Alabama, I am indebted to its librarian, Dr. W. Stanley Hoole. I am also indebted to his staff, especially to Mr. Charles E. Beard, Mrs. Addie Coleman, Mr. Joseph A. Jackson, Mrs. W. E. Lamont, Mr. Dereck S. Milsom, and Mrs. Jane P. Temple for their many kindnesses; to Harold Ober Associates for permission to quote from the unpublished letters and papers of Scott and Zelda Fitzgerald; to Mr. William Frederick of the Mercantile-Safe Deposit and Trust Company of Baltimore, Maryland, for permission to quote from the unpublished letters of H. L. Mencken; to Mrs. George Jean Nathan for permission to quote from the unpublished letters of George Jean Nathan; to Mr. Edwin Castagna, director of the Enoch Pratt Free Library, for giving me access to the Mencken and Fitzgerald materials there and to the members of his staff for their aid; to Mr. William Dix, librarian of Princeton University, for permission to use the Fitzgerald, Mencken, and Sylvia Beach collections in the Firestone Library, and to his staff for their assistance, particularly to Dr. Howard C. Rice, Mr. Alexander P. Clark, Mrs. Alden Randall, Miss Julie Hudson, Mr. Alfred Bush, and Mr. Charles Green; to Mr. George H. Healy, curator of rare books at Cornell University Library for permission to use the Nathan materials there; to Mr. William H. Bond of the Houghton Library, for allowing me to quote from the Fitzgerald materials by permission of Harvard College Library; to Mr. David R. Watkins, chief reference librarian of the Beinecke Library for access to the Fitzgerald and Van Vechten materials in the Yale University Library; to Mr. Milo B. Howard, director of the Department of Archives and History of the State of Alabama, for allowing me to use the Sayre and Fitzgerald papers there, and to his staff, especially Mrs. Glenn Allen Jones for her many courtesies.

For permission to quote from copyrighted and other material I am indebted to: Houghton Mifflin Company for *The Far Side of Paradise*, © 1951 by Arthur Mizener; Charles Scribner's Sons for *This Side of Paradise*, © 1920, *The Beautiful and Damned*, © 1922, *The Great Gatsby*, © 1925, *Tender Is the Night*, © 1934, *The Last Tycoon*, © 1941, by F. Scott Fitzgerald, all copyrighted Charles Scribner's Sons; Harold Ober Associates Incorporated for *Save Me the Waltz*, © 1932, by Zelda Fitzgerald; Charles Scribner's Sons for *The Letters of F. Scott Fitzgerald*, © 1963 by Frances Scott Fitzgerald Lanahan, for *Scott Fitzgerald's Letters to His Daughter*, © 1965 by Frances Scott Fitzgerald Lanahan, for *Scott Fitzgerald* by Andrew Turnbull, © 1962 by Andrew Turnbull; Alfred A. Knopf, Inc., *Letters of H. L. Mencken*, © 1961; excerpts from *The Crack-Up* by F. Scott Fitzgerald, Copyright 1934, 1936, by Esquire Incorporated. Copyright 1945 by New Directions Publishing Corporation. Reprinted by permission of New Directions Publishing Corporation; New American Library, *The Best Times: An Informal Memoir* by John Dos Passos, © 1966 by John Dos Passos; Prentice-Hall, *The Movies, Mr. Griffith and Me* by Lillian Gish and Ann Pinchot, © 1969 by Lillian Gish; *On Reflection* by Helen Hayes with Sanford Dody, © 1968 by Helen Hayes and Sanford Dody. Reprinted by permission of the publisher, M. Evans and Company; *The Princeton University Library Chronicle*, © 1964, for "(Signed) F. S. F." by Dale Warren; *The New Yorker*, excerpts from "Living Well Is the Best Revenge" by Calvin Tomkins (July 28, 1962), © 1962 and "Sheila Graham and Scott Fitzgerald" by Edmund Wilson (July 24, 1957), © 1957. Used by permission; *Saturday Review*, excerpt from "Trade Winds" column by Bennett Cerf (August 16, 1947), © 1947. Used by permission; *Time*, The Weekly News-magazine, excerpt from "Work of a Wife" (April 9, 1934) and "Obituary of Zelda Sayre Fitzgerald" (March 15, 1948), Copyright Time Inc. Reprinted by permission from *Time*, The Weekly Newsmagazine; *Saturday Evening Post*, excerpt from "One Hundred False Starts" (March 4, 1933), © 1933 The Curtis Publishing Co. Reprinted with permission of *Saturday Evening Post*; and to *Comment* Magazine, *Atlanta* Magazine, *The Birmingham News*, and *The Montgomery Advertiser* for permission to quote from their files.

I am deeply appreciative of the kindness of Mrs. Harry M. Ridgeway, Mrs. Newman Smith, Mr. and Mrs. George Mark Wood, and Mr. Alex Sartwell for turning over to me their notes on the Fitzgeralds, and to Rebecca Franklin (Mrs. Ward Morehouse) to quote from her *Manhattan Diary* and to the following persons for answering my queries and giving me permission to quote from their letters or for supplying vital information: Miss Betty Adler, Mrs. B. F. Austen, Mrs. Fred Ball, Mr. Waverly Barbe, Dr. Carlos Baker, the late Mrs. Minor W. Brinson, Dr. Matthew J. Bruccoli, Mr. James M. Cain, Mr. C. Lawton Campbell, Miss Virginia Cody, Miss Joan Crawford, Dr. S. H. Darden, Mr. John Dos Passos, Dr. Oscar Forel, Professor Guy J. Forgue, Mr. and Mrs. William Forshaw, Mrs. Elizabeth S. Fritz, Mr. Hobart Fulton, Miss Lillian Gish, Mr. and Mrs. Frederick Gunster, Judge and Mrs. Robert Harwood, Mr. Milo B. Howard, Mr. Thomas Horan, Admiral Edouard Jozan, Judge John P. Kohn, Dr. John Kuehl, Mrs. Grace Gunter Lane, Professor André LeVot, Mrs. Dorothy Maner, Mrs. Willey Gayle Martin, Mr. Paul McLendon, Dr. Marjorie Hope Nicolson, Mrs. Nash Read, Mrs. Charles P. Rogers, Mrs. Vaughan Hill Robison, Mr. Noble H. Seay, Mrs. C. Grove Smith (the Fitzgeralds' daughter, Scottie, formerly Mrs. Samuel J. Lanahan), Mrs. Mary Lee Stapp, Mrs. Ann Hooper Stavrolakis, Mr. Donald Ogden Stewart, Mr. Hudson Strode, Mrs. Felix M. T. Tankersley, Mrs. Jane P. Temple, Mrs. Eugenia McGough Tuttle, Mr. Dale Warren, Mr. Robert Penn Warren, Mrs. Katherine Whitfield Wolf, and Mr. Sydenham Moore Wilkinson.

Additional thanks must also go to Miss Betty Adler, Dr. Matthew J. Bruccoli, Dr. Oscar Forel, Mr. William Forshaw, Professor André LeVot, Professor J. B. McMinn, Miss Caroline Lyla Plath, Mrs. C. Grove Smith, Mrs. Newman Smith, Mr. Hudson Strode, Mr. J. R. Travis, and Mr. Edmund Wilson for reading and criticizing the manuscript for me; to Mrs. Elizabeth M. Lee, Mr. Michael Lee, and Miss Camilla Mayfield for typing, proofreading, and correcting it. In conclusion, I am deeply grateful to Mr. Richard Tucker Kennedy, senior editor of Delacorte Press, and to my agent, Mr. Lurton Blassingame, for their constant encouragement and help.

Index